Battle for the Bocage, Normandy 1944

Battle for the Bocage, Normandy 1944

Point 103, Tilly-sur-Seulles and Villers-Bocage

Tim Saunders

Pen & Sword
MILITARY

First published in Great Britain in 2021 by
PEN & SWORD MILITARY
An imprint of
Pen & Sword Books Ltd
47 Church Street
Barnsley
South Yorkshire
S70 2AS

Copyright © Tim Saunders, 2021

ISBN 978-1-52678-423-0

Typeset by Concept, Huddersfield HD4 5JL.
Printed and bound in England by CPI Group (UK) Ltd, Croydon, CR0 4YY.

Pen & Sword Books Limited incorporates the imprints of Atlas, Archaeology,
Aviation, Discovery, Family History, Fiction, History, Maritime, Military,
Military Classics, Politics, Select, Transport, True Crime, Air World,
Frontline Publishing, Leo Cooper, Remember When, Seaforth Publishing,
The Praetorian Press, Wharncliffe Local History, Wharncliffe Transport,
Wharncliffe True Crime and White Owl.

For a complete list of Pen & Sword titles please contact
PEN & SWORD BOOKS LIMITED
47 Church Street, Barnsley, South Yorkshire, S70 2AS, England
E-mail: enquiries@pen-and-sword.co.uk
Website: www.pen-and-sword.co.uk

Contents

Acknowledgements

Writing during the COVID-19 pandemic was particularly challenging, as the normal sources of detail – the war diaries and documents held by The National Archives and regimental headquarters – were simply not available. I am, however, immensely grateful to the various internet forums and their members who have made their specialist knowledge and archive materials available to me. Without them and the individuals named below I would have been twiddling my thumbs!

Richard Hone, his library and encyclopaedic knowledge of weapons, vehicles and equipment has, as ever, been of the greatest assistance in answering a daily stream of questions. In short, he has been a constant source of help and advice with the text, images and captions.

Another friend and colleague, Lieutenant Colonel Andrew Duff, with the commitment of a good regimental infantry officer in 'lockdown', patiently scanned pages of his regiment's history to ensure that I did justice to the 2nd Battalion, Essex Regiment. I did not have to try too hard to achieve this, as the powerful events at Essex Wood very much speak for themselves and after almost five years of war they illustrate the enduring quality of the oft-maligned county regiments of the British army. He also provided an illuminating sketch of the traffic issues in the beachhead during mid-June 1944.

I would also like to thank fellow members of the International Guild of Battlefield Guides who have been equally as generous as ever with their help and advice. Without them and the cast above, this book could not have been written.

Tim Saunders
Warminster, 2020

Introduction

'We must be able to concentrate armour and push fairly strong armoured columns rapidly inland to secure important ground. Such columns will form firm bases in enemy territory from which to develop offensive action in all directions ... offensive eagerness is not only necessary in the soldier; it is essential in the officer, and especially in the senior officer and commander.'
[Montgomery's notes for his pre-invasion briefings]

Montgomery did not like Lieutenant General Morgan's COSSAC plan and set about revising and upscaling it. While he and his newly-assembled 21st Army Group staff were beginning the process, the ill-fated Anzio landing took place, of which Churchill memorably said: 'I had hoped that we were hurling a wildcat onto the shore, but all we got was a stranded whale.' Montgomery's revised plan envisaged German panzer divisions being fixed against the British Second Army, but it was criticized for being 'overly defensive'. Consequently, under pressure to justify his strategy and reassure political and military leaders that the Allied armies would not become another 'whale', ambitious objectives were inserted. Chief of these was to establish 'firm bases' at Évrecy and Villers-Bocage on D-Day, some 18 miles inland and more than 9 miles forward of the main D-Day objective. They were demonstrably offensive and were further rationalized as a measure to disrupt enemy counter-attacks against the lodgement. How seriously Montgomery took these objectives has been much debated and is a source of much criticism of his handling of the campaign. Nonetheless, for XXX Corps and the formations under its command, Villers-Bocage was an objective that above all shaped the conduct of the battle inland for two weeks after D-Day.

The first part of this book examines General Sir Miles Dempsey's aims for Second Army to make rapid progress south into the interior of Normandy in the seven days following D-Day. Even beyond the first week of the campaign, it is quite clear from the grouping of veteran formations, including the 7th Armoured Division, the first such division ashore, that General Montgomery's intention continued to be to use XXX Corps to make his advance south. Meanwhile, I Corps astride the Orne and Caen remained relatively static, holding a long line, in contrast to the effort and resources devoted to a determined effort to get south to Villers-Bocage for almost two weeks after D-Day.

Using the ebb and flow of battle in the area of Point 103, Tilly-sur-Seulles and west to la Belle Épine, the conduct of operations by two veteran formations –

8 Armoured Brigade and the 50th Northumbrian Infantry Division – is charted. Against these are balanced the operations of the 12th *Hitlerjugend* SS Panzer Division and 130th *Panzer Lehr* Division. This will demonstrate that the slow tempo of British operations and the arrival of these two highly-capable panzer divisions did much to thwart XXX Corps' attempts to establish a position 20 miles inland, on the high ground around Villers-Bocage. This included the 7th Armoured Division's attempt to exploit the Caumont Gap and outflank the stubborn defences around Tilly in Operation PERCH.

The second part of the book concentrates on the resulting protracted struggle in the bocage or hedgerow country and the 50th Division's struggle to capture the ruins of Tilly and the villages to the west. During this period, a continuing theme is the struggle by both infantry and armoured forces to come to terms with the bocage. This challenge held veterans of the desert war in North Africa in its grip until new tactics started to emerge towards the end of the period covered by this book. One veteran Yorkshire infantryman writing in his personal diary went so far as to write: 'I wish we were back in the good old desert.'

A point that needs addressing at the very start of the book is the question of the presence or absence of Tigers with *Panzer Lehr* in the Point 103 and Tilly area. It is a seemingly intractable issue, as indicated by the quotation marks I have used when referring to 'Tiger Hill'.

Panzer Lehr's order of battle has the 316th *Funklenk* Company equipped with Tigers: five King Tigers and three Tiger Is. These were conversions of early-production models for use with the Borgward remote-control demolition tanks and had more room in the turret and fewer rounds of ammunition. The King Tigers were so unreliable that they were withdrawn and *Sturmgeschütz* IIIs were issued in lieu, but other than British 'sightings' there is little evidence of their presence in Normandy either. Even if the Tigers were present, just three of them could not, as reported, have been in so many different places at the same time! A Tiger that could have been belonged to the 316th *Funklenk* Company was found abandoned near Amiens, a considerable distance to the east.

It is worth noting that German practice was for vehicles and equipment to be taken on strength of a division when it was issued to them from the factory and is consequently shown in returns, whether or not in this case the Tigers were actually fighting in Normandy.

A company of Tigers of 101 *Schwere* SS Panzer *Abteilung*, as is very well known, arrived near Villers-Bocage after a circuitous march on its tracks from Versailles in time to confront the 7th Armoured Division in Operation PERCH on 13 June 1944.

As Point 103 is known to veterans as 'Tiger Hill' and 'Tigers' are so frequently mentioned in the accounts given by those who fought the battle, I have decided to leave such references in any quotations I have used as not only is the presence of Tigers still debated but it gives a distinct flavour of the time. There was a definite 'Tiger phobia' among the Allies that saw panzers being consistently reported as

A Panzer IV with *Schürzen* fitted to its sides and around its turret.

Tigers. The fact that the Panzer IV had 'bazooka plates' (*Schürzen*) fitted, which gave the turret a rounded look similar to the Tigers, plus the long 75mm gun and its prominent muzzle brake did not help recognition either![1] When the side plates were lost in battle, those around the Panzer IV's turret tended to remain in place.

I have similarly commented on the other 'phobias' of the day – the '88' and the 'sniper' – at appropriate points in the story.

As is my normal practice, I have used the ranks held at the time by the individuals who fought the battles. For instance, Brigadier 'Speedy' Bredin was a major and second-in-command of 1 Dorsets, and Lieutenant Colonel Stanley Christopherson was also a major, squadron leader and took over as commanding officer of the Sherwood Rangers Yeomanry, still as a major during the fighting on Point 103.

The map on pp. xvi–xvii has been included to help readers with the many grid references quoted in the various war diaries. These are of course referenced in the text and on the accompanying maps, but maps as a whole are essential military history tools.

With regard to British unit abbreviations, I have employed the style most commonly found in contemporary documents. For example, the 6th Durham Light Infantry were ubiquitously referred to as 6 DLI, while more straightforwardly the 1st Dorsets was referred to as 1 Dorsets.

In some cases, particularly in the west of the area, the reader trying to locate the likes of Grainville and L'Oraille will not find them on a modern map; they are still there, but under a different name. It is, however, relatively easy to reconcile the maps in this book with modern maps as few roads have changed.

Timeline

The area south of Bayeux in which XXX Corps fought after the first couple of days following the landings was sizeable, and with the 50th Division having four brigades of infantry and an armoured brigade under command with the 7th Armoured Division superimposed for some days, there was a lot of action in different parts of the area.

6 June: D-Day. Landing of the 50th Northumbrian Division. Assault landing by 69 and 231 brigades, supported by elements of 8 Armoured Brigade. Advance inland by follow-on brigades: 56 and 151 brigades.

7 June: Bayeux liberated, and operations conducted to clear the very large divisional area. Orders finally given for 8 Armoured Brigade's exploitation to Villers-Bocage given late pm.

8 June: Fighting to clear western part of the divisional area and link beachhead with First US Army's. Pm: 8 Armoured Brigade begin their advance to Villers-Bocage on two routes but blocked at Putot by the 12th *Hitlerjugend* SS Panzer Division. Armour reaches Point 103 and infantry fighting in Audrieu.

9 June: 8 Armoured Brigade's hold on Point 103 consolidated. Exploitation to and capture of Saint-Pierre. Arrival of leading elements of the 130th *Panzer Lehr* Division and they attack 151 Brigade on the axis of the Bayeux road but quickly go over to the defensive when 8 Armoured Brigade advances on Saint-Pierre.

10 June: Counter-attacks against Saint-Pierre held by 8 DLI and 24th Lancers. Heavy attacks by *Panzer Lehr* all day and night on Point 103. 7th Armoured Division advance south towards Tilly; reached Bucelles. 56 Brigade advance south along the Aure valley including Bernières-Bocage. 2 Essex secure Juaye-Mondaye and reach Point 112.

11 June: 7th Armoured Division advances south towards Tilly and Lingèvres. 2 Gloucesters break into the town but unable to secure it and withdraw. 231 Brigade advance south to la Belle Épine, where 2 Devons were heavily counter-attacked. 6 Green Howards supported by 4th/7th Dragoon Guards attack Cristot from Point 103 area, but the village remained in the hands of the *Hitlerjugend*. 2 Essex attack orchards outside Verrières.

12 June: The 7th Armoured Division resumes attack on Tilly but it was broken off in order to redeploy the division west to exploit the Caumont Gap (Operation PERCH). 22 Armoured Brigade begin the march south to Villers-Bocage and leaguer north of Livry for the night. The 1st Dorsets finally relieved on Point 103 by the 5th East Yorks.

13 June: Leading tanks of 22 Armoured Brigade reach Villers-Bocage and Point 213. Counter-attack by Michael Wittmann and Tigers of 101 *Schwere* SS Panzer Battalion. Villers-Bocage occupied by the 4 CLY and 1/7th Queens but abandoned and 22 Armoured Brigade withdrew to the Island Position onto the high ground west of the town. 6 DLI attempt attack to bypass Tilly to the west but fail.

14 June: 151 and 231 brigades attack on the frontage of Verrières, Lingèvres and la Senaudière. 22 Armoured Brigade fight in the Island Position but withdraw overnight.

15 June: A quiet day on the 50th Division's front.

16 June: 151 Brigade's attacks on Verrières and Lingèvres and 231 Brigade attack la Senaudière.

17 June: 2 Essex begin first phase of their attack on Tilly-sur-Seulles.

18 June: 69 Brigade attempt to expand their lodgement. 2 Essex and 6 DLI make progress, as does 49th Division south of Saint-Pierre. With Tilly becoming a salient, *Panzer Lehr* withdraws overnight.

19 June: Tilly in British hands. Attack by 231 Brigade on Hottot and Château Cordlion.

50th (Northumbrian) Infantry Division
Main combat elements post D Day

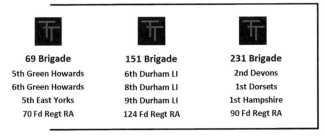

69 Brigade	**151 Brigade**	**231 Brigade**
5th Green Howards	6th Durham LI	2nd Devons
6th Green Howards	8th Durham LI	1st Dorsets
5th East Yorks	9th Durham LI	1st Hampshire
70 Fd Regt RA	124 Fd Regt RA	90 Fd Regt RA

Div Tps and Atts		
61st Recce Regt		
2nd Cheshire (MG)		
C Sqn 141 Regt RAC	**156 Ind Brigade**	**8 Armd Brigade**
C Sqn 22nd W Dragoons	2nd Essex	4th/7th DG
N. Hussars A/Tk Regt	2nd S Wales Border	Sherwood Rangers
73 A/Tk Regt	2nd Gloucester	24th Lancers
25 Lt AA Regt		147 Fd Regt RA (SP)

Glossary of Terms

Abbreviations abound in war diaries and accounts. The main ones are listed here, but in an army, where combat training had priority over staff work, many non-standard and local variations have been used. The following list will help:

2iC	Second-in-Command
A1 Echelon	Immediate replenishment of combat supplies
A2 Echelon	Further back planned replenishment of combat supplies
Adjt	Adjutant, a unit's commanding officer's staff officer
Adv	Advance
AGRA	Army Group Royal Artillery, a corps' artillery 'division', heavy, medium and field regiments plus anti-aircraft guns
Amn	Ammunition
AP	Armour Piercing
APDS	Armour Piercing Discarding Sabot, anti-tank ammunition
Assy Area	Assembly area, where troops regroup (e.g. tanks, infantry and gunners) for an operation prior to moving to the FUP
A/Tk	(+ variants) Anti-tank
AVRE	Armoured Vehicle Royal Engineer
Axis	The central direction of advance
B Echelon	The entry point of combat supplies into a unit's logistic infrastructure
BCR	Battle Casualty Replacement
Bde	Brigade (British) equivalent to a US or German regiment
Bn	Battalion
Br	Bridge
Bty	Battery
Cas	Casualties
Casevac	Casualty evacuation
CCP	Casualty Clearing Post
C in C	Commander in Chief
Civ	Civilian
CL	Centre Line or axis of advance
CO	Commanding Officer*

*Today the distinction between CO and OC is well-defined, with the former commanding a unit such as a battalion and the latter a sub-unit such as a company, but in many British Second World War memoirs and documents they are transposed or used inconsistently.

Co-ax	Coaxial machinegun mounted in tanks alongside the main armament
Conc	Concentrate, also Concentration Area, where units assigned to an operation gather before moving forward to the assy area
Comd	Command
Coord	Coordinate
Coy	Company
Cpl	Corporal
CPO	Command Post Officer (artillery)
CSM	Company Sergeant Major
D Day	The day on which an operation begins
Dem	Demolition
Dets	Detachments
DF	Defensive fire, pre-planned artillery, mortar or medium machinegun target areas on likely enemy approaches, etc.
Div	Division
DP	Distribution point (logistic)
DR	Dispatch rider also 'Don R' or 'Don Romeo'
Ech	Echelon, normally referring to fighting echelon and logistic echelons of a unit
En	Enemy
Enfilade	Fire from a flank
Fd Regt	Field Regiment RA
FOB	Forward officer Bombardment – naval gunfire
FOO	Forward Observation Officer - artillery
FUP	Forming Up Place
Fwd	Forward
Gd	Guard typically advanced, flank or rear guard
Gr	Grenadier
H-hour	The hour (time) at which an operation starts
HE	High Explosive
Inf	Infantry
Int	Intelligence
KIA	Killed in action
KO	Knocked out
LAD	Light Aid Detachment
LCA	Landing Craft Assault
LCpl	Lance Corporal
LCT	Landing Craft Tank
Ldr	Leader
Line	Field telephone wire
MG	Machine gun
MMG	Medium machine gun

MSR	Main Supply Route
O Group	Orders group, the assembly of subordinate commanders for the issue of orders
OC	Officer Commanding
OP	Observation Post
P Hour	Time of a parachute drop
PIAT	Projector Infantry Anti-Tank
Pl	Platoon
Posn	Position
Pt	Point
Pte	Private (rank)
Pz	Panzer
RAP	Regimental Aid Post
Rd	Road
Regt *or* Rgt	Regiment
RHA	Royal Horse Artillery
RMO	Regimental Medical Officer
RSO	Regimental Signals Officer
RV	Rendezvous point
SA	Small Arms
SB	Stretcher bearer
Sec *or* Sect	Section
Shellrep	Report of enemy shelling, used to locate enemy batteries
Sgt	Sergeant
Sitrep	Situation Report
SL	Start Line
Smk	Smoke
SP	Self Propelled
Sub-unit	Company, squadron or battery sized unit
Sups	Supplies
Sqn	Squadron
Tac	Tactical, usually used in the context of a tactical headquarters
Tgt	Target
Tk	Tank
Tp	Troop
Tpt	Transport
Unit	An infantry battalion or a British artillery or armoured regiment
Wef	With effect
WIA	Wounded in action
X Rds	Crossroads
Yd/yds	Yards

A busy scene in the Second Army's rear area.

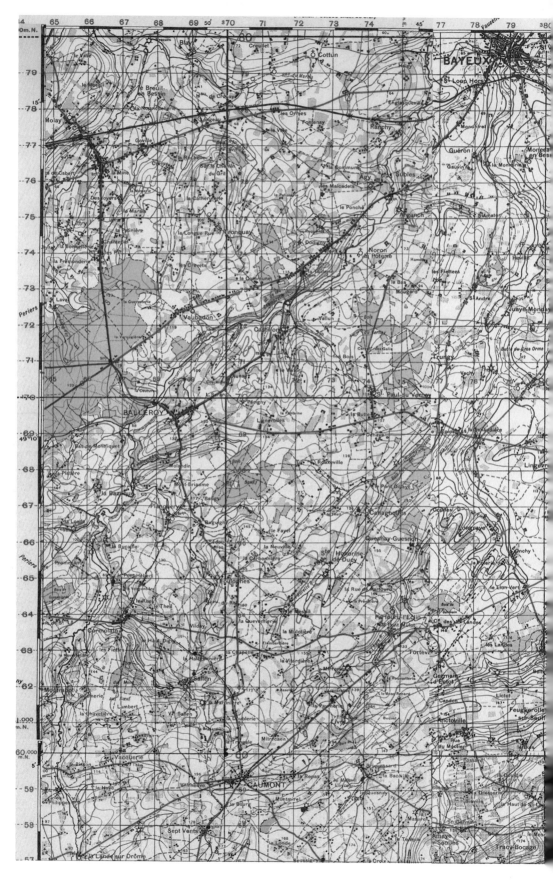

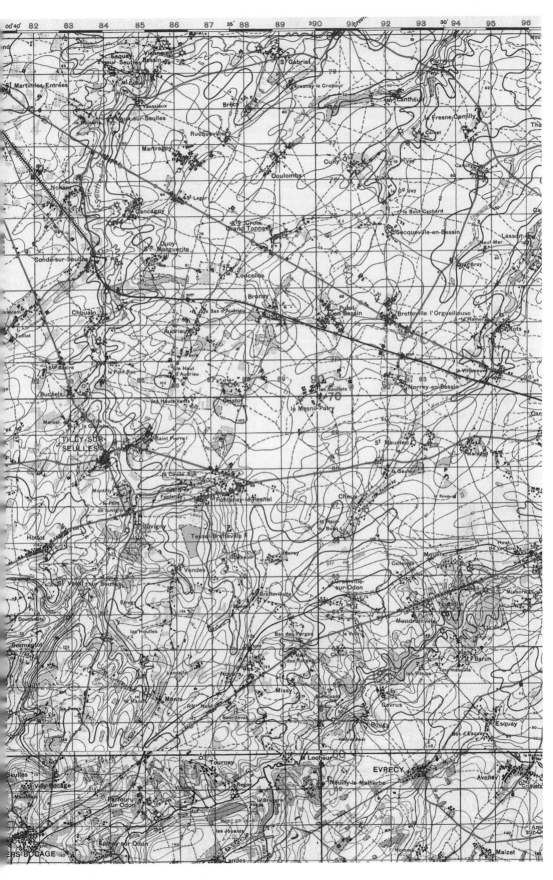

Inland from the beaches. A 22 Armoured Brigade halftrack passes a military police traffic point.

Chapter One

Planning and Preparations

In the dark days of 1940 Winston Churchill ordered the raising of a Combined Operations headquarters, with one of its tasks being to study 'the problems associated with returning to the Continent'. Significant work, however, did not begin until 1942 following the agreement with the USA over the Germany first policy. Lieutenant General Sir Frederick Morgan, who had formed a good working relationship with senior American officers as the commander I Corps in the Mediterranean, was much to his surprise appointed as Chief of Staff Supreme Allied Commander (COSSAC (Designate)) in March 1943.[1]

Under General Morgan's leadership, a tri-service, principally Anglo-American COSSAC staff, assembled in Norfolk House, London, and began serious planning only months in advance of the QUADRANT Conference held in Canada during August 1943. Allied leaders approved his appreciation, outline plan and that the location for the invasion of North-West Europe would be Normandy. With a target date of May 1944, the COSSAC planners worked to a very tight schedule to elaborate the plan for the enormous undertaking and prepare for its execution.

The plan for OVERLORD that COSSAC developed was based on the resources and lift, both sea and air, which were to be available on 1 May 1944. A corps of the US First Army was to land over three beaches (Sword, Juno and Gold) with three divisions, one each of US, British and Canadian troops. When Montgomery was shown the plan by Churchill in North Africa on New Year's Eve 1943, he did not like it and delivered a closely-argued critique to the prime minister the following morning.

On assumption of command of 21st Army Group he addressed his concerns, not least the narrow frontage of the landing at just 15 miles, and the small scale of the undertaking in comparison to the likely German reaction. General Morgan had been beset by both national and service agendas, which had limited the resources that were made available for his plan but with absolute priority now afforded to OVERLORD, the scale of the amphibious operation was expanded. This involved increasing the landings to five divisions, with the insertion of Omaha and Utah beaches and dropping three rather than one airborne division on a frontage of some 70 miles. The trade-off was that an extra month of preparation was required, pushing D-Day back to early June 1944.

In his campaign plan Montgomery aimed to seize and maintain the initiative in order to pre-empt the inevitable German counter-strokes. Fully aware that he

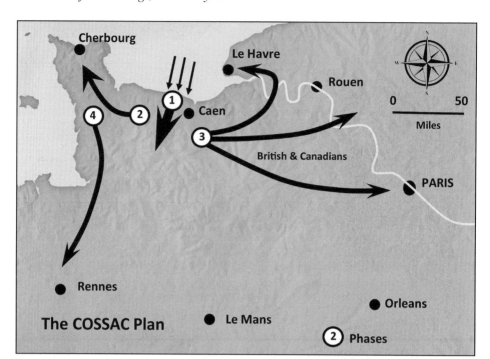

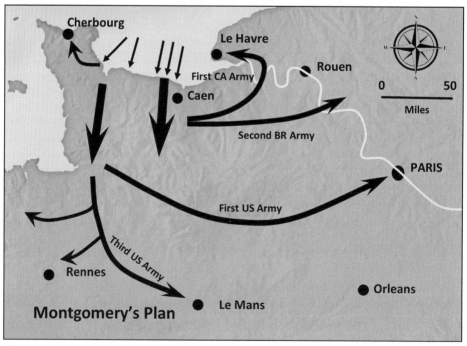

The contrasting plans.

Lieutenant General Sir Frederick Morgan.

needed a deep-water, all-weather port that could handle the tonnages required by the two armies that would grow to 1 million men, General Bradley's US First Army's highest priority was securing Cherbourg. A second advance by his army was to be directed south on St Lô, but the main responsibility for operations to cover the capture of Cherbourg was that of General Dempsey's British Second Army, which was to draw and fix German panzer formations against the eastern part of the lodgement. With the news from Anzio in mind, to achieve this, General Dempsey's D-Day divisions were required to advance rapidly and seize key terrain around the village of Évrecy (I Corps) and the town of Villers-Bocage (XXX Corps). It was expected that if these objectives were seized on D-Day and fully secured by D+3 or D+4, they would disrupt both German defences and counter-attacks, create room in the beachhead for the build-up and provide a basis for an early break-out.

In a letter Montgomery explained his concept to his army commanders Bradley and Dempsey:

1. In Operation OVERLORD an uncertain factor is the speed at which the enemy will be able to concentrate his mobile and armoured divisions against us for counter-attack.

   On our part we must watch the situation carefully, and must not get our main bodies so stretched that they would be unable to hold against

General Montgomery, commander of 21st Army Group.

determined counter-attack; on the other hand, having seized the initiative by our initial landing, we must ensure that we keep it.

2. The best way to interfere with the enemy concentrations and counter-measures will be to push forward fairly powerful armoured-force thrusts on the afternoon of D-Day.

If two such forces, each consisting of an Armd Bde Group, were pushed forward on each Army front to carefully chosen areas, it would be very difficult for the enemy to interfere with our build-up; from the areas so occupied, patrols and recces would be pushed <u>further</u> afield, and this would tend to delay enemy movement towards the lodgement area.

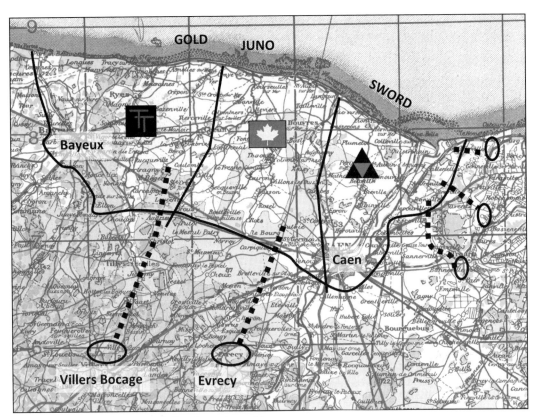

The D-Day objective including forward patrol bases.

      The whole effect of such aggressive tactics would be to retain the initiative ourselves and to cause alarm in the minds of the enemy.

3. To be successful, such tactics must be adopted on D-Day; to wait till D plus 1 would be to lose the opportunity, and also to lose the initiative.

      Armoured units and brigades must be concentrated quickly as soon as ever the situation allows after the initial landing on D-Day; this may not be too easy, but plans to effect such concentrations must be made and every effort made to carry them out; speed and boldness are then required, and the armoured thrusts must force their way inland.

4. The result of such tactics will be the establishment of firm bases well in advance of our own main bodies; if their location is carefully thought out, the enemy will be unable to by-pass them. I am prepared to accept almost any risk in order to carry out these tactics. I would risk even the total loss of the armoured brigade groups – which in any event is not really possible; the delay they would cause to the enemy before they could be destroyed would be quite enough to give us time to get our main bodies well ashore and re-organised for strong offensive action.

      And as the main bodies move forward their task will be simplified by the fact that armoured forces are holding firm on important areas in front.

5. Army Commanders will consider the problem in the light of the above remarks and will inform me of their plans to carry out these tactics.[2]

The result of these armoured thrusts was referred to as 'patrol bases' *vis* paragraph 2 above in most accounts.

In Lieutenant General Bucknall's XXX Corps' operation order, Montgomery's instruction was framed as 'Exploit as far as VILLERS-BOCAGE 8157 with a strong forward body containing armour and commanded by Commander 8 Armoured Brigade' (code-word PENDA) and that subsequently 'The maximum amount of offensive action by mobile forces will be carried out in front of these firm bases.'[3]

Phase 2 of XXX Corps' plan (code-word PARTRIDGE) would see '7th Armoured Division, with 56 Infantry Brigade under command, advancing from its assembly area is to join 8 Armoured Brigade in the area of VILLERS-BOCAGE' during D+3/D+4, which would fully secure the firm base.

Festung Europa

One of the attractions of Lower Normandy at the time when COSSAC recommended it as the place to invade was that it was relatively lightly defended. In late 1943, however, with the certainty of Allied invasion of North-West Europe, Hitler had issued *Führerbefehl* 51, which gave impetus to the building of the Atlantic Wall otherwise known as Fortress Europe or *Festung Europa*:

> All signs point to an offensive on the Western Front no later than spring, and perhaps earlier.
>
> For that reason, I can no longer justify the further weakening of the West in favour of other theatres of war. I have therefore decided to strengthen the defences in the West, particularly at places where we shall launch our long-range [V-weapon] war against England. For those are the very points at which the enemy must and will attack: there – unless all indications are misleading – the decisive invasion battle will be fought.

Along with the orders came a new Army Group commander. At the same time that Montgomery and Eisenhower returned from the Mediterranean, *Feldmarschall* Rommel took up the post of Inspector General of the Atlantic Wall. His responsibilities extended beyond his own Army Group B in Northern France and Belgium covering both the Atlantic and the North Sea coasts. What he saw failed to impress him, despite the best efforts of the Todt labour organization and its much-publicized works around the Pas-de-Calais. Building on his experience of operating against the Allies with air superiority in the Mediterranean, Rommel assessed that he would have to defeat the enemy invasion on the beaches. To that end, with incredible vigour, Rommel set about constructing what he described as a 'devil's garden' of defences. He drove his soldiers and workers hard and, at times, despite supply difficulties, they worked in shifts twenty-four hours a day. In six months, they laid the majority of the 1.2 million tons of steel and poured 17.3 million cubic yards of concrete used in the construction of *Festung Europa* and produced a crust of mutually-supporting defended localities. All along the coast, these localities were surrounded by more than 4 million anti-tank and

Feldmarschall Rommel conducting an inspection of the Atlantic Wall during the winter of 1943–44.

anti-personnel mines, while on the beaches, 500,000 obstacles of various types were constructed.

In the run-up to the invasion, German commanders had a spirited debate over the role and location of the panzer divisions. Rommel, having felt the lash of Allied air fighter-bombers in the Mediterranean, believed that the panzer divisions would be unable to assemble and make a timely move to battle while subjected to Allied air interdiction sorties. Rather than having the panzer divisions located in the centre of France, Rommel advocated a 'string of pearls' deployment just inland from the beaches, from where the panzers could counter-attack at the crucial time and place, early in the battle, while the Allies struggled to establish a beachhead. Although 'penny packeting' is contrary to the credo of any armoured commander, he argued that this deployment would defeat the invasion. Senior panzer commanders, with their Eastern Front experience, disagreed and both sides vigorously lobbied Hitler. The result was that the Führer partly supported both sides, satisfying neither, and insisted that his personal authority was required before any panzer formation was redeployed or committed to battle. Rommel had, however, successfully argued the case for control of three of the eight panzer formations in the west, with the remainder split between Panzer Group West and I SS Panzer Corps. Consequently, there was no coherent plan for the panzers. It is no wonder that von Rundstedt complained: 'As C-in-C West, the only authority I had was to change the guard at my front gate.' Milton Shulman, having studied the German chain of command, wrote:

> When the invasion began there was, therefore, neither enough armour to push the Allies back off the beaches in the first few hours, nor was there an adequate striking force to act as an armoured reserve later on. No better

design for a successful Allied landing could have been achieved than this [German] failure to concentrate the armour in the West along one unified and determined course.

Thanks to ULTRA, the radio intercepts that were decrypted at Bletchley Park, the Allies were monitoring large parts of this debate. Not only that, they had Field Marshal von Rundstedt's full appreciation and plan for the defence of Normandy that he had sent to Berlin via the Lorenz attachment.[4] Other decrypts, along with SOE and Resistance information, indicated movement of troops into north-western France. Among the enemy formations identified was the arrival of

the *Panzer Lehr* armoured division from Germany into an area north of the Loire aboard thirty-five trains between 3 and 9 May, while others moved forward to the coast. Of great importance was the location of the 352nd Infantry Division which had been identified inland at St Lô, but there was doubt as to its location as D-Day approached. Brigadier 'Bill' Williams, Montgomery's senior intelligence officer, wrote in a highly-classified summary just before D-Day:

Panzer Lehr divisional badge.

The evidence about 352nd Division is flimsy. For some time now in other areas coastal divisions have been narrowing their sectors while divisions, the role of which had hitherto been read as layback, have nosed forward into the gap provided by the reduced responsibility of the coastal divisions. 711th Division on the extreme left of Fifteenth Army is a case in point, for it is apparent that elements of 346th Division have eased themselves into its former holding on the right just west of the Seine. The evidence that the same has happened on the left in the case of the 716th Division is slender indeed. A single soldier from 352nd Division is reported to have been making for Arromanches in March. That 716th Division has followed the pattern of coastal readjustments is not substantiated; yet it should not be surprising if we discovered that it had two regiments in the line and one in reserve, while on its left 352nd Division had one regiment up and two to play.

Williams was nearly correct. It was actually two regiments up in the Omaha sector and one in play, which was LXXXIV Corps reserve, *Kampfgruppe* Meyer. The 352nd Division was a newly-formed field grade division rather than a lower establishment and lower-quality coastal division, and as such it would be a problem for the 50th Division as its right flank overlapped into the Gold Beach area.

Monty's Men

Second Army that was going to execute Montgomery's great design was a mixed bag of troops. On the one hand there were the Mediterranean veterans, including the 50th Infantry Division and 8 Armoured Brigade, which Montgomery had brought back with him, and on the other there were formations that had only trained and retrained since 1939, plus those who had not been out of the UK since 1940. Montgomery explained:

> The army then in England lacked battle experience and had tended to become theoretical rather than practical. Officers did not understand those tricks of the battlefield which mean so much to junior leaders and which save so many lives. In the last resort the battle is won by the initiative and skill of regimental officers and men, and without these assets you fail – however good the higher command. Some very experienced fighting formations had returned to England, however, from the Mediterranean theatre at the end of the Sicily campaign. By exchanging officers between these formations and those which had never left the country, I tried to spread such battle experience as was available over the widest possible area. Again, this was unpopular, but was more readily accepted when I had explained the reason.[5]

Where possible this was achieved by swapping commanders between battalions of the same regiment but where this was not possible, for example, reluctant senior NCOs from the 50th Northumbrian Division found themselves transferred to what they regarded as 'alien battalions' of, for instance, 43rd Wessex Division.

50th Division's units had returned from the Mediterranean understrength; consequently, the loss of experienced officers and NCOs plus an influx of replacements meant that the division was not as 'veteran' as was often assumed. For instance, in the case of 1 Dorsets of 231 Brigade, only a third of each infantry platoon had fought in Sicily and Italy.

It wasn't just individuals that were moved but formations as well. In the case of the latter, 231 Brigade (also Mediterranean veterans) joined the 50th Division, along with a fourth infantry brigade, 56 Brigade. This temporary attachment of a fourth brigade was due to the extent of the division's tasks, which included linking up with US V Corps 10 miles to the west near Port-en-Bessin. In the case of 8 Armoured Brigade they lost two experienced armoured regiments and, left with just the veteran Nottinghamshire Sherwood Rangers Yeomanry, they were joined by the 4th/7th Dragoon Guards who fought in 1940, and the war-raised

Formation badges: 50th Division, 8 Armoured Brigade and 56 Infantry Brigade.

24th Lancers. In addition, there were some exchanges of manpower. Once again, this brigade was not as veteran as commonly supposed.

Preparations for the Invasion

When the 50th Division and 8 Brigade reassembled after their disembarkation leave the emphasis was on taking in replacements and drawing new vehicles, weapons and equipment to replace those left in the Mediterranean. All that changed, however, when Montgomery replaced his veteran formations in key roles. The 49th Division, which had been earmarked for the assault on Gold Beach, were replaced by the 50th Division, which had carried out the assault landing on Sicily six months earlier and 231 Brigade had made a second assault landing on the toe of Italy at Pizzo. Trips to Scottish lochs for landing craft familiarization at the Combined Operations Training Centre told the veterans as well as any 'Most Secret' briefing that they would again be at the forefront of the action.

Amphibiousness of a different kind awaited four of 8 Armoured Brigade's squadrons, two each from the Sherwood Rangers Yeomanry (SRY) and the 4th/7th Dragoon Guards (4th/7th DG): an introduction to the DD Tank. Second Lieutenant Stuart Hills of C Squadron of the SRY was among them:

> Soon news came through that C Squadron, of which I was part, and B Squadron would undergo some special tank training for the invasion. There appeared to be considerable secrecy and mystery surrounding this training, which suggested that it might not be too savoury. Each squadron consisted of four HQ tanks and four troops each of three tanks, of which mine, No. 4 Troop, was one ... Our destination for this training turned out to be the seafront at Great Yarmouth, where we took over a row of boarding houses. Here we learned to our considerable surprise that we were to train on tanks which would swim – a somewhat alarming prospect as we tried to imagine tanks being launched thousands of yards from the shore and waddling in like so many overgrown ducks to attack the beaches of Europe in support of the infantry.
>
> The training tank was a Valentine as the Shermans were not yet ready. In anything other than in calm conditions, the Valentine would ship water alarmingly and its bilge pump could barely cope. Fortunately, we never had to take it to sea, but inevitably there were accidents. Once, a driver misheard an order to form line abreast as one to deflate. The tank sank in the middle of the lake, although all the crew escaped. Unsurprisingly, there were many grumbles from men who thought that 'being a bloody sailor in a bloody tank' was taking patriotism too far, but requests for danger pay, which was enjoyed by numerous navy personnel, was turned down by an unsympathetic War Office. I perched precariously on my bridge at the back of the tank, which was certainly better than sitting inside it, and peered over the canvas screen. I realised fairly quickly that the screen might protect me from the salt spray, but not from a German bullet or shell.[6]

A Valentine DD Tank with its screen down.

Launching a Valentine DD from an LCT (Landing Craft Tank).

Meanwhile, 1 Dorsets reassembled after leave in Essex, in camps and billets around Halstead. Major 'Speedy' Bredin wrote:

> At the end of February, the Battalion moved to Southwold, and our training had already begun to acquire a fairly strong 'combined operations' flavour; we realised we were 'for it' again … Early in March the Battalion took part in an exercise (known as BULLOCK[7]) to demonstrate the types of obstacles likely to be encountered on a hostile coast, and the latest mechanical methods to overcome them.
>
> The next move was to the Combined Training Centre on Inveraray Loch. It had been decided, 'on a high level', that the 50th Division were to take the place of another formation in the assault in Operation OVERLORD. It immediately became obvious that the 231st Brigade would be, for the third time, an assault brigade – and so it was.
>
> Time was considered to be short, so our course at Inveraray was rather rushed through – it was just as well we had been through that sort of thing twice before. We started with lectures and craft training, followed by 'Dryshod' exercises on the 17th March … More ambitious waterborne exercises followed the 'Dryshod' ones, notably 'Exercise NEWTON BA' and 'Exercise ARDNO'. The last-named, carried out on the 22nd March, was a brigade exercise, designed to approximate roughly to our operational task.[8]

After their abbreviated amphibious training package, 231 Brigade joined the rest of the division and the armoured brigade in and around the New Forest, near the Force G embarkation points on Southampton Water. 8th Battalion, Durham Light Infantry, was in the tented Toothill Camp near Romsey. Major Lewis recorded that

> General Montgomery was continually seeking to improve the standard of training in the divisions which made up 21st Army Group. He gave them no respite; formations like 50th Division, with years of battle experience, put in long, hard days of training alongside divisions which had not been overseas. On April 17th the 8th Battalion took part in Exercise SMASH, which had been designed primarily to test the naval plan for the landing and handling of the Beach Groups. The infantry did not go aboard the landing craft but were guided by men of the Beach Groups through dummy minefields on the Dorset coast and so to an assembly area inland, near to Swanage. There followed a long, strenuous advance when the marching troops of 50th Division were driven really hard as they had been in North Africa and Sicily. Several mock battles were fought, and the exercise was watched by General Montgomery and the senior Naval and Air Commanders, who seemed pleased with what they saw and the many lessons which had been learned.[9]

As assault troops, the divisional group received numerous visitors as D-Day approached. Private Bill Willis of 2 Devons was in a camp adjacent to Lord

Montague's palace at Beaulieu when General Montgomery came on one of his stage-managed visits:

> We were ordered to close in around Monty who stood up in his car and looking down on us, spoke to us in his clipped voice that we knew well from newsreels. But the older soldiers – veterans – amongst us didn't like being talked down to in this way. There was muttering in the crowd around Monty that was silenced by glowers from the sergeant majors but afterwards as he drove around the camp he was booed and jeered by some. I suppose they didn't fancy their chances of surviving another assault landing and him telling us what he expected was the final straw.

As on his previous visit to the battalion in Italy, where a 'glum' was seen off by the promise of a return to England, Montgomery restored morale by ordering railway warrants for the battalion, which saw the Devons home on an unexpected weekend leave. Shortly afterwards, a very different style of visit from General Eisenhower completed the restoration of morale. Private David Powis recalled the Supreme Commander's visit:

> The General chatted to each man in turn of the front row, and even spoke through the ranks to those in the rear, jesting about their being stuck out of sight at the back, and causing laughter and comical answers to be given by them, which he shared with the addition of his own witty replies. He continued along the Brigade in a similar manner for some considerable time,

A typical scene from one of Montgomery's pre-invasion visits.

then made a very impressive speech to all the 231 Brigade before responding to our salute and making his departure.

Many said afterwards how much they liked the American General and were glad that he had been chosen to take over as Supreme Commander.[10]

The stage-managed 'three cheers' of a Montgomery visit were overtaken by spontaneous applause from the assembled brigade as Eisenhower drove off.

In April, many of 1 Dorsets had the strange experience of conducting live firing assaults on the country surrounding their home towns and villages along Studland Bay, while 1 Hampshires, during 50th Division/Task Force G's final rehearsal, Exercise FABIUS in early May, attacked the Hampshire coast at Hayling Island. In this period the brigade

saw a good deal of our affiliated armour, the Sherwood Rangers (Notts Yeomanry), an experienced armoured regiment, who had seen service in the

Exercise FABIUS: Shermans disembarking without enemy interference or a rough sea.

desert and in Italy. The gunners of 90 Field Regiment were unfortunately too busy most of the time – what with trying to get the SP guns into LCTs and, having succeeded in doing that, trying to fire them from the moving craft.

With the arrival of May, orders marked 'BIGOT TOP SECRET' came down the chain of command and reached brigade level. Maps of the actual coast with bogus names were initially circulated to allow planning while retaining some security. The D-Day secret was, however, safe as the prohibited area along the south coast and the capture and turning of German spies had both been highly effective. As Lieutenant Colonel 'Cosmo' Nevill, who commanded 2 Devons, recalled:

> On May 10th the three COs attended a secret conference in the brigade briefing room. The brigade commander described the plan for D-Day and gave the outline plan for the brigade. These preliminary details were given well in advance to allow time for COs to study maps, air photos, and the mass of information which was constantly coming in.
>
> Conference followed conference: the CO and the battalion intelligence officer were to be seen daily, coming and going, tightly clasping weighty briefcases as if their lives depended on their security, which in fact they did.[11]

Plans for the Advance to Villers-Bocage

Before they could execute their advance to Villers-Bocage, 8 Armoured Brigade with four squadrons of Duplex Drive Shermans was to lead the 50th Division's assault brigades ashore on Gold Beach. They would subsequently support the division's advance to objectives which included Bayeux, points along the N13 Caen-Bayeux road, the Longues-sur-Mer Battery and link up with the Americans south of Port-en-Bessin. After that, on receipt of the code-word YAR issued by 50th Division, the brigade and those units that would come under command would concentrate for the advance on Villers-Bocage at a point designated depending on the situation. Brigadier Cracroft described the PENDA plan:

> During the planning of the invasion of Normandy I was warned that as soon as the initial objectives had been obtained, I should be put in command of a Mobile Column to exploit, as an independent force, with the objective of capturing the centre of communications at VILLERS-BOCAGE. I was asked to submit a plan. I had maps and air photographs to work from.
>
> In making my plans I took into consideration the following factors:
>
> a. I wanted one or two intermediate objectives which I could hold tactically whilst I regrouped my forces if necessary.
> b. I wanted two lines of advance, so that, if opposition or obstacles were met on one, I could switch to the other.
> c. I wanted to avoid using main roads because I thought that on these I was likely to run head-on into enemy reinforcements moving forward and should get involved in battles which would divert me from my objective.

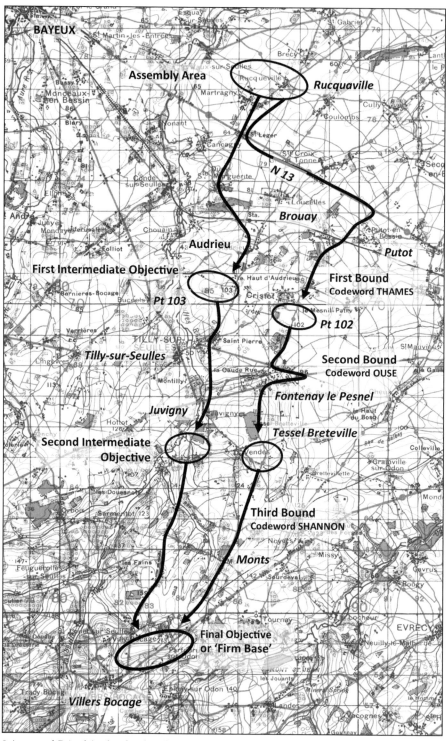

8 Armoured Brigade's plan for the advance to Villers-Bocage.

Brigadier Cracroft, commander of 8 Armoured Brigade.

d. I thought that by staying as far forward as possible I should have a shorter distance to go and a shorter line of communication to keep open.

Accordingly, I recommended my start line should be the main road BAYEUX-CAEN. My intermediate objectives were to be:

I. Points 103 and 102.
II. The TESSEL-BRETTEVILLE feature.
III. High ground north-east of VILLERS-BOCAGE.

My axis of advance was to be:

Right Road:	COULOMBS	Left Road:	BRONAY
	LOUCELLES		CRISTOT
	AUDRIEU		FONTENAY-LE-PESNEL
	JUVIGNY		VILLERS-BOCAGE
	VILLERS-BOCAGE		

This plan was approved, and decided that the Mobile Column should be formed as soon as possible after the D-Day objectives had been captured.[12]

A transcript of 8 Armoured Brigade's operation order is in Appendix II.

The Bocage Country

While there were pockets of thick country across the Second Army's area, particularly around villages and in river valleys, south and south-east of Bayeux lay the eastern extension of the bocage or hedgerow country. It was into this difficult ground that 8 Armoured Brigade would be launched. The 4th/7th Dragoon Guards' historian describes the ground in which they and the infantry fought:

> The country was never anything else but close, consisting of a mass of small fields, interspersed with high thick hedges, often formed on thick earthen banks; a large proportion of the fields themselves are orchards with small bushy apple trees set close together; most of the roads are sunken country lanes, very narrow and bounded on either side by high hedges.[13]

The impact of the bocage on the conduct of operations, particularly where armour was concerned, was as follows:

> Rarely could a tank see more than 400 yards and was absolutely ideal for defence and when it was resolutely defended ... one German machine-gunner and a couple of snipers [isolated riflemen] could prevent an entire battalion moving a hundred yards between one hedge and the next until they were either killed by a direct hit (and as it was usually impossible to spot them, this was unlikely), or they were physically dug out of their hiding places in a hand-to-hand fight.
>
> In conditions such as these, not only were the odds against the attacker and casualties high in proportion, but it was extremely difficult for a tank to watch out for its infantry even when moving with them.

The Normandy bocage: a patchwork of small fields divided by hedges and banks.

Embarkation

Finally, the long wait was over and orders were written and ready for dissemination, as recalled by Colonel Nevill:

> On Monday May 29th, all invasion troops were confined to their camps. Each camp was surrounded by barbed wire, and large numbers of security police effectively stopped all contact with the outside world. At this moment, every man was let into the secret of the plan for D-Day, with the exception of two facts – where the landing was going to take place and the actual date ... However, everyone deduced that the landing would be made in France, because we were issued with French money.

The plan to embark the troops aboard Task Force G efficiently and quickly was, if anything, more complicated than the actual landing plan! Organizing the arrival of units with their vehicles, stores and equipment at the correct landing craft in the reverse order to the assault required excellent staff work by the Combined Operations planners.

The commanding officer of 2 Devons described his battalion's by now well-rehearsed embarkation:

> At 1030 hours on the morning of 31st May the Battalion assault group, complete with all representatives of the supporting arms, fell in for the last time. The move in MT from the camp to Southampton went without a hitch. We were driven straight to the quay alongside which HMS *Glenroy* was lying ready to receive us. Tea was served to all ranks in the shed while the adjutant handed the many forms and detailed lists to the Embarkation Staff. Embarkation was completed in record time; each serial [landing craft load] was received on board by our Assistant Military Liaison Officer, and by the ship's Master at Arms; a Royal Marine acted as guide who not only led the serial to their correct deck, but also showed each commander the quickest way to the LCA [Landing Craft Assault] allotted to him. The efficiency with which the troops were received and stowed on board demonstrated the value of the close liaison which had been established with the officers and ratings of HMS *Glenroy*.

Once on board their landing ships and craft and at anchor out in the Solent, final details were revealed to all, including maps with the correct names and the latest air photographs. Private Powis recalled that

> One photograph was taken at such a low level that we could clearly see into a house with a distinct view of the pictures hanging over the bed, in a house situated to the rear of the beach area we were intending to land on ... Another photograph taken when the tide was high showed a horse-drawn cart ... on the beach ... this gave us comforting information that the fairly narrow stretch of dry beach could not be mined.

Shermans embarking on LCTs. The tank in the centre is dragging a Porpoise reserve ammunition sledge on board.

The DD tanks of 8 Armoured Brigade were among the last part of Force G to embark, in their case aboard Landing Craft Tank. Major Christopherson, one of the SRY's DD squadron commanders, wrote:

> The weather at the beginning of June was extremely cold and unpleasant, and we all kept wondering whether there would be a postponement. Sometimes I hoped there would be – a kind of urge to put off the evil hour – and at other times I had a longing to get cracking and to get the thing started. The answer was not long in coming. In the afternoon of Sunday June 4, the word came and quickly swept round the camp. We gathered our possessions, loaded what petrol, ammunition and food we immediately needed on our tanks and consigned the rest to the lorries of B Echelon. Then we moved in column out of the gate and down to the quay, where the LCTs waited for us.[14]

With a window in the poor weather that had delayed the invasion by twenty-four hours, forecast for the following morning, the invasion fleet sailed. Colonel Nevill described the scene:

> ... at 6 PM on June 5th, Force G (50th Division) weighed anchor and sailed west down the Solent. There was no hooting of ships' sirens; no cheering crowds as in the last war ... It was just like another rehearsal. The ships moved off in their allotted places. The Divisional Commander's ship HMS *Bulolo* led the field, followed by the Brigade Commander's frigate HMS *Nith*. We were third.
>
> ... In the distance out to sea, two immense fleets could be seen moving eastwards up the Channel. These were two more divisions linking up for the assault: truly a noble sight.

One of the Gold Beach air photographs complete with Germans on the beach.

As darkness fell, the ships of the various naval forces sailing from port all along the south coast converged on Point Zulu, the entry to the five swept lanes south across the Channel. Major Christopherson was aboard a rolling LCT:

> We talked quietly among ourselves and tried to snatch a few moments of sleep, but the tension and growing sense of excitement and anticipation made this impossible. The night was cold and the sea still quite choppy as the flat-bottomed LCT lost any protection from the English coast and began to slide about on the surface of the waves in mid-Channel. Many of us still felt sea-sick, despite the pills we had been issued to counter this, and we had by now been so long at sea that our sense of disorientation had grown. Mugs of hot soup were passed around and these gave us a momentary warmth. All of us were looking forward to the moment when we could leave the ships and sea behind us and get back onto dry land. Indeed, that anticipation overcame any accompanying nervousness about the prospect of going into action.

With the throb of marine diesel engines all around them, Task Force G headed to the enemy-held coast of Normandy.

Tank landing craft of Force G at anchor in the Solent waiting to go. In the centre is an 8 Armoured Brigade 17-pounder Firefly.

Chapter Two

D-Day: 6 June 1944

This chapter provides an overview of the 50th Division's operations to land on Gold Beach and their fight 8.5 miles inland on D-Day, but it focuses on the events that shaped the delay in launching 8 Armoured Brigade's mobile columns south to Villers-Bocage. It will be recalled that Montgomery's direction to his army commanders read: 'To be successful, such tactics must be adopted on D-Day; to wait till D plus 1 would be to lose the opportunity, and also to lose the initiative.'

After an uncomfortable and, for many, a sleepless night, the landing ships anchored 6 miles out to sea, between 0430 and 0510 hours, still before dawn. An hour later in the first light of day, the guns of the naval Bombardment Force opened fire on enemy gun batteries. For the infantry the first of the day's difficult tasks came at 0545 hours: the disembarkation from the 'mother ships' into the diminutive Landing Craft Assault (LCA). Heavily laden with full fighting order, climbing down the soaking wet scrambling nets and timing the jump into LCAs, which were being thrown around by the heavy seas, was no easy matter. Major Mott of C Company, 1 Hampshires, recalled the process of leaving HMT *Empire Arquebus*:

> We were called up over the blower: 'Serial 2042 – to your boat station – No. 4 boat station – Port side – now' and I led my boatload consisting mainly of coy HQ and an assault rifle section up to our LCA. All our heavy kit had been preloaded and needed a quick check before we could report all correct. Final goodbyes and good lucks before we were lowered into a lumpy sea … Everything was ominously quiet.

Second Lieutenant Holdsworth of 2 Devons was one of the unlucky ones who had to use a scrambling net to reach his LCA:

> Clambering down the side of the ship, hand over hand, gripping a suspended rope scrambling was, for me, if not the rest of the platoon, a particularly unpleasant and frightening experience. I had no head for heights, and I hated the sea. Without the military paraphernalia which we carried, it would have been bad enough. With it, it was like playing a team game of Russian roulette. Rifles, pouches, packs and bayonet scabbards each took their part in offering the chance of a speedy death by getting caught in the ropes or on someone else. And, to further complicate our individual balancing acts, the rope net which we held onto so grimly had a nasty habit of swaying against

LCAs assembling in front of the 'mother ships' during training in calm weather was easy, but off the coast of Normandy on D-Day it was a very different matter.

the movement of the ship and of becoming more slippery the nearer we got to the assault craft which were bobbing around like corks on the sea below us.

... Each of the craft carried a platoon of thirty men or their equivalent in supporting arms and staff ... In all I suppose it took some fifteen landing craft to carry the Devons to their mission.

In daylight the craft of the assault force formed up and began the hour-long transit to the beach. The leading landing craft passed through the line of bombarding ships, where the rolling blast of the 6in to 15in naval guns could be felt as much as heard. Years later one Dorset soldier commented: 'We had been told about the bombardment and the aim "to drench the beach with fire" but I had no idea it would be like this – it seemed to me at the time nothing could survive the pounding – how wrong I was.' This was just the beginning. The naval gunfire paused only long enough for flights of medium bombers to hit the coast, but due to the weather conditions three seconds were added to their bomb run, which placed the bombs too far inland to be useful.

The timings for the assault were as follows:

(1) H-hour 0725.
(2) Sunrise minus 40 [i.e. nautical twilight, 0530 hours] – preparatory bombardment of coast defences by RN. [0610 Strikes by medium bombers.]

(3) From H minus 60 [0625 hours] – preparatory bombardment by RN, SP [self-propelled] artillery and RAF [fighter-bombers].

(4) H minus 5 – DD squadrons arrive at firing positions on the beach.

(5) H-hour – armoured assault teams land.

(6) H plus 5 – leading companies of assault battalions land.

(7) H plus 20 – reserve companies of assault battalions land.

(8) H plus 45 – H plus 60 – reserve battalions of assault brigades land.

(9) H plus 60 – H plus 90 – armoured regiment, less DD squadrons land.

(10) H plus 60 – H plus 120 – SP artillery lands.

(11) H plus 120 – 47 (RM) CDO lands.[1]

At H-35 minutes, ninety-six 25-pounders, four regiments' worth of the Royal Artillery's guns, were conducting a run-in shoot from a range of 10,000 yards, all a part of drenching the beaches with fire. The self-propelled Sextons were aboard standard LCTs each adapted to carry two vehicles with sufficient ammunition to fire during the run-in ashore and then to come into action promptly once on dry land. They specifically engaged the beach and defences where the armour and infantry were to land. Checking fire just before H-hour, they sheared off to the rear of the flotilla of landing craft for their own landing at H+60 minutes. For the

The landing table for 231 Brigade bound for Jig Sector of Gold Beach. 69 Brigade, landing on King Sector, would have had a similar table.

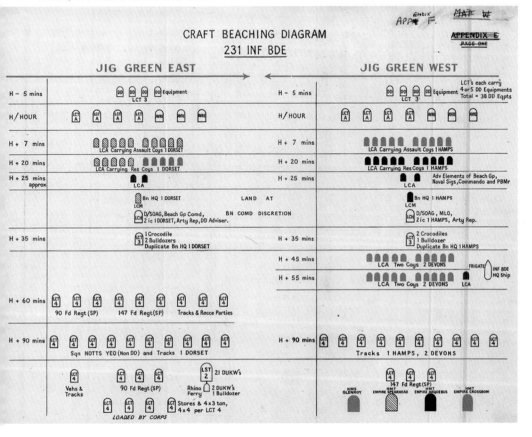

bombardment on Jig Beach, 147 (Essex Yeomanry) Field Regiment had an allocation of 3,800 rounds for the run-in. Sergeant Major Jack Villader Brown recalled:

> Everybody opened up, the noise was horrific, it was ear-shattering. In
> that running shoot, the guns got so hot the blokes could hardly handle
> them. Grease was running out of the breech-blocks and the empty cartridge
> cases were being thrown over the side. Each gun fired between 150 and
> 200 rounds – as soon as one's gone, you put another one in. We didn't have
> time to be afraid, you don't get time to think.[2]

The launch carrying 147 Regiment's Forward Observation Officer broke down.
Consequently, the significant German strongpoint *Wiederstandsnest* at Le Hamel
[WN-37], which enfiladed Jig Beach, was not engaged as planned. Instead, 147's
guns were taken under command of 90 Regiment in the shoot on the far less
significant WN-36. This early failure compounded by later misses by the Air
Force led to the assault infantry facing a protracted, unsupported battle against an
unsuppressed enemy in well-prepared positions. This was one of the root causes
of delays that prevented the advance by 8 Armoured Brigade on Villers-Bocage
on D-Day.

Meanwhile, as the assault flotilla approached the coast, the DD tanks aboard
the LCTs were prepared to be launched between 3,000 yards from the coast, but
such was the sea state that swimming this distance was clearly impractical. Troop
commander Stuart Hills explained:

> It quickly became clear to all of us that this would court disaster. The
> roughness of the sea, and the slow pace at which we would crawl through it,

A Sexton self-propelled 25-pounder gun of the 86th Field Regiment (Hertfordshire Yeomanry)
preserved at Ver-sur-Mer.

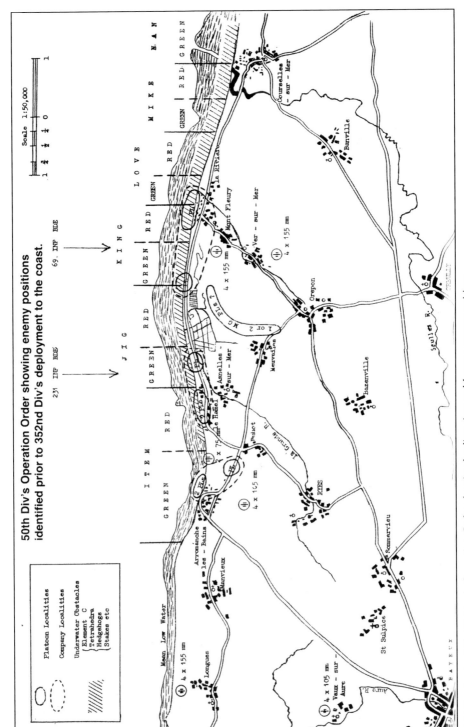

Gold Beach: the 50th Division's Operation Order showing landing sites and known enemy positions.

meant that we would simply be in the water for too long – and the longer we were there, the more chance there was of being struck by a wave that would swamp us, run down by another craft or even hit by German fire. (On Sword, a DD tank was run down by the LCT it had just left with the loss of most of its crew.) Furthermore, as we deployed towards the assault run, the planned discipline of the formation began to fragment. Through no fault of their own, some ships and craft began to lag behind, while others forced their way forward. To launch too far out risked not only sinking or being run down but also late arrival on the beach where the infantry so badly needed our protection.

As the assault force closed on Gold Beach, the bombardment reached its crescendo, with the inclusion of Hunt- and Fleet-class destroyers, plus specialist naval fire support craft. The bombardment was effective in doing much to undermine German morale, damage field defences and wire and detonating mines. However, even a direct hit on a concrete casemate by all but the heaviest shells did little damage, other than to the nerves of the occupants.

The Final Approach

With Force 6 winds and a heavy sea, the DD tanks were delayed and rather than a squadron's worth of fifteen Shermans coming in as an organized flotilla ahead of the engineers and each of the division's four assault battalions, depleted squadrons came in over a period of minutes. Some LCTs launched their DDs 800 yards out and the tanks swam in; others were dropped in close enough to wade ashore with their screens up, while some were landed on the beach. Lieutenant Hills was among those to be launched:

> The critical moment of launching was now upon us. I could see two AVRE Churchills[3] brewing up on the beach – the tanks had been completely destroyed, and their crews killed, by 88mm shells[4] which had ignited the explosives they had been carrying to clear obstacles – and I wondered if this would not soon be our fate too. We were the front tank on the LCT, poised at the top of the ramp and clearly silhouetted, a perfect target for the German gunners ...
>
> I gave the order, 'Go, go, go.' Geoff Storey moved into gear and we lumbered slowly down the ramp and flopped into the sea. Geoff engaged the propellers and we were on our way. I was still standing in my bridge position on the back of the tank, feeling terribly exposed and trying to peer over the canvas screen, while at the same time issuing orders to the driver and crew. The sea was rough and the struts holding the screen were hard-pressed to do their job properly; possibly the screen itself had been damaged by one of the shells. At any rate, without it we would not be able to keep afloat for long. We had gone about 50 to 70 yards in the water towards the beach when it became clear that something was seriously wrong and it certainly was not just the canvas screen: the tank was shipping water from the bottom. In the

driver's compartment, Geoff Storey was already knee-deep, and he shouted, 'We're taking water fast.' Arthur Reddish slipped into the co-driver's compartment and engaged the bilge pump . . .

It was clear that we had no chance whatsoever of making it to the beach. The Sherman DD tank was about to become the Sherman submarine. I gave the order to bail out or abandon ship. Corporal Footitt had the presence of mind to pull the ripcord to inflate our yellow rubber dinghy . . . The tank was now virtually awash, and we did not have long. I frantically scrabbled about inside the turret to retrieve my map-case, but without success. Trying to work quickly and calmly in a sinking tank is hard at any time and with shells dropping close by impossible.

Hills' tank was one of eight Sherwood Rangers Yeomanry DD tanks that failed to reach the beach.

69 Brigade heading for King Beach had the village of Ver-sur-Mer and the holiday shacks on its western edge to guide their craft into the correct place for landing, but 231 Brigade had low sand dunes bereft of landmarks to steer for. Consequently, they landed around 800 yards east of where they should have been. Contributory factors were a strong breeze and current that sent them to the east, and probably in subsequent landing serials a desire to avoid the fire emanating from the unsuppressed WN-37 strongpoint.

On King the 4th/7th DG lost five out of thirty tanks but the unexpected appearance of the DD tanks on the beach had the desired effect on German morale and did much to suppress the enemy defences while the engineer's breaching teams came ashore at H-hour, followed by the infantry at H+5 minutes. The 4th/7th DG DDs knocked out a bunker housing an 88mm gun that was picking off armoured vehicles on the beach.

There was, however, a problem on Jig Beach and that was that in WN-37 at Le Hamel, which it will be recalled had been missed by the bombardment, contained a 1939-vintage Polish 77mm (75mm) anti-tank gun that enfiladed and dominated the 1,700 yards of the beach.[5] Its first victims were the specialist armour of the 79th Armoured Division, which lost three of its six vehicles to flanking shots. Major Mott landed with his company of Hampshiremen five minutes after the engineers:

We had the word to get ready and tension was at its peak when the ramp went out. I was with the second in command of the company, a captain. He went out with me close behind. We were in the sea to the tops of our thighs, floundering ashore with other assault platoons to left and right of us. Mortar bombs and shells were erupting in the sand and I could hear the burp of Spandau light machine guns through the din. There were no shouts, only the occasional cry as men were hit and went down.

The beach was filled with half-bent running figures and we knew from experience that the safest place was to get as near to Jerry as we could. A near one blasted sand over me and my radio went dead, riddled with shrapnel.

A sweet rancid smell, never forgotten, was everywhere; it was the smell of burned explosive, torn flesh and ruptured earth.

High up on the beach a flail tank was knocked out; I saw B Company's Headquarters group take cover behind it just as a shell scored a direct hit on them. They were gone in a blast of smoke out of which came cartwheeling through the air a torn shrieking body of a stretcher-bearer with the red cross on his arm clearly discernible.

The Hampshires landed around the battered WN-36 and, having dashed across the fire-raked beach, a company was pinned down in the sand dunes and the commanding officer seriously wounded. The Dorsets, on the other hand, touched down further east around the lightly-defended point, landing out of the

Men of 1 Dorsets photographed by an illicit camera in their LCA on their way to Jig Beach.

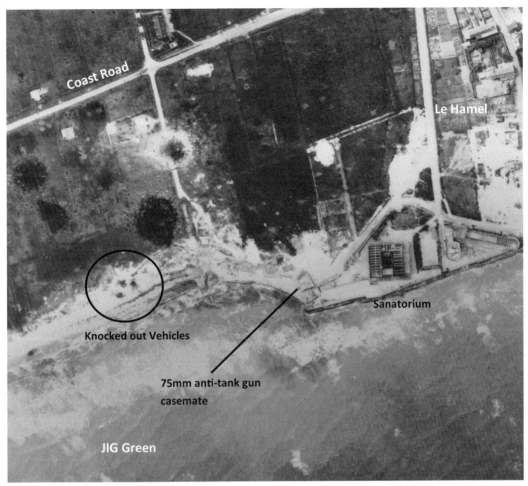

Coast Road

Le Hamel

Sanatorium

Knocked out Vehicles

75mm anti-tank gun
casemate

JIG Green

An air photograph taken on D-Day showing the strongpoint of WN-37 and three knocked-out vehicles of the 79th Armoured Division's Breaching Team 1.

worst of the fire, and were across the beach and into the dunes with few casualties. The beach here was backed by an extensive marsh, so the companies turned right and made their way through the dunes to take WN-36 but when they arrived, they found it was already in the hands of the Hampshires.

The result of the mislanding and the work of the WN-37 anti-tank gun was a difficulty in getting vehicles off the beach through a single viable exit, thus denying 231 Brigade's infantry all-arms support for vital hours and delaying progress inland.

On King Beach, 69 Brigade's assault battalions, 6 Green Howards and 5th East Yorks, were ashore, with the 5th fighting in Ver-sur-Mer, while just to the west of the village, Sergeant Major Stanley Hollis of the Green Howards' D Company was earning D-Day's only Victoria Cross. Advancing from the beach, on his own he promptly cleared the Mont Fleury Battery, which had been effectively suppressed by the naval bombardment but was showing signs of coming back into action. The reserve battalion, 7 Green Howards, came ashore at 0815 hours and

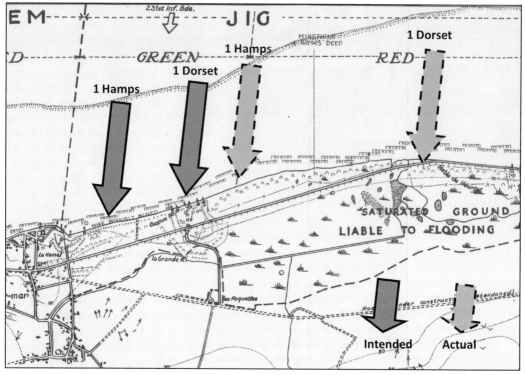

Intended and actual landing of 231 Brigade.

was advancing inland, with the Shermans of the 4th/7th DG seen climbing Meuvaines Ridge. The brigade made such good progress that an air observation post aircraft thought they could not possibly be British and engaged with naval gunfire. Fortunately, the error was quickly realized.

However, no such progress was being made by 231 Brigade. Their commander, Brigadier Stanier, seeing the problem with the anti-tank gun at WN-37

The anti-tank casemate at WM-37, Le Hamel.

on the western end of Jig Beach, redirected the remainder of the tanks and other vehicles, including the Sextons, to land around the point on King Sector. So as not to disrupt 69 Brigade and to take their own objectives, the units would follow the single narrow embanked road across the marsh to the area of WN-36. As ill luck would have it, compounding their problems, a very large shell or bomb had hit it and when the leading vehicles reached it, they were brought to an immediate halt! A monumental traffic jam resulted, with commanders and vehicles essential for the all-arms battle stuck in it, only getting past the crater with difficulty. This left the Dorsets' and Hampshires' company commanders to revise their plans.

With the companies swinging right, the Hampshires heading for Le Hamel and the 77mm gun that was still causing problems, and the Dorsets heading further inland for Asnelles, the reserve battalion, 2 Devons, landed. Instead of the well-ordered beach with signs and military police, there was the crack of bullets and the explosion of mortar bombs. One company joined the Hampshire company in the dunes and the remaining three left the beach on a single track at WN-36 and began their advance inland up the valley of la Grande Rivière. They,

The crater in the lateral road and the traffic jams back onto the beach.

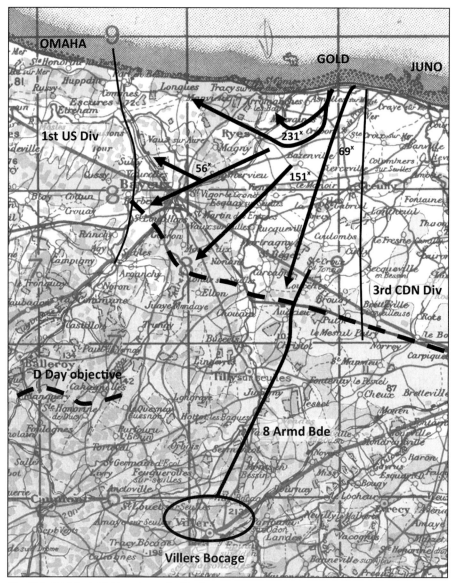

The 50th Division's D-Day plan and objectives.

however, came under mortar fire and promptly ran into a local German counter-attack coming from the opposite direction, so it was not until 1120 hours that the Devons began their advance on Ryes. The ambitious timetable for the day had already slipped by two hours.

With progress being made by 69 Brigade, 151 (Durham) Brigade's landing on King Beach was only slightly delayed, with the main body coming ashore between 1030 and 1200 hours.[6] The 8th Durham Light Infantry's (8 DLI's) historian wrote:

> ... the Battalion HQ ship ran in towards King Beach closely followed by the LCI [Landing Craft Infantry] carrying A and B Companies. The two leading craft were unable to run up right onto the beaches because of wrecked assault craft and partly submerged tanks which blocked the way. As the ramps touched down Lt Col Lidwill led the way ashore through a very rough choppy sea. The men followed, wading up to the waist with rifles and Brens held high above the head. They landed fairly dry thanks to the waterproof anti-gas trousers with which every man had been issued.[7]

The Afternoon's Fighting

151 Brigade was almost complete in its assembly area at Meuvaines by 1330 hours. Their task was to come up into line with 69 Brigade and advance in a south-westerly direction towards their objectives beyond the N13 and the railway line on the River Seulles south of Bayeux.

Following a passage of lines through the right flank of 69 Brigade, they began their advance at 1530 hours. The divisional war diary records that '... some opposition was encountered, and the advance was slow.'

Meanwhile, the squadron of 4th/7th DG was still in support of 69 Brigade's advance south. Lieutenant Trasenster, a troop commander aboard a Sherman nicknamed 'Winchester' recalled:

> Then we continued our advance skirting Crépon village then onto Creully where for the first time 'Winchester' was hit by an armour-piercing round knocking off our spare bogey, eight foot of Willets' aerial and the troop pennant, also a chunk of armour was gouged out near my head!
>
> Another enemy tank missed us at 100 yards as we were approaching the river bridge [the Seulles at Creully]. By putting down smoke bombs, one of which miraculously landed on the bridge, we got to cover and our supporting infantry, 7 Green Howards, who cleared Creully very rapidly. My troop Corporal and I drove through the eerily deserted street. As soon as we got through Creully the Squadron advanced towards the ridge ... Then we really hit trouble; nine tanks were knocked out in about as many minutes from an anti-tank gun in front.

This was a platoon at least of *Sturmgeschütz* belonging to the 352nd Division. This battalion had been sent west before dawn to counter-attack the American airborne landings around Carentan but had been recalled to block the advance from Gold Beach, which posed the Germans a greater threat. After running the gauntlet of Allied aircraft, they had arrived south of Creully sometime after 1600 hours. Lieutenant Trasenster continued:

> To add to the confusion, HMS *Orion* opened fire with several broadsides. The infantry and tank crews out of their tanks were massacred. Ten of the

regiment were killed and sixteen were wounded. However, the regiment had penetrated about 6 miles inland at the cost of nineteen tanks and twenty-four casualties. Reg Cox saw the tank his brother was driving blown up and explode 20 yards in front of us. Lipscombe's tank was brewed and all the crew were wounded.

69 Brigade advanced a further 1.5 miles before culminating short of the village of Rucqueville as evening drew on, more than 2 miles short of their D-Day objective.

Meanwhile, 231 Brigade was stalled just a couple of miles inland. The essence of the problem was that in advancing to the west they were clearing through the Germans' defended crust and crucially they were engaged in an infantry action with negligible all-arms support. The Hampshires were fighting along the coast towards Arromanches and by 1400 hours had reached St Côme-de-Fresné and the Dorsets alongside them had ground to a halt on Point 54. The Devons advancing on Ryes were meeting stiff opposition and the assembly area for 56 Brigade was still under fire. The tempo of operations, however, speeded up noticeably when, for example, the Dorsets' battalion headquarters, an artillery forward observer and a squadron of SRY tanks finally shook themselves free from the traffic jams and swept through Point 54 to their final objective. With the capture of Ryes the next phase of the battle could begin, but in the western part of its area the 50th Division was now hours behind schedule.

Of the two follow-on brigades, 151 was ashore with only moderate delays advanced from the area of Ver-sur-Mer and Meuvaines at 1530 hours. To secure the division's next objectives as quickly as possible, the brigade's plan was for 9th Battalion, Durham Light Infantry (9 DLI) to advance on the right with 6 DLI on its left and 8 DLI following in reserve. Both of the leading battalions were spearheaded by a mobile column, consisting of carrier, mortar and anti-tank platoons, a platoon of 2 Cheshires' machine guns, a rifle company mounted on bicycles, sniper and pioneer sections and an FOO (Forward Observation Officer) of the 86th Field Regiment, plus a squadron of 4th/7th DG.

Lieutenant Kirk commanding 6 DLI's Carrier Platoon described the advance: 'Although the country was open, we were not able to move as freely as we had appreciated from aerial photographs because most of the hedgerows had tree trunks in them and were usually carrier obstacles.'

The advance of the mobile column was slow, with congested roads and narrow village streets, which were difficult for Shermans to negotiate, being the chief problems encountered rather than much opposition from the enemy. Kirk continued:

When we got to Villiers-le-Sec, we met a few pockets but, when we turned our not inconsiderable fire power on, they quickly left. I found the greatest difficulty in stopping the tanks once they had started firing as they were both blind and deaf. I tried rapping on the turret with my pistol-butt, but it did not have much effect.[8]

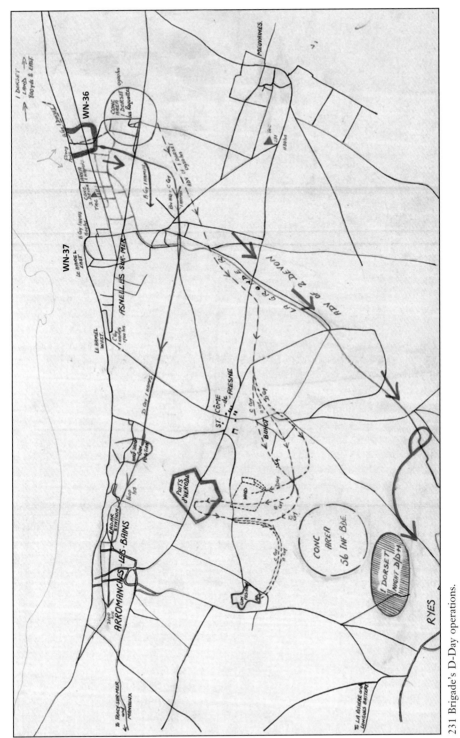

231 Brigade's D-Day operations.

US Army self-propelled (SP) 155mm guns attached to the 50th Division coming ashore on Gold Beach on the afternoon of D-Day. The largest SP guns that the Royal Artillery had were the 25-pounder Sextons.

In Esquay-sur-Seulles some opposition was encountered, but it was 'easily dealt with and prisoners taken were found to be Russians from the 642nd Ost Battalion who quickly surrendered and were obviously pleased to be out of the war.'

The mobile columns pressed on, reaching the N13 Caen/Bayeux Road, but with Brigadier Senior and his tactical headquarters being captured near Bazenville during the afternoon,[9] in the resulting hiatus in command the advance stalled. General Graham visited 151 Brigade's headquarters and called off any further advance and the leading battalions dug in at Esquay and Sommervieu, short of the Phase III line. The mobile spearheads fell back from the N13.

After circling in its landing craft off the beach 56 Brigade was finally able to begin its landing at 1130 hours, but the anti-tank gun and defences in WN-37 were still active so they landed on King Beach. The brigade started to concentrate at Butot at 1600 hours, with the Dorsets having concluded their action above them on Point 54 and the Devons still fighting their way up the valley to their objective of Ryes. The village was reported clear at 1735 but prisoners taken were reported as being from the field grade I Battalion 916 Grenadier Regiment from the 352nd Division rather than coastal troops. Brigadier Pepper ordered 56 Brigade's advance on Bayeux, some 4.5 miles inland, to begin at 1745 hours.[10] However, the progress of 2 Essex supported by a squadron of the SRY was slow and the brigade only reported advancing through Ryes and the Devons' patrols around la Rossière at 1930 hours. Elements of the brigade reached Bayeux as dusk fell but, with the commander not relishing the prospect of a fight in a built-up area at night, he withdrew them and ordered the resumption of operations to capture Bayeux and close up to the D-Day objective the following morning. This was an unfortunate delay as the city was all but unoccupied by the enemy. Further west, the South Wales Borderers were one of the very few battalions to reach their D-Day objective on 6 June.

Infantry of 69 Brigade following the advance inland from King Beach.

By nightfall the 50th Division was substantially ashore, having broken through Hitler's vaunted Atlantic Wall and had advanced some 8 miles inland. As we have seen, they had, however, fallen short of Montgomery's ambitious D-Day objective beyond the N13. The principal reasons for this were as follows:

- The failure to engage defences (WN-37) at Le Hamel and the resulting German anti-tank fire enfilading the beach east to the Point.
- Sundry delays in getting 231 Brigade's armour and other support vehicles off the beach due to landing on a sector backed by the marsh, with only one exit, which was under fire.
- The presence of field grade enemy troops in Le Hamel, on Point 54 and defending Ryes.
- The loss of commander 151 Brigade, leading to a lack of drive to keep battalions moving forward to their objectives.

Not only had objectives not been reached, but some elements of 8 Armoured Brigade were delayed coming ashore. From H+90 minutes the landing was

running behind schedule, initially due to uncleared beach obstacles and numerous drowned vehicles and sunken craft. Subsequently, crowding on the beach and exits caused further delays. One of the victims of this was the third tank unit of 8 Armoured Brigade, the war-raised 24th Lancers. Their advance party got ashore reasonably on time, but the precarious business of offloading the Shermans onto the barely seaworthy Rhino Ferries in the still heavy seas was a nightmare and when they eventually approached the surf off King Sector, the first ferry was waved off by the Royal Navy Beach Master. By nightfall on D-Day, rather than the whole regiment being ashore and ready for battle, only the Lancers' B Squadron and sundry elements of others

The cap badge of the 24th Lancers.

had been landed. Thus, another key part of Brigadier Cracroft's command had been badly delayed and was unlikely to be immediately available for the advance to Villers-Bocage the following day.

The 7th Armoured Division's disembarkation that was to have got under way in earnest on the evening of D-Day had also yet to start.

The German Reaction

While the coastal divisions were struggling to contain the Allies on the beaches, the 21st Panzer Division, the only armour that Rommel had been allowed to move forward to within easy counter-attacking distance of the coast, was in action around Caen.[11] The other panzer divisions within striking distance of the coast were *Panzer Lehr* and the 12th *Hitlerjugend* SS Panzer divisions, but they both waited for most of the day for orders to move. Allied intelligence summaries warned of the likely arrival of these formations in the invasion area on D-Day, but in practice they could not be deployed to battle without Hitler's authority. Despite being stood to ready to move since the early hours of 6 June, orders to march to the battle area were not issued until early afternoon and when they came the *Hitlerjugend* was directed off the pre-recced routes to the coast in the Caen area. This caused significant delay, necessitating the revision of movement tables. They marched at 1600 hours and soon found that Allied aircraft were waiting to interdict them on their 70-mile march to battle. HQ I SS Panzer Corps, however, was still not in contact with *Panzer Lehr* at 1800 hours. Consequently, this elite division only began its march as darkness fell.

Panzer Lehr was made up of veteran commanders and soldiers from the German Army Panzer School, but for the young soldiers of the *Hitlerjugend* their first experience of a full air onslaught was a nasty shock. Riding in a truck, *Sturmmann* Pock of 25 *Panzergrenadiers*, which was leading the division's main body west, recorded in his diary:

General Fritz Bayerlein, commander of *Panzer Lehr*.

> The number of our vehicles knocked out kept growing. They sat where they were hit, burnt out. Grenades are scattered about, shells, all types of ammunition, amongst them dead soldiers.
>
> The march became more and more dangerous. The pastures and fields were ploughed by bomb craters. We increasingly realise that the enemy, as far as matériel is concerned, seems to be far superior to us.

Hitlerjugend Sd.Kfz.251 Hanomag half-tracks pass a victim of Allied air attack.

Beginning its move overnight, *Panzer Lehr* made good progress towards Thury-Harcourt, still well south of the battle area, under cover of darkness, with leading elements arriving in the town around dawn on 7 June.

If British commanders had been able to exploit the opportunity granted to them by the delay in ordering the two panzer divisions to march and had established the patrol bases at Villers-Bocage and Évrecy on D-Day, the subsequent conduct of the battle on the Second Army's front could have been very different.

Infantry Mobility

The British battalions in infantry divisions had sufficient transport for command, control and administration, prime movers for mortars and anti-tank guns, plus a carrier platoon. There was no organic transport to move the soldiers of the rifle platoons. When a move of time and/or distance dictated, Troop Carrying Vehicles (TCVs) were allocated from the parent division's RASC company.

British battalions' equipment tables included sufficient bicycles for an infantry company and other specialists. For the latter, to make up for the lack of their vehicles during the initial phase of the D-Day landings, apart from the infantry company, being mounted on bicycles was to help keep up with the projected speed of the advance inland from the beach. This had been practised during the FABIUS D-Day rehearsal exercises.

In the reality of battle, however, very few of the battalions' follow-on companies made anything but incidental use of their bicycles. On D-Day some of their landing craft could not cross sand bars and most bikes in this case were lost before they got to the beach, while others, finding the beach under fire, dropped the bikes and ran for the cover of the dunes.

Those battalions that got their bicycles ashore from D-Day onwards struggled with them through tank-rutted tracks and mud before abandoning them, normally within a maximum of twenty-four hours of being ashore.

Planned bicycle moves in the immediate aftermath of D-Day were either carried out on foot or by vehicle shuttle. The lucky ones rode in the few trucks available.

The one successful use of bicycles on D-Day was that of 6 Commando's Cycle Troop, who reached Pegasus Bridge a good hour before the rest of 1st SS Brigade and two hours before Lord Lovat's almost ceremonial arrival!

A rare picture of infantry bicycles in use in Normandy.

Chapter Three

D+1: 7 June 1944

Operations by 50th Division to complete their D-Day tasks resumed shortly after dawn, with the units and sub-units that were to form 8 Armoured Brigade's mobile column still grouped as they had been the previous evening under other headquarters. There seemed to be little concern in the British chain of command about the failure to start establishing the firm base at Villers-Bocage as planned for the previous day. Nor is there much evidence of urgency to 'get on with it'. It has been argued that the far from satisfactory situation at Omaha was absorbing Montgomery's attention and the arrival of a substantial part of the *Hitlerjugend* Panzer Division around Caen was the focus of General Dempsey and I Corps. For Major General Graham's 50th Division attention was on the substantial number of Germans still present, active or otherwise, in the 100 square miles of his area of responsibility and the lack of link-up with the Americans.

As far as 151 Brigade was concerned there was little opposition to the battalion's mobile columns, which resumed their advance and reached their objectives on the River Aure south of Bayeux within three hours at 0815 hours. The marching troops following them closed up an hour later and were quickly digging in.

69 Brigade was also in action having halted some way north of the N13 the previous evening, but they became bogged down in mines and wire clearing a Luftwaffe radio station at Le Park, just short of the N13 to the west of St Léger.

There was, however, no such speedy conclusion for 56 Brigade in Bayeux to match that of 151 Brigade. Moving forward at 0830 hours, the Essex with the SRY under command were delayed by mines and snipers, but the only serious but brief enemy opposition in the city was near the station. The Gloucesters eventually reached the centre of the city at 1230 hours, where the main problem was the exuberance of the French population at their liberation, without too much damage! It was only at 1800 hours that the two battalions were secure on their D-Day objectives south-west of the city and the SRY could be released back to 8 Armoured Brigade.

Behind the two leading brigades, in the considerable ground across which the 50th Division had advanced, there were still plenty of Germans who had been bypassed or simply gone to ground. Some readily surrendered to passing troops and were easily dealt with, but other substantial or dogged pockets needed more determined action. With the Hampshires clearing the Arromanches area, the only uncommitted battalion the division had available was the 1 Dorsets, who had taken over Ryes from the Devons at 0530 hours in order to release that

8 Armoured Brigade Shermans in Bayeux's narrow streets.

battalion for its attack on the Longues-sur-Mer Battery. Their first skirmish came as a result of the padre and a burial party of D Company who were combing the wood to the west of Point 54 for the battalion's dead. Thirty Germans including an officer were taken prisoner 'after a short sharp action'.

Mopping up at Bazenville

Shortly before midday the battalion was called upon for an altogether more serious operation. According to the battalion's D-Day report, they were

> ... ordered to send a Coy gp [company group] to mop up the enemy in the area BAZENVILLE 8782 and LA CROIX 8781. B Coy (Maj P. Chilton MC) with under command dets carrier pl and mortar platoon and sp [supported] by a Sqn SHERWOOD RANGERS, left the area to carry out this task.

This body of enemy in company strength had been missed by 69 Brigade being in some thick country between their two axes of advance the previous afternoon. Though it was not known at the time, they were miscellaneous gunners of the 352nd Division, infantry of 916 Regiment and elements of *Kampfgruppe* Meyer (915 GR) which had arrived too late the previous afternoon to put up a coherent fight.

The 24th Lancers' war diary records that 'B Squadron together with eight tanks of A Squadron were used during the day for mopping-up operations in the BAZENVILLE area.' However, there is no record of this in the Dorsets' war diary. It is possible that as this was a company operation and Major Chilton was wounded on 14 June, a full account was not available for writing up the report or the tanks were providing a wider screen of fire support.

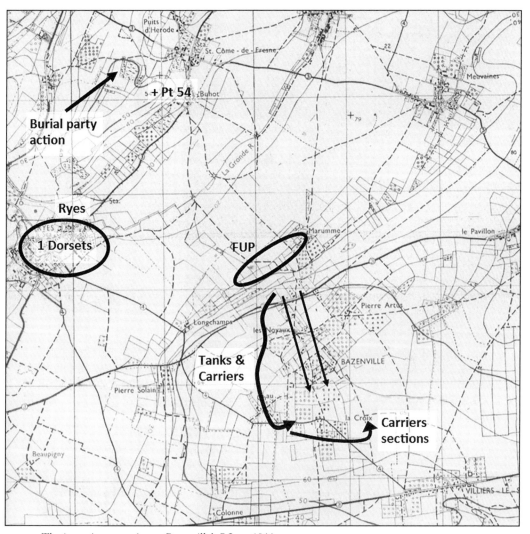

The 'mopping-up action at Bazenville', 7 June 1944.

B Company left Ryes to march the mile to their assembly area at 1215 hours, where they were joined by a troop of Shermans of C Squadron of the SRY, which had been sent back from Bayeux. Major Chilton's plan was to advance south from the Sommervieu-Crépon road into the straggling village and orchards around the two settlements. In thick country the infantry was to lead, with their 3in mortar section in support, ready to take on points of resistance. The SRY troop and carrier platoon were to remain in the open country to the right along with the two carrier sections, keeping abreast with the advance and engaging the enemy from a flank as necessary.

Dorset Regiment cap badge.

According to an entry in the Dorsets' war diary, at 1400 hours a German 'who gave himself up to the SHERWOOD RANGERS' states 'there is 1 coy enemy area LA CROIX to west of road.' This meant that the first phase of the attack would in effect be an advance to contact over 800 yards through Bazenville, its orchards and paddocks to La Croix, the last portion of which had a convenient north-south road through the orchards for use as an axis of advance.

There is little detail of the actual attack, but it is recorded in the war diary at 1630 hours that the attack was successful. Given the nature of the ground, this represents very good progress. In the final phase the tanks remained on the right flank, while the sections of the carrier platoon deployed to the east of the area in more open country. From the left flank they acted as cut-offs, covering likely enemy escape routes with their Bren guns. Reportedly they 'had a very good shoot'.

By 1730 hours the Dorsets' B Company was reorganizing, but they came under fire directed at the Shermans on the edge of the village, which killed Lieutenant Mayes. During the clearance of the area in detail the Dorsets counted forty enemy dead and took seventy prisoners. Among the items found was Brigadier Senior's armoured car and all the papers and codes lost the previous day. It later transpired that the brigadier had, although wounded, escaped during the confusion caused by B Company's attack and after lying up for some time rejoined the division, but such were his injuries, he was evacuated.

Most of the two Dorsets killed and twelve wounded during 7 June were in D Company around Point 54.

By the end of the 7th the immediate divisional rear area was reasonably secure, but Germans were still appearing days later. One example is the clearance of the area west of Arromanches, which was not as thorough as it could have been with the focus very much on the early stages of the building of the Mulberry harbour. Brigadier Walter of the Port Construction Force, which came ashore during D+1, recorded that:

> We ended the day by bivouacking in a wood to the west of Arromanches as dusk was falling. We dispersed early next morning [8 June] but about mid-morning there came sounds of battle from the west of the town. Later it transpired that a party of about sixty Germans had emerged from underground passages below where we had bivouacked the night before and were engaged by such Port Construction Force troops as could be mustered who, with the aid of a tank killed some but took forty-seven prisoners.

Further west during the course of the 7th, the Devons of 231 Brigade captured the Longues-sur-Mer Battery, 47 Commando attacked Port-en-Bessin and the South Wales Borderers closed up to the army boundary on the River Drôme, but there was no sign of the Americans from Omaha Beach. The link-up would only take place on the evening of 8 June.

With their B Squadron ashore and in action, the rest of the 24th Lancers were still waiting to land. They had been badly delayed the previous day by

One of the gun casemates of the Longues-sur-Mer battery.

sundry problems, most of which had eased by D+1 but not the state of the sea. 8 Armoured Brigade's war diary states:

Tanks of the 24th Lancers began to land during the day and by the evening [the remaining] two squadrons less Regimental Headquarters had landed and assembled in area 8984. Lt Col WAC Anderson, commanding 24th Lancers, reported during the afternoon that in general the LSTs would not close the beach and the sea was too heavy for tanks to land from Rhino Ferries.

This simple statement belies a whole host of difficulties. The sea was too rough to land the tanks via the Rhino Ferries, of which few were still operational as most were to be seen washed up on the beaches by the waves. The American captains of the landing ships tank (LSTs) were reluctant to go into the beach to land the tanks as this meant remaining stranded and vulnerable on the beach until floated off by the next tide. Beach masters were also reluctant as beached LSTs took up valuable space on the beaches. After terse conversations with the skippers, the LSTs were eventually run up onto the beach and the tanks disembarked and de-waterproofed. Due to the depth of the water, a fair number of smaller vehicles were drowned during landing.

With smaller vehicles of the 61st Recce Regiment it was still necessary to bring the LSTs in towards the beach and use a combination of ramp and Rhino Ferry. As recalled by Corporal Don Aiken of B Squadron, the process of landing was far from straightforward:

The LST dropped anchor and the remaining Rhino was untied from the side of the ship and made its way round the bows, ready to be attached to the gangway which projected forwards when the bow doors opened. It was then

An LST discharging tanks and soft-skin vehicles onto a Rhino Ferry in calm seas following D-Day.

discovered that the coupling gear had been smashed and this sparked off a frenzied burst of activity to try to tie the units together with ropes. However, ropes are flexible by necessity, and the choppy seas made it almost impossible to hold both units in line; but with the aid of a couple of small motorboats, pushing away like tug boats, they became near enough to go for it and our Troop made the transfer across.

Soon we were running in to the beach and the Rhino bottomed out. The light armoured car (Recce Car) in which I was a crew member was the first to drive off, and in my elevated position in the turret I felt like a submarine commander, especially when we suddenly dropped into a bomb hole which was concealed beneath the water and only the turret was left exposed. The Beach Party had been well trained for this situation and had the de-waterproofing area completely organised and running smoothly.

German Plans and Movements

The German intention had always been to counter-attack an Allied landing in its early stages, while it was at its most vulnerable. The success of OVERLORD's deception plans, however, had caused OKW to hold its hand for vital hours on 6 June, but on D+1 the Germans intended to launch that counter-attack with the three panzer divisions but there was a twofold problem. The first was that while the leading elements of the *Hitlerjugend* and *Panzer Lehr* had reached the edge of the battle area, both divisions were strung out on routes of march that had pass times of some ten hours.[1] The second was Allied air power. General Fritz

Bayerlein, commanding *Panzer Lehr*, recalled the first attacks of Allied fighter-bombers:

> Our motorised columns were coiling along the road towards the invasion beaches. Then something happened that left us in a daze. Spurts of fire flickered along the column and splashes of dust on the road. Everyone was piling out of the vehicles and scuttling for the surrounding fields. Several vehicles were already in flames. This attack ceased as suddenly as it had crashed on us fifteen minutes before. The men started drifting back to the column again, pale and shaky and wondering how they had survived this fiery rain of bullets. This had been our first experience of fighter-bombers. The column of march was now completely disorganised, and every man was on his own, to pull out of this blazing column as best he could. And it was none too soon, because an hour later the whole thing started all over again, only much worse this time. When the attack was over, the road was strewn with smashed anti-tank guns (the pride of our division), flaming vehicles and charred implements of war.

Bayerlein later explained the practical difficulties of movement:

> The nights were very short in France in June 44. We could move a maximum of only 10 or 12 km per hour and could cover a total of only 60 to 70km during the hours of darkness. As we had 140km to cover to reach the coast, we had to move during the day and, as a result, suffered heavy losses from the

Bombing up an RAF Typhoon fighter-bomber, which was still operating from a UK airfield at the time.

air. I proposed that we rest during the day and resume the march the next evening, but *Generaloberst* Dollmann, who underestimated the Allied air forces, said we had to keep moving. (This problem of time of movement was another good reason why the Division should have been nearer the coast.)[2]

It took two days and one night to reach the Caen front ...

He complained to General Dollman that on 7 June

... by noon it was terrible; every vehicle was covered with tree branches and moved along hedges and the edges of woods. Road junctions were bombed, and a bridge knocked out. By the end of the day I had lost forty trucks carrying panzer fuel, and ninety other vehicles. Five of my Panzers were knocked out, and eighty-four half-tracks, prime movers and self-propelled guns.

For a panzer division that had not come into action these were heavy losses and mirrored those in the *Hitlerjugend*. SS *Brigadeführer* Fritz Krämer, Chief of Staff I SS Panzer Corps, under which the two panzer divisions were to operate, commented that 'the impossibility of daytime marches was pointed out. Seventh

Panzer Lehr on the march by day had to dash from cover to cover, slowing the rate of progress to the beachhead.

Army made it clear that it was essential to carry out counter-attacks by the corps as soon as possible.' Krämer went on to complain that even though daylight movement under Allied air supremacy was obviously impossible, it took days for his superior headquarters to realize this and revise their orders accordingly!

In the afternoon of 7 June, the *Hitlerjugend*'s leading regiment, 25 *Panzergrenadiers*, commanded by *Oberführer* Kurt 'Panzer' Meyer, launched its attack north-west of Caen against the 3rd Canadian Division. The resulting battle centred on the Abbey d'Ardenne and Buron area had the characteristics of a meeting engagement, the intensity of which shocked the soldiers of both sides. The *Hitlerjugend*'s second regiment, 26 *Panzergrenadiers*, was still south-east of Caen moving painfully slowly and would not be ready to join the attack until the following day.

Concentration of 8 Armoured Brigade

When C Squadron of 4th/7th DG became available during the afternoon of 7 June Brigadier Cracroft ordered a reconnaissance of the route south to Point 103. They reached the railway line west of Audrieu Station, but as they attempted to cross it, two Shermans of the leading troop were knocked out.

Headquarters 50th Division was only able to issue the code-word YAR for the units that were to join Brigadier Cracroft's mobile column at 2230 hours on 7 June. This was some twenty-eight hours after it had been hoped to issue it! The force was to assemble in the Brécy-Rucqueville area, to the rear of 69 Brigade, by first light but even this proved over-optimistic. For instance, the RASC trucks to pick up the Dorsets did not arrive until well after dawn; consequently, they didn't leave Ryes until 0810 hours.

The force was to consist of the following units under the command of 8 Armoured Brigade:

> 4th/7th Dragoon Guards
> Sherwood Ranger Yeomanry
> 24th Lancers
> 147 Field Regiment RA (SP) Essex Yeomanry
> Detachment 168th Light Field Ambulance

Attached from 50th Division:

> 61 Reconnaissance Regiment[3]
> A Company 1 Dorsets (on cycles) [*sic*, the whole of 1 Dorset]
> 288 Anti-Tank Battery (Northumberland Hussars)
> A Company 2 Cheshires (MG), less one platoon
> 86 Field Regiment RA
> RE Reconnaissance Party

Of the Dorsets, Brigadier Cracroft wrote:

> As my Motor Battalion 12 KRRC had been excluded from the earlier [landing craft] loading tables, a battalion from 231 Brigade, 1 Dorsets, were

allotted to me for this role and quite magnificently did they carry it out, although they had never worked with armour before and the nearest that they came to a Motor Battalion in the matter of equipment was to have one company (A) equipped with cycles. Their CO [Lieutenant Colonel Norrie] joined my Tac HQ[4] on the morning of the 8th and not long afterward the remainder of the Battalion moved into the assembly area at RUCQUE-VILLE, where they came under my command.

The fact that the Dorsets, rather than having half-tracks for the whole battalion, only had a company mounted on bicycles was not too much of a disadvantage as south of the railway line they would be entering the true bocage of steep valleys and small fields surrounded by banks and hedges! Cracroft commented on the ground south to Point 103: 'The country on this line was very thick and very

Shermans of 4th/7th DG in Normandy.

built-up, and it was apparent that we should need considerable infantry support to get the tanks through it.'

Orders for the advance were changed in detail as all three armoured regiments were available. The armoured cars of the 61st Recce Regiment would lead on the right route via Point 103 (nicknamed CONGO), with the 24th Lancers advancing on the left route (nicknamed ISEL) via Point 102; the tanks were supported by the Dorsets' A Company on their bicycles (see map on page 16). Both columns had artillery OPs to provide firepower. The SRY followed and the

An air photo of the initial ground across which the columns were to advance. Note the increase of hedgerows south of the N13.

4th/7th DG were in the centre behind the brigade's Tac HQ with the remainder of the Dorsets.

H-hour for the advance was 1000 hours and the start line was the railway but from the beginning there were difficulties, not least because 69 Brigade had not advanced south of the N13 in the Loucelles area, let alone to the railway line. With enemy clearly present, H-hour was delayed and eventually fixed as midday. As the operation began, Brigadier Cracroft recalled that 'I thought at this time that there was probably only a thin crust of German defence and that if I could once break through there would be no further organised resistance.' How wrong one can be!

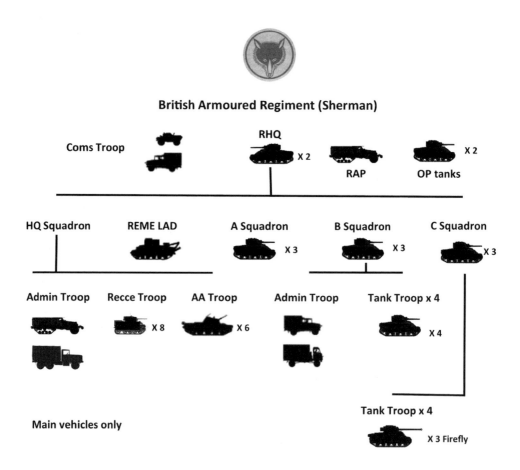

British Armoured Regiment (Sherman)

Coms Troop

RHQ
X 2

RAP

OP tanks
X 2

HQ Squadron   REME LAD   A Squadron   X 3   B Squadron   X 3   C Squadron   X 3

Admin Troop   Recce Troop   X 8   AA Troop   X 6   Admin Troop   Tank Troop x 4   X 4

Tank Troop x 4

Main vehicles only

X 3 Firefly

Chapter Four

The Advance Begins

'Wiping up a few straggling schoolboys with pistols.'
[Brigadier Cracroft][1]

With uncertainty as to the situation ahead of them, at midday 8 Armoured Brigade's advance guard finally started to move forward and cross the N13 east of St Léger. A brief entry in 8 Armoured Brigade's war diary records 'Opposition was met on the right at LOUCELLES (8773) and at the left at BROUAY (8872).' It was readily apparent that Germans were holding ground south of the N13, particularly around Loucelles and Brouay.[2] The adjutant of the Dorsets, still waiting in the assembly area at Rucqueville, said that 'it has become evident that 8 Armd Bde will have to fight its way fwd to Pt 103.'

Fighting had already been under way at Brouay since before dawn. Elements of *Panzer Lehr*, the infantry of II Battalion, 902 *Panzergrenadier* Regiment, had arrived in the area during the course of the night of 7/8 June and attacked 6 Green Howards, supported by its own heavy weapons company and infantry gun platoon. It, however, lacked artillery and armoured support from other parts of the division. The reason for this is that thanks to the lack of sustained workable communications with I SS Panzer Corps, General Bayerlein was still unaware that Bayeux had been captured and that the Allies had closed up to the Caen-Bayeux railway line. This lack of situational awareness meant that his division was deployed for the route of march rather than battle. Consequently, the first units of the division in action were not grouped for combat when they became aware of the presence of 69 Brigade in Brouay. The remainder of *Panzer Lehr*, including I/902 *Panzergrenadiers*, was still strung out back south to Thury-Harcourt and beyond and would take another night's march to arrive in any force. Bayerlein commented: 'Owing to the air attacks, my troops just trickled through with the artillery lagging behind them.'

Another factor, according to Bayerlein, was that his division was ordered to 'take Bretteville-l'Orgueilleuse and break through to the coast at Courseulles-sur-Mer' but this, as he explained, was changed during the afternoon of 8 June:

I was told not to attack toward Courseulles-sur-Mer, but to withdraw to Tilly-sur-Seulles and attack toward Bayeux. These orders show confused thinking. Had we actually gone through Bretteville-l'Orgueilleuse, I believe *Pz Lehr* and 12 SS Pz Divs could have cut through to the coast. Dietrich, however, was afraid the British would drive in behind us, and of course we would have suffered heavily from naval shelling and air attack. The British had advanced beyond Bayeux and our left flank would have been in danger.

This all added time to operations as staff re-planned and issued revised orders and routes. If there had been greater clarity the *Hitlerjugend* would not have been overextended west, launching almost individual battalion attacks, and Bayerlein's units would have made a properly coordinated attack. The Germans were, as Guderian said, 'feeling with the fingers, not hitting with the fist'.

The initial attack by *Panzer Lehr* on the village of Brouay was beaten off with the help of British artillery and naval gunfire. *Oberscharführer* Kesslar of 10th Company, 26 SS *Panzergrenadiers*, which had been advancing through the woods near Château de Brouay, came on the aftermath of a naval gunfire strike:

> The enemy had virtually cut to pieces units of *Panzer Lehr* with heavy artillery. The SPWs [Hanomag half-tracks] and equipment had been ripped apart and next to them lay pieces of our comrades. Others hung from the trees. A dreadful silence covered all.

During the morning a British Auster air observation post aircraft[3] was active over the Brouay area calling for fire from the medium guns of XXX Corps' Army Group Royal Artillery (AGRA) and naval gunfire.[4] For the German soldier fighting in Normandy, a second reality, alongside Allied air power, was very quickly apparent: the crushing weight of their enemy's artillery, both naval and land-based.

Sturmbannführer Olböter's III Armoured Battalion of 26 SS *Panzergrenadiers* had arrived later in the morning into the same area as II/902 *Panzergrenadiers*

An Auster air observation post aircraft. From early on in the invasion they operated from grass strips in the beachhead.

thanks to a lack of clarity regarding the interdivisional boundary and assembly areas. The SS promptly renewed the attack, but despite it being properly supported with artillery and panzers, the Green Howards of 69 Brigade held the young grenadiers of the *Hitlerjugend*, who were fighting their first battle. The SS dug in to the south of the railway line.

Morning of 8 June: attacks of 26 SS *Panzergrenadiers* and pm, initial moves of 8 Armoured Brigade.

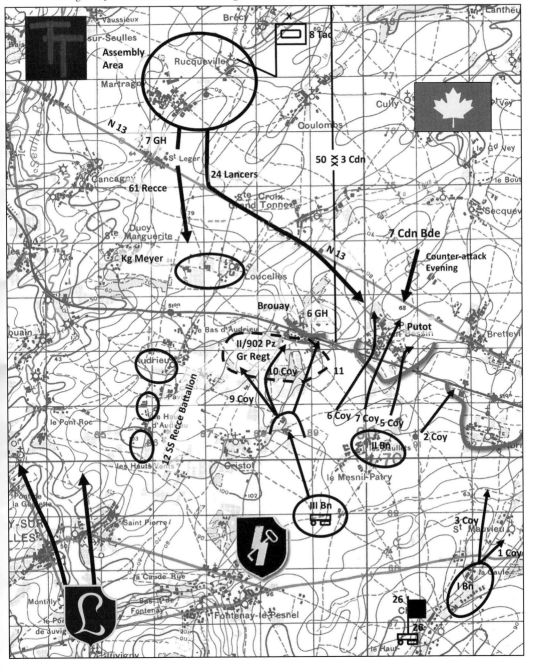

The Initial Advance of 8 Armoured Brigade

The armoured cars of 61st Recce Regiment and A Squadron of the 24th Lancers began their advance to the railway crossings south of Loucelles at 1400 hours. Major Brownrigg, the regimental second-in-command, recalled that

> A Squadron and a squadron of tanks were ordered to capture a piece of high ground 2 miles outside the bridgehead perimeter [Point 103]. One imagined the enemy tightly penning in the bulge, so that any move forward of the FDLs [Forward Defence Lines] would draw a rain of fire. In fact, the move out was completely peaceful but after about half a mile A Squadron was held

The advance of the 24th Lancers and the action at Putot.

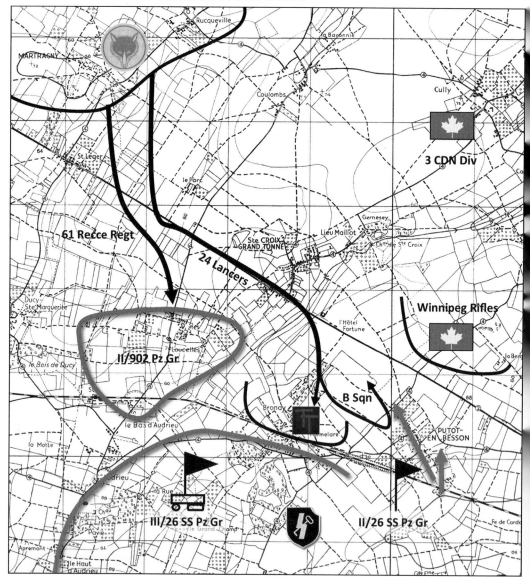

Mark II Daimler armoured car as used by the squadrons of recce regiments.

up by isolated parties of the enemy and lots of snipers. We were being pressed by Brigade to get on: 'Use your big friends and push on'[5] kept coming over the air to me in the rear link [radio to brigade HQ].

However, with A Squadron fanning out, they had not gone far beyond the N13 when they ran into trouble. Trooper Derek Edmonds recalled:

Our troop of four carriers did our bit, we entered a wood from open ground and the lead carrier was fired on from a Jerry machine-gun nest at the side of the road, the Corporal in charge was wounded, he threw a Mills bomb at the Jerries, they threw it back and he threw it back, where it exploded, we retired to the beginning of the wood, the Corporal lolling back, wounded, we saw some more Jerries on the other side of the hedge about to fire and one of our chaps got him first, we then withdrew further back. My part was to report back and yell out '*Er geben si sich*', which meant 'Surrender yourselves'. Remember the Reconnaissance role was to draw fire, retire and report back, which is what we did. The Corporal got the MM for that episode.

The Lancers' A Squadron was also under fire as they moved forward to Loucelles and the surrounding woods. Trooper Midgely, who was driving the squadron's

(*Left*) The cap badge of the Reconnaissance Corps RAC.

(*Right*) The tactical sign painted on all recce regiment vehicles. '41' painted on a green-over-blue background donates an infantry division's recce regiment.

Humber armoured car, was following his commander's tank at a distance of 20 yards when they came under artillery fire. He recalled: 'I can remember the first shell that landed nearby; the shrill scream and the immediate reaction inside the car; visor down, hood hatch closed, into reverse and away.' Corporal Don Aitken commented: 'The German opposition was stronger than we had anticipated.'

With anti-tank guns deterring the Shermans from moving forward and with the demands of brigade to 'get moving' ringing in his headset, as recalled by Sergeant Roy Howard, the 61st's commanding officer motored forward:

> Colonel Mount came forward in his Bren-gun carrier to assess the situation. He then drove up to my Light Recce Car and gave me orders to drive forward and go through the village at speed and await the arrival of the rest of the armoured column about a mile beyond the village [Loucelles] in a small wood. His order was 'Show the tanks how it should be done.' Normally I would have had the support of my Troop Commander in his heavy Recce Car but his 37mm gun had jammed and his turret was out of action, so it would have been a single-vehicle operation armed with only one Bren gun. I had to dismount and was standing examining the map with Col. Mount when he collapsed in his carrier, struck in the hip by a sniper's bullet.

Major Brownrigg heard over the radio:

> . . . the ominous words come over the air from the CO's operator: 'My Sunray has been hit.' He had been standing up his full 6 feet plus in his carrier giving orders to the tanks when he was shot at very short range through the thigh. This was a tremendous loss to the Regiment.

The orders for a relieved Sergeant Howard's drive through Loucelles were cancelled, followed by orders for the Recce Regiment to pull back, but there was a problem. Major Brownrigg explained:

> The Brigadier had decided to concentrate on our route, and to relieve us with an armoured regiment. There was one awful moment; two sections of carriers had been sent to clear the village ahead from the rear. This meant a

wide detour, but we got through on the air to recall them. To our horror we found that the message had reached only one section. As the armoured regiment entered the village shooting all their weapons right, left and centre, the other section of carriers motored straight through the fire, from the reverse direction, with the officer standing up in the leading carrier and looking distinctly surprised. No one was hurt.

Along with the 61st, A Squadron of the 24th Lancers were pulled back. Corporal Don Aitken recounted that

... we advanced some distance towards Villers-Bocage before we were eventually given the order to 'harbour' down for the night and we drove into a tree-lined field, concealing the vehicles around the perimeter. I had no idea what our position was, and what the situation was around us.

In thick bocage country in the presence of an established enemy, the 61st Recce Regiment was returned to the command of the 50th Division.

Route ISEL: Putot-en-Bessin

B and C squadrons of the 24th Lancers on the left of Martigny crossed the N13 and headed for the railway crossing in the village of Brouay. Leonard Wills recorded that 'The operation fell into place like an exercise on the North York Moors. It was almost unrealistic and gave us a great confidence in our training with calm cool voices on the wireless net, but this was for real.'

The reality of war was not long in coming. Two tank commanders were shot and killed by German infantry concealed in long grass, trees and hedgerows that surrounded Putot and what is more the enemy was clearly in the area in strength.

The results of the sundry delays in launching 8 Armoured Brigade's advance south to Villers-Bocage were now being reaped. Time, some thirty-six hours, had given the Germans the opportunity to recover from their own delay in committing *Panzer Lehr* and the 12th SS Panzer Division on D-Day. In the case of the *Hitlerjugend* their 25 SS *Panzergrenadiers* were in action against the Canadians north-west of Caen on 7 June (D+1). During the night of 7/8 June 26 SS *Panzer-grenadiers* had extended their division's front and *Sturmbannführer* Siebken's II Battalion had attacked 7 Canadian Brigade's positions in the village of Putot at 0630 hours. They advanced, covered across the open ground by artillery and smoke, led by the regiment's recce company, but as they attempted to cross the railway line into Putot, they came under small-arms fire. It was abundantly clear that the village was strongly held and a protracted fight resulted. It wasn't until the young *panzergrenadiers* had cleared the village and surrounding orchards and reorganization had taken place that, in the early afternoon, II Battalion was starting to advance north to the N13. At that point the 24th Lancers appeared.

Lieutenant Wareham, mounted in a Stuart light tank, was with the regimental second-in-command Major Jones of the Winnipeg Rifles somewhere north of Brouay when they were stopped. Without either tank or artillery support, the

Winnipegs were struggling to withdraw their men from the village and contain the Germans. The Lancers should, of course, have been heading for Brouay, but if Putot remained in enemy hands the village on their left flank would have been a considerable problem. Consequently, the Lancers' B Squadron was ordered to advance into the orchards and paddocks to the north-west of the village and with reports that 'Eighteen Tommy panzers are attacking', quickly climbed the SS command nets.

With grenades and small-arms fire being aimed at the Shermans, they were clearly at close quarters with the *panzergrenadiers*. The saving grace was that with the *Hitlerjugend* on the offensive they had few *Panzerfausts* and therefore little means of knocking out the tanks. Equally, however, the Lancers had no infantry support to clear the enemy in detail or to hold any ground they gained. Their war diary recorded:

> A particularly active enemy position was found at PUTOT-EN-BESSIN and in the late afternoon the Regiment advanced and attacked this position. The position was found to be strongly held by three battalions [*sic*] of a *panzergrenadier* regiment of the *Hitlerjugend* Division; numbers of whose infantry had hidden themselves … After inflicting heavy casualties and

A well-camouflaged *Hitlerjugend* Pak 41 75mm anti-tank gun.

taking approximately forty prisoners the Regiment withdrew from this position and later were ordered to concentrate again in the MARTRAGNY area.

What the Lancers do not mention is that their withdrawal was probably prompted by the arrival of the *Hitlerjugend*'s anti-tank guns and an armoured patrol from the Recce Battalion. In an exchange of fire with the German 75mm anti-tank guns the Shermans scored some hits, but also lost men and tanks before they fell back. Among those damaged was the second-in-command's tank which was hit in the rear, smashing one of the engines.[6] *Oberscharführer* Dargel of II Battalion recorded: 'Half an hour later our armoured reconnaissance vehicles arrived from the direction of Putot. The enemy tanks probably mistook them for panzers and withdrew. Afterwards, I met four of my men without their helmets and belts. They had escaped from captivity.'

The Winnipeg Rifles' war diary records that 'Armd sp was requested by us but did not materialise', but the intervention of the Lancers, while not restoring the situation at Putot, had checked any idea of an advance by II/26 *Panzergrenadiers*. In the late afternoon the *Hitlerjugend* infantry were dug in among the orchards and their presence effectively blocked the way south to Point 102. Putot was recaptured with a properly-supported attack by the Canadians that evening.

With the *panzergrenadiers* of III/26 SS *Panzergrenadiers* dug in beyond the railway at Brouay, recce confirmed that Route ISEL was firmly blocked. Consequently, with the enemy denying him the way south to Point 102, Brigadier Cracroft revised his plan:

> On the left 24 Lancers ran into very strong opposition in the area PUTOT-EN-BESSIN. The country here was very thick and the enemy appeared to have a number of anti-tank guns; we lost tanks and in spite of every effort to outflank the village it became apparent that further advance without infantry support would not be possible. Unfortunately, I had no infantry for this task and accordingly I decided to abandon the attempt to break out on this axis and to concentrate all my efforts on the axis LOUCELLES-Pt. 103 ...
>
> At about 1600 hrs I therefore moved 1 Dorsets into LOUCELLES to replace 61 Recce Regt who were unsuitable for the dismounted fighting which was now necessary. As soon as this regrouping had taken place the advance continued and we succeeded in capturing the crossing over the railway south of LOUCELLES.

Route CONGO: Loucelles

The Germans in Loucelles and the surrounding woods were reported by *Sturmbannführer* Bremer, commander of the *Hitlerjugend*'s reconnaissance battalion, to be a mix of the remnants of *Kampfgruppe* Meyer and *Panzer Lehr*. Having already halted the advance by 61st Recce Regiment on Route CONGO, this mixed group of infantry had put up a remarkably good fight, but now they would be attacked by a battalion of infantry and a regiment of tanks.

A paper cutting from the *Reading Advertiser* describing the action of Corporal Wells near Loucelles, and a photograph of Sergeant Charlie Wells, B Squadron, 61st Recce Regiment.

Timed at 1600 hours, the Dorsets' war diary records the orders they were given:

Battalion, led by A Company mounted on bicycles, moves from assembly area, on route ST. LÉGER – LOUCELLES – Railway crossing 869728 – AUDRIEU, with the intention of seizing the high ground north of VILLERS-BOCAGE, in order to prevent enemy advance north from the PINCON ridge 8446, and control roads passing through VILLERS-BOCAGE.

With the tanks of 4th/7th DG in support, Major Jones and A Company advanced through the retiring 61st Recce Regiment and had by 1800 hours captured Loucelles and were clearing up the remnants of *Kampfgruppe* Meyer in the woods. B Company was meanwhile pushing forward towards the railway line: 'A Company passed through LOUCELLES, encountering no opposition at first, but were held up at Railway crossing 869728 by machine-gun fire at the crossing and from station 300 yards west up the line.'

Every attempt to reach the two crossing-points of the railway was met with heavy fire from II/902 *Panzergrenadiers* of *Panzer Lehr*. For example, C Squadron 4th/7th DG made a recce of a crossing further west with a view to continuing to Pt 103, but though they had reached the railway without difficulty, two tanks of the leading troop had been knocked out trying to cross it. Eventually, the

'Machine gun at railway crossing was dealt with by 11 Platoon, but fire from station and AUDRIEU itself held up B Company's further advance.'

To help overcome the enemy in the station, 4th/7th DGs advanced. Their war diary notes: 'Heavy mortar fire was encountered just north of the railway when the tanks came out of a narrow valley on to more open low-lying ground.' Lieutenant Wide, one of the C Squadron troop leaders, was leading the squadron towards the railway line. As he approached Audrieu railway station his Sherman came under anti-tank fire and was hit twice. His driver and co-driver were both killed, but the tank continued to drive on towards a steep railway cutting. Nonetheless, Lieutenant Wide and his turret crew continued to fire at the enemy gun with high-explosive shells. Just before the Sherman tumbled into the cutting, he and his surviving crew bailed out and made their way across a field under machine-gun fire to a wood, which it transpired was still full of German infantry, probably some of those ejected from Loucelles. According to his Military Cross citation, Lieutenant Wide 'piloted his men through enemy lines and returned to his squadron on foot some four hours later'. He later ruefully recalled his commanding officer's enthusiastic reassurance that he was 'not to worry as they would have a new tank for him by morning'. Three tanks were knocked out, including the 147 Regiment's OP Sherman of the supporting battery commander.

Lieutenant Wide MC,
C Squadron, 4th/7th DG.

Point 103

With Route CONGO south to Point 103 also blocked, Brigadier Cracroft again revised his plan. The brigade's war diary recorded that

> At 1800 hours the Sherwood Rangers Yeomanry were given the task of out-flanking the opposition in LOUCELLES by moving to Point 103 by the best route they could find west of AUDRIEU (8671). They crossed the rail-way at 861727, met little opposition and gained their objective, Point 103.

As dusk fell, the SRY slipped across the railway and reported that the 'regiment moved with remarkable speed'. Major Christopherson, commanding A Squadron, recalled:

> We encountered en route certain anti-tank guns, which we bypassed, and snipers as usual compelled all tank commanders to keep their heads down, but we arrived at our destination without a casualty, except for Victor Verner, one of my troop commanders, who was hit in the head by a sniper and eventually died from his wound … His death was a grave loss to the squadron.
>
> On arrival at Point 103, the squadron took up fire positions in the trees overlooking St Pierre, which appeared to be deserted by the civilians and Germans. As no infantry had arrived, John Bethell-Fox, one of my troop commanders and Keith Douglas,[7] my second-in-command, climbed down the hill into the village, but had the greatest difficulty in making contact with any of the civilians who had all taken refuge in the cellars. They eventually persuaded an old Frenchman to come out of hiding; he told them that there were Germans in the village and tanks in the vicinity; then, thinking dis-cretion the better part of valour, they beat a retreat back to their tanks, but on turning a corner they came face-to-face with a German patrol under an officer. Such an unexpected meeting caused alarm and surprise on both sides and they turned about and made for their respective bases. Keith, however, managed to empty his revolver in the direction of the enemy, but did not wait to ascertain the damage.

They were, however, very much on their own.

Audrieu

The Point 103 feature may have been in the brigade's hands, but the tanks were extremely vulnerable, particularly at night, without infantry. C and D companies of the Dorsets, along with some of 4th/7th DGs' Shermans, followed suit and crossed the railway further to the right and advanced across some open ground. This was made possible by a heavy artillery and naval bombardment on the station and le Bas d'Audrieu, which was controlled by a forward observation officer of 147 Field Regiment.[8] The Dorsets claim that this was the initiative of Colonel Norrie, but it could equally well have been requested by the SRY or, more likely, given the level of fire support, directed by brigade headquarters.

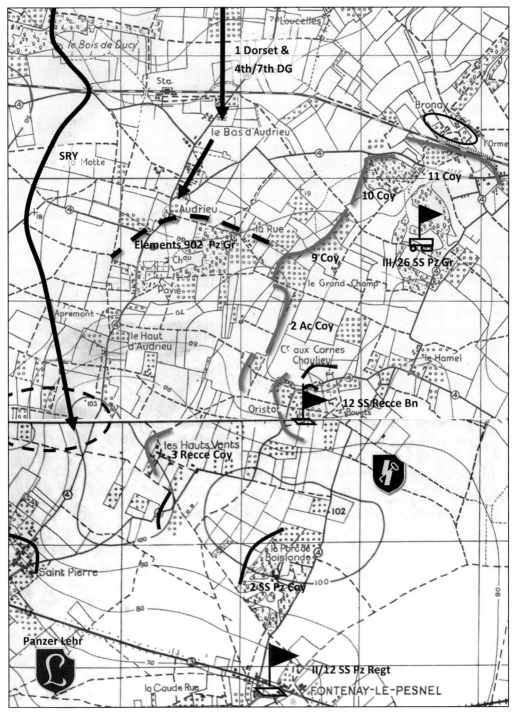

The evening of 8 June 1944, showing the SRY's route to Point 103, progress of the Dorsets and German positions.

Lieutenant Colonel Norrie,
commanding officer of
1 Dorsets.

However, the Dorsets, being on foot, had not been able to go as far to the right as the tanks and, probably not benefiting from the element of surprise, were soon under fire from the hedgerows and buildings at the outskirts of the series of hamlets that make up Audrieu. As noted by Brigadier Cracroft: 'By dark we had advanced into the northern outskirts of AUDRIEU.'

The enemy here, so far not having received the attentions of Allied naval gunfire, were fresh and they were also determined soldiers of the *Hitlerjugend*'s III/26 *Panzergrenadiers* and men of the 12th SS Reconnaissance Battalion. This latter unit covered their division's left flank, occupying positions facing west along the very road that 8 Armoured Brigade was planning to use in its advance to Point 103 via Audrieu.

In contrast to the British concept of light recce, observe and report, German reconnaissance battalions were all-arms units that were prepared to fight, with punch for both attack and defence. Indeed, as in this case, thanks to the long front the *Hitlerjugend* was required to hold, it was used as an additional *Kampfgruppe*.

With the Dorsets and 4th/7th DG across the railway and clearing le Bas d'Audrieu, *Oberscharführer* Kesslau recalled that

> ... a Sherman tank, followed by a Bren gun carrier, approached from le Bas d'Audrieu. We let them through our own lines. *Unterscharführer* Spary tried to knock out the tank with a *Panzerfaust*, but he was spotted by its commander, fired on with a machine pistol and wounded. Recognising its desperate situation, the tank drove at full speed into the garden of the railwayman's cottage, and was forced to a stop there, with nowhere to go.

The carrier had followed it, like a foal would its mother, and was also forced to surrender. The tank was a command tank with a dummy gun.[9] The crew, together with their maps, was sent to the Battalion command post.

The fighting in Audrieu went on into the night with the Dorsets holding the northern part of the village and the SS the southern. The Dorsets' report concludes that 'This was an extremely ticklish business and C Coy were unfortunate in losing the Coy 2 i/c Capt TUCKER who was leading a patrol.' He was leading a patrol near an enemy position in the Audrieu church. The Dorsets who lost their tank support when the Shermans of the 4th/7th DG withdrew to leaguer up for the night at Loucelles, but the artillery remained on call and fired several 'Uncle targets'[10] to break up enemy movements likely to herald a counter-attack.

Obersturmführer Hubert Meyer recorded in his divisional history that

During these attacks, Audrieu and Cristot were under artillery fire. At 2000 hours Audrieu came under the most concentrated artillery fire which included ships' artillery. Within one hour, the village was destroyed. Around 2100 hours the fire was shifted to the château gardens south of the village where the headquarter staff and the headquarter company of 12 SS Reconnaissance Battalion were located. They were shot to pieces. The fire attack lasted exactly one hour. Then there was a pause of five minutes, apparently to tempt the men to leave cover and retrieve the wounded. It was followed by another fire attack of twenty minutes. Most of the losses were incurred during that period. Based on the report by a British colonel who visited the

Sturmbannführer Bremer, commander of the *Hitlerjugend*'s recce battalion.

then chief of the staff company, *Hauptsturmführer* Gerd Frhr. von Reitzenstein in captivity, the fire attack was carried out by three artillery regiments [Mike Target] and two cruisers. The remains of the companies in action near Audrieu were pulled back; a number of armoured personnel carriers and a 7.5cm anti-tank gun were destroyed. The battalion was forced to abandon its previous lines in the face of high losses and the constant pressure of the superior enemy … It withdrew to the line south-west of Château Brouay-western edge of Cristot, western edge of Les Hauts Vents to the area 500m north-east of St Pierre. The Battalion command post was moved to the area south of Cristot … *Sturmbannführer* Bremer, wounded in the shoulder, then handed over the *Abteilung* to *Hauptsturmführer* von Reitzenstein.

Meanwhile, with the Dorsets unable to reach Point 103, 8 Armoured Brigade had no uncommitted infantry, so Major Martin, commander of A Company, 2 Cheshires, and his machine guns were called upon:

> All that night, the Dorsets battled away in Audrieu and as there was nothing for my company to do, I went to sleep. Shortly after midnight, I was ordered to report to the Brigadier. He told me that a squadron of Sherwood Foresters [*sic*], by following a circuitous route, had reached Point 103 – a dominant feature south of Le Haut d'Audrieu, the southernmost hamlet. My company was to move across country to join them. We had a nightmare journey through enemy territory. By 0230 hours, we were up on Point 103.

It would seem, however, that with the Dorsets in Audrieu holding their attention, the SS Recce Battalion was not fully aware of the SRY's position at Point 103, as Brigadier Cracroft commented 'it was held without opposition during the night 8–9 Junc.'

With prisoners from *Kampfgruppe* Meyer (352nd Division), *Panzer Lehr* and the *Hitlerjugend* being questioned and passed on to the headquarters of the 50th Division, it was more than apparent that if 8 Armoured Brigade were to reach their objective on the high ground north of Villers-Bocage, they were going to have to fight hard to get there.

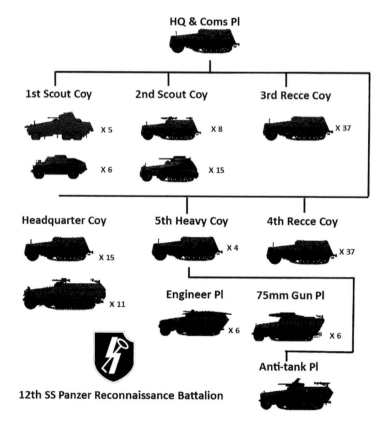

Chapter Five

Advance to Point 103 and Saint-Pierre

'The 50th Division Bayerlein. Our very special friends from Africa!'
[Field Marshal Rommel, night of 8/9 June]

Having secured his first intermediate objective of Point 103, albeit tenuously, and overnight received an additional infantry battalion that he requested, Brigadier Cracroft again recast his plan. The Dorsets and 4th/7th DG were to continue to advance through the straggling hamlets of Audrieu to Point 103. He decided, however, to slip 24th Lancers and 8th Durham Light Infantry (8 DLI) south, by crossing the railway further west on the same route that the SRY had used the previous evening and which was reported to be still undefended. This gave the brigade sufficient force to advance south on its second bound via the village of Saint-Pierre to Juvigny (see map on page 16).

In full daylight, the SRY found that Point 103 was not an ideal defensive position and that the enemy which had been absent in significant numbers the previous evening were now all too evident. Major Martin of 2 Cheshires recalled:

At first light, German tanks approached from the south and engaged the forward tanks of the Sherwood Foresters [*sic*], knocking some of them out. The remainder withdrew to the reverse slope of Point 103, leaving my two platoons totally isolated.

The enemy tanks stood off about 120 yards away, hull down, and began shelling our bank with high explosive, causing casualties. On several occasions, when the Tigers cruised too far forward, with turrets open, our [Vickers] machine-gunners fired at them to make them close down.

The SRY's war diary summarizes:

We held Point 103 throughout the day, in face of considerable anti-tank gunfire. There appeared to be also about fourteen enemy tanks in the neighbourhood of ST. PIERRE. Although the ground on Point 103 gave some cover from view by various belts of trees, it was almost impossible to take up a good hull-down position to engage enemy tanks.

Captain Douglas and Lieutenant Bethell-Fox, out on another patrol, came to a stream which was defended by a strong enemy group. They got out of

Vickers guns of 2 Cheshires preparing for action in the Normandy campaign.

their tanks to complete their reconnaissance on foot. As Captain Douglas was running along a ditch, he was killed by a mortar shell.

Meanwhile, as the commanding officers of the Lancers and DLI planed their advance to Point 103, the Dorsets and 4th/7th DG were fighting in Audrieu. Colonel Norrie's plan, which he had given out during orders at 0600 hours, was to resume the fight through the village, which also had the benefit of covering the noise of the Lancers' tracks. C and D companies were to continue to battle their way through the houses, paddocks and orchards with the tanks of A and C squadrons providing support. Meanwhile, A Company, with B Squadron's Shermans would take a route out to the west and attack le Haut d'Audrieu. Battalion headquarters and B Company (reserve) were to follow C and D companies.

At 0845 hours the Dorsets' advance began, but there was nothing like the amount of opposition there had been the previous evening. The *Hitlerjugend*'s recce battalion had withdrawn east overnight, leaving behind outposts, which fell back after firing a few shots. B Company passed through C and D companies and cleared the Château d'Audrieu and the group of houses known as Pavie. During the advance, the 4th/7th DG knocked out what they claimed to have been an SP gun. This, however, is unlikely; it was more probably an armoured car or a Sd.Kfz.250 half-track mounting a gun. The Dorsets occupied the string of hamlets from the railway line south to le Haut d'Audrieu and 'the Commanding

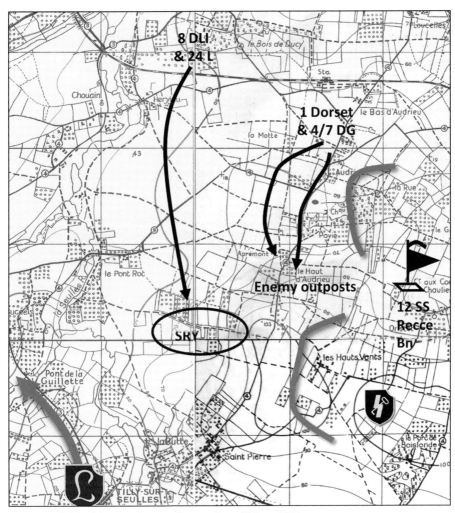

8 Armoured Brigade's operations on the morning of 9 June 1944.

Officer and the company commanders went forward to Point 103 to carry out a reconnaissance.' In the close country, however, there was a problem. Major Bredin, the battalion's second-in-command, described the issue confronting him:

> Odd parties of enemy, including some Spandau groups, were hovering about on our flanks particularly on the left (the east), and Audrieu appeared to be full of 'fifth column' rumours of enemy infiltration. 'Hundreds of Germans' approaching from all directions was the commonest story. To counteract all this, and to be more concentrated for our move forward to occupy Point 103, the Second-in-Command decided to close up Battalion Head-quarters and the rear companies (C and D) on to B Company at Pavie.

A view across the eastern part of the broad plateau that is Point 103.

As C and D companies moved forward vacating le Bas d'Audrieu and the main village, the *Hitlerjugend* infiltrated behind them and Major Bredin found himself conducting an unusual tactical variant: 'This movement was carried out on the lines of a "withdrawal forward", covered by rear parties including carriers. There were one or two minor encounters and awkward moments.'

Corporal Redpath of C Company covering the left flank of the battalion was awarded the Military Medal for his part in the fighting that morning. His citation reads that he

> ... was in command of a section that was doing flank protection. Spandaus and snipers were constantly firing at him and at one time he was under both HE and MG fire from a tank for over four hours.
>
> Despite this his behaviour was outstanding in a ticklish situation, and he set a fine example of steadiness, cheering his section on by showing great leadership under very trying conditions.

War Crimes

Arriving at Château d'Audrieu, Major Bredin was taken to see a grizzly sight behind the badly damaged château buildings.

From the outset, the Canadians and SS troopers of the *Hitlerjugend* waged their own bitter fight with scant regard for the rules of war on either side. It was,

The Military Medal, awarded for acts of gallantry and devotion to duty under fire.

however, the scene of a mass execution upon which the Dorsets stumbled at Château d'Audrieu on the morning of 9 June 1944.

During 8 June a considerable number of prisoners had been taken by the *Hitlerjugend* and approximately 100 were executed at various times and places that day on the insistence of *Obersturmführer* Wilhelm Mohnke, who had already been implicated in murders of prisoners in incidents dating back to 1940 at Wormhout. Approximately sixty prisoners, mainly Canadians from the Winnipeg Rifles who had been taken in Putot, and two British soldiers had been escorted to the château, the headquarters of the *Hitlerjugend*'s recce battalion, presumably because *Sturmbannführer* Bremer could speak fluent English.[1] He was personally questioning the prisoners and when he was finished with them, he sent them over to the Eastern Front veteran *Scharführer* Stunn, who was to oversee their executions. The first batch of prisoners were shot in the back of the neck, but two of the next group turned just before they were shot to stare their executioners in the face, which greatly disturbed the young SS troopers. Consequently, the next three Canadians were ordered to lie on the ground and were shot in the back of the head. In all, some forty prisoners were executed in this manner. However,

Château d'Audrieu after post-war repairs had been carried out.

when a very heavy bombardment fell on the château area, heralding the renewed attempt by 8 Armoured Brigade to cross the railway, the remaining thirteen prisoners were simply machine-gunned. Due to the pressure they were under, the Recce Battalion on the night of 8/9 June withdrew from the area of the château before they had the opportunity to conceal their crime. When the British

A postcard of pre-war Audrieu, which was a patchwork of paddocks and buildings.

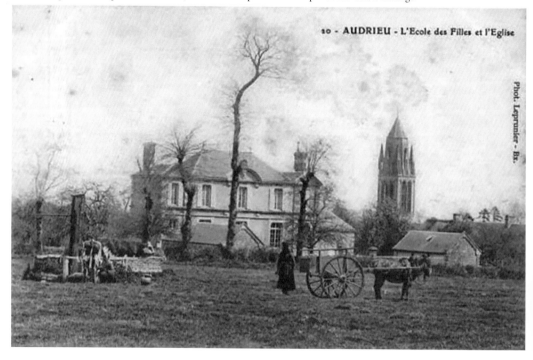

10 - AUDRIEU - L'Ecole des Filles et l'Eglise

Phot. Leprunier - Bx.

advanced past the château the following day, Major Bredin was shown the bodies by Monique Level, the daughter of the château's owner. He wrote: 'We saw them with our own eyes laid out in rows behind the château …'

Attempts were made to stop the executions of prisoners, but for some time this did not prevent the casual battlefield killings at the point of capture by both sides.[2] Eventually, it was realized that the killing of prisoners benefited neither side and was officially frowned upon but was never entirely stamped out.

The Mobile Column

Meanwhile, the Lancers and DLI were preparing a column for the swing out to the west. The plan was that the Recce troop's ten Honey light tanks would lead, with the DLI's C, B and A companies, in that order, mounted on the Lancers' Shermans. D Company would follow on their bicycles along with the battalion's support weapons in their carriers.

At 0930 hours, the Recce Troop crossed the railway and was moving tactically by bounds. Just an hour later the column halted 1,000 yards short of Point 103, and at 1100 hours with the brigade's tactical headquarters and 147 (Essex Yeomanry) Field Regiment's Sexton self-propelled 25-pounders came up to join them. Brigadier Cracroft wrote: '… we motored quickly forward onto Pt 103, meeting no opposition. The enemy were so surprised at this manoeuvre that only a few shots were fired at us from AUDRIEU and LE HAUT D'AUDRIEU as we advanced.'

It wasn't entirely plain sailing for all parts of the column, as 8 DLI's historian records that

> D Company brought up the rear on their bicycles, or it would be more accurate to say pushing their bicycles. As the column did not keep to the roads but moved over undulating cornfields the going was too bad for bicycles, and exasperated D Company men had to push them all the way. This caused some ribald amusement to the other companies who had up to this point rather envied D Company in their mobile role.

With the Lancers and DLI halted, the brigadier went on forward to carry out a reconnaissance and summoned his commanding officers to an observation post overlooking the next bound for orders.

With the guns moving forward to support the advance down the second bound, Brigadier Cracroft kept 8 DLI and the Lancers in positions on Point 103 prepared to resume the advance south on Route CONGO until 4th/7th DG was ordered up onto the feature to take over its defence. By 1300 hours, the Dragoons, an additional troop of tank destroyers and 147 Field

Durham Light Infantry cap badge.

Regiment joined the Cheshires' A (MG) Company on the broad plateau of
Point 103. Major Martin, with the two platoons of machine guns on the feature,
recalled that

> The situation was precarious, because if the enemy put in a determined
> attack from the south, he would be right on top of us before encountering
> our tanks or anti-tank guns. So were very cheered when soon after
> midday, recce parties from 1 Dorsets arrived to say that Audrieu was being
> cleared and the Battalion would soon come to join us.

He would, however, have to wait until the evening as the situation on Route
CONGO was far from straightforward. In the meantime, the Lancers' war diary
describes what it was like to be on the crest of Point 103 waiting for the attack on
Saint-Pierre:

> The Regiment remained in this position during the day and engaged self-
> propelled guns and dug-in German heavy tanks which continually shelled
> the position with High Explosive and – when opportunity offered – with
> armour-piercing. The position was also subjected to heavy mortar fire day
> and night. The Germans were found to be using flashless 88mm guns which
> made their position extremely difficult to locate.[3] Most useful support was
> given to the Regiment while holding this position by our artillery observa-
> tion post.

This British conversion of the M10 Tank Destroyer mounts a 17-pounder gun and has an out-of-
action cover for the open turret top erected.

The Germans were not, however, having things their own way. Two troops of 288 Anti-Tank Battery were in action

with three six-pounders each, deployed along the forward edge of the field with the muzzles poking through gaps in the hedge, and Lieutenant May's two M10s were sitting at the far side of the field keeping a lookout to the north. The battle proceeded throughout the day, and although the enemy fire was accurate, casualties were light. Hitting back at such extreme range made observation of results difficult but at least six enemy tanks and self-propelled guns were definitely destroyed. The Battery claimed two German 'Panther' tanks,[4] one hit by Sergeant Thompson's M10 and another knocked out with four rounds of [discarding] sabot, a new and effective anti-tank projectile, fired from Sergeant Joyce's gun. Lieutenant Brameld, commanding No. 2 troop, borrowed from one of the Armoured Regiments a Firefly and scored several hits on at least two more Panthers.[5]

Other long-range hits were reported, with one being variously recorded as a Tiger or a *Sturmgeschütz*. Another was hit on the engine deck by an HE round at 4,000 yards.

The 4th/7th DGs' war diary records its fighting strength: 'Regiment had 39 tanks fit [i.e. a loss of twenty-five Shermans in three days]. Casualties two officers killed, six wounded; eight Other Ranks killed, seventeen wounded and seven missing.'

Meanwhile, having been relieved by 4th/7th DG, the SRY were back in the assembly area at Martigny, where in the short hours of summer darkness they would carry out repairs, replenish fuel and ammunition and get a couple of hours' sleep before dawn at 0430 hours.

Forward on Point 103, the replenishment of the 24th Lancers in daylight before they launched their attack was a totally different matter, as explained by the Lancers' padre Mark Green:

We got A1 Echelon,[6] the most forward soft vehicles, into an orchard on Point 103 and established the Regiment Aid Post there. All the time things were unpleasant, the enemy was mortaring us, and our tanks grouped on and around Point 103 seemed to be having quite a battle. Casualties came in in pretty large numbers, including Bertie Garai, who had had a pretty horrible time, with his driver killed outright and his crew all wounded. I got the crews of the Echelon vehicles on to the job of brewing up water so that we could give the wounded some tea. One of our boys, Carter, came in with a leg blown off, and the Doctor worked on him for over an hour (later I heard he was doing well in England).

Various episodes come back, but there is no sequence about them; one man whom I had prepared in England for confirmation, gibbering like an idiot, bomb-happy; the Doctor doing a blood transfusion in the rain, with a gas-cape rigged up for shelter and the bottles of plasma and bits of tubing lashed to a tree trunk; other Regimental Aid Posts on Point 103 all filled to overflowing with wounded men lying on the ground; so the evening wore on, punctuated every few minutes by a whizzing noise, an explosion, and more casualties, sometimes in our own orchard. It seemed to be a desperate problem to get the wounded evacuated back to the Advance Dressing Station – not nearly enough ambulances. I suppose we had something to eat, probably numerous cups of tea, hard biscuits and chocolate, and endless cigarettes.

Panzer Lehr Advances on Bayeux

From the crest of Point 103, throughout the day considerable movement of enemy vehicles and panzers was visible northwards from Tilley-sur-Seulles towards Bayeux and from Juvigny eastwards. This was the bulk of *Panzer Lehr* deploying and, in the case of the northward movement, launching an attack on Bayeux.

I SS Panzer Corps' plan for 9 June was to renew the attack northwards. On the right flank, 26 SS *Panzergrenadiers* attacked Norrey but the main German effort, benefiting from poor weather in the UK that grounded most Allied aircraft, lay with *Panzer Lehr*, which directed its attack west of the River Seulles towards Bayeux. This attack fell on 151 Brigade and 6 DLI in particular, whose A Company was dug in astride the road to the north of Jerusalem crossroads. They were occupying trenches that had been dug by the Germans presumably prior to D-Day. Major Atkinson, commanding the battalion, commented that 'We only had to alter them, so they faced in the opposite direction.'

One of the unique features of the division's *panzergrenadiers* is that they wore the short double-breasted assault gun tunic rather than the usual longer M36/40 jacket.

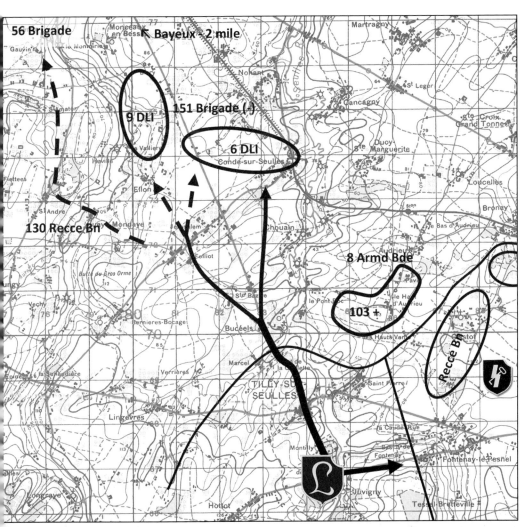

The situation around midday, 9 June.

The advance of some 6 miles north from Tilly-sur-Seulles was led by Major von Fallois' 130th Recce Battalion, which would then cross the River Aure to cover the left flank of the advance on Bayeux. The main attack was to be delivered by Major Prinz von Schönburg-Waldenburg's fifty Panzer IVs of II Battalion, 130th Panzer Regiment, supported by I Battalion, 901 *Panzergrenadiers*. The first objective was the village of Ellon and the surrounding high ground, just 3 miles from Bayeux, which would be a good jumping-off point for an attack on the city.

From positions up on Point 103, the panzers and the infantry were spotted moving north out of Tilly and were engaged by British artillery but, moving swiftly and well dispersed, the formation was not badly hit and forged on towards Ellon to the west of the Tilly-Bayeux road.[7] By midday the panzers had passed Jerusalem and were approaching their first objective, while 130th Recce Battalion, having less artillery fire to contend with, was progressing north on the western side of the River Aure towards Guéron.

The continuing German advance was reported by observers on Point 103, but with no tanks available to 151 Brigade, divisional headquarters hurriedly deployed two self-propelled anti-tank batteries. The 289th held eight 6-pounders and four M10 tank destroyers and the 234th a dozen M10s.[8] These vehicles, mounting at this stage in the campaign a mixture of 3in and 17-pounder guns, were designed for defensive action. They would normally be deployed as a mobile force in support of a gun-line established by the towed 6-pounders of the infantry and the towed 6- and 17-pounders of an anti-tank regiment's towed troops and batteries.[9] Without these guns the six 6-pounders of 6 DLI's anti-tank platoon would have been unlikely to have halted the panzers.

As far as 6 DLI were concerned, the first reports of enemy recce probing forward came during late morning from a standing patrol at the Drouet/Jerusalem crossroads. Around midday a Panzer IV, with infantry, approached A Company's positions astride the Tilly-Bayeux road. Private Lodge described the action:

> We could hear them coming ... but the tank was coming straight down the road ... Our officer issued sticky bombs ... We were supposed to run out and stick it on the side of the tank and that used to knock the tank out. We thought, 'There's no tank going to get that near.' ... On the opposite side of the road, we had the Cheshires with their machine guns and our own anti-tank 6-pounder. 'Crack!' Our 6-pounder knocked the first one out ... I can just still remember the first one, because I was up with my rifle waiting for someone bailing out and there was nobody bailed out. The fellow next to me pulled me down and said, 'If you don't want your head blown off, get down here.'

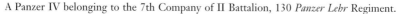

A Panzer IV belonging to the 7th Company of II Battalion, 130 *Panzer Lehr* Regiment.

At 1430 hours, German armoured cars and infantry opened fire on A Company, initiating a fire-fight designed to cover a right flanking move using the hedgerows. This took the *panzergrenadiers* into B Company's field of fire. Well camouflaged, the company withheld its fire until the Germans were at a range of less than 100 yards and then opened fire with Vickers and Bren machine guns. The enemy infantry was driven back, and this part of the battle had subsided by 1600 hours.

At 1720 hours enemy tanks were reported heading towards A and B companies' position and were engaged by artillery and mortars. Despite this, in the hedgerows and orchards along the line of the stream forward of B Company's position, Lieutenant Scott, commanding the company's forward platoon, reported that a tank was infiltrating into the position. The panzer was promptly engaged by

Panzer Lehr's attack on 151 Brigade, 9 June 1944.

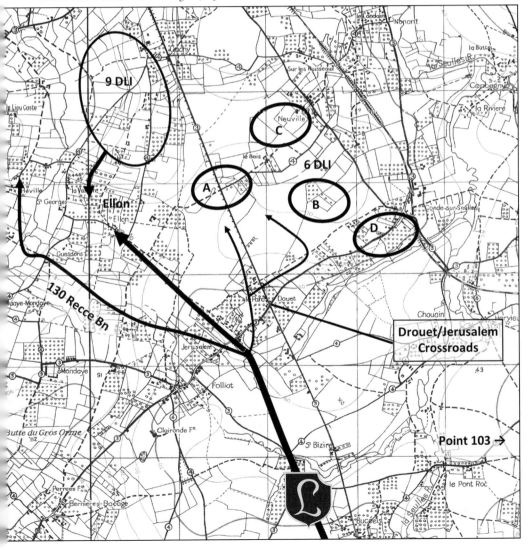

Private Wheatley of 6 DLI in action with a Bren gun near Drouet during June 1944. The censor has unusually obliterated the 'Durham LI' shoulder title but not the divisional flash.

one of 6 DLI's anti-tank sections, but the shot ricocheted off the turret. In return fire, the 6-pounder, which in firing had revealed its position, was destroyed by another tank. The second of the section's guns continued to fire at a group of six Panzer IVs that were forming up in the orchards 600 yards in front of them.

This was clearly a dangerous situation, and without a Royal Artillery forward observation officer (FOO) of their own, they had passed details to A Company's FOO who was himself under fire. Lance Corporal Ware, the B Company signal detachment commander, coolly passed the firing data but by the time the fire control orders had reached the ships of the Royal Navy bombardment force, the fast-moving panzers were less than 300 yards away. Ware recalled that the first

shell came over from the ships at sea . . . We thought it was going to take our heads off . . . The first shot was a direct hit on a tank. It was fantastic to see and then there was salvo after salvo fired after that. The infantry lads were standing up cheering. It was really fantastic what the Navy did that day.

B Company was soon reinforced by a section of the M10 tank destroyers, but one was eventually knocked out and the other immobilized by running over one of the DLI's own mines as it manoeuvred to take a shot.

Attacks on A Company were similarly broken up by artillery and naval gunfire. Major Atkinson later wrote in a report:

> The success of the last two days was reflected in the magnificent spirit of the men. Some were under fire for the first time and had certainly been shaken by the appearance of the first troop of tanks on our front but the first-class shooting of the artillery and anti-tank guns soon restored confidence.

Meanwhile, to the west of the Tilly-Bayeux road, the village of Ellon was under attack. It was held by forward elements of 9 DLI who were driven out by a superior force. Fighting in the village was over quickly and the *panzergrenadiers* now felt the full fury of the Allied artillery: two field regiments plus mortars. Panzer platoon commander Lieutenant Balko wrote:

> The enemy's artillery fire concentrated on the village and it increased in intensity. Shells of all sizes rained down on houses and panzers without stopping. Heavy mortar rounds smashed into the road sending splinters of steel slicing through the air, crashing against our panzers. The 7th and 8th companies' panzers continued through the village to its northern edge. The grenadiers followed, rounding up prisoners and sending them back. When Ellon was finally cleared of enemy, we in the 5th Company along with the 6th stayed in the village and when the artillery fire lifted we dismounted and looked at the damage to our panzers; antennas and bazooka plates had been ripped off and track guards crushed like eggshells.

The situation for the Germans was, however, deteriorating elsewhere on *Panzer Lehr*'s battlefield. The increasing numbers of British troops reported in Audrieu and arriving on Point 103 had been of growing concern to headquarters I SS Panzer Corps since midday, but when the attack on Saint-Pierre and its bridge over the Seulles developed, there was a threat of break-out. Orders were given to suspend the advance on Bayeux and to send back the 7th and 8th panzer companies to counter-attack. Similarly, eastward movement towards Fontenay was turned around. The German intent at this stage was to resume the attack on Bayeux once the situation south of Point 103 had been resolved. However, as reports of the scale of Allied operations climbed through the German chain of command, Bayerlein was ordered to halt the advance and withdraw to defensive positions on the line Verrières, Tilly and linking up with the *Hitlerjugend* near Cristot. The events on Point 103 had drawn the teeth of *Panzer Lehr*'s counter-stroke. 9 DLI recorded that C Company retook Ellon from the retiring Germans, supported by their carrier platoon providing mobile fire-power and artillery.

Of the result of the day's fighting, Major Ritgen of 130 Panzer Regiment said '… the only classic armoured attack conducted by the *Panzer Lehr* in Normandy was at an end. At the same time, the attempt to thwart the enemy that had landed back into the sea and regain the initiative finally failed.'

The Attack on Saint-Pierre

The capture of the village of Saint-Pierre was to be the first stage of the next bound south to Villers-Bocage. During the early afternoon Major Dunn of 8 DLI,[10] Lieutenant Colonel Anderson of the 24th Lancers and the commanding officer of 147 Field Regiment assembled on Point 103 to produce their plan for an advance to Point 111, the high ground east of Juvigny (Objective Ouise). Captain English recalled:

Captain English.

> The village was surrounded by very thick hedgerows and bushy trees, but it was possible to see a little of St Pierre from Point 103, and when Major Dunn had carried out a reconnaissance, he gave out his orders from an orchard on the feature. The plan was to attack with C and D Companies forward. On reaching the village C Company was to swing right-handed to take up a position round the church and the bridge over the River Seulles, covering the western exits. D Company was to push through the village and hold a position astride the road leading to Fontenay-le-Pesnel; this was to be the limit of advance. A and B Companies were to be called forward when the leading companies had reached their objectives. The 24th Lancers would protect the open left flank. Concentrations on the village would be fired by 147 Field Regiment for fifteen minutes before the advance commenced.

The attack started well at 1745 hours, with the Cheshires joining the barrage with an indirect machine-gun shoot on the village. C Company advanced downhill behind what was described as 'a rather ineffectual smoke screen', with D Company following, all supported by the Shermans of the Lancers' C Squadron. The remaining squadrons remained on the high ground in overwatch. The Germans in and around Saint-Pierre held their fire until the companies had almost reached the village. Machine guns and mortars caused casualties in C Company as they sought cover and returned the fire. The wounded included C Company commander Major Laybourne. D Company had, meanwhile, moved up and, having won the fire-fight with the assistance of the Lancers' tanks firing high-explosive shell and adding fire from their hull and co-ax machine guns, the two companies forced their way into the village. Captain English wrote:

> Fierce fighting broke out in the back gardens and orchards of cottages, Brens and Sten guns being used at close range. After a short but fierce fight the two companies broke the German hold on St. Pierre, drove the enemy from the village and gained their objectives. The rest of the Battalion saw the red and

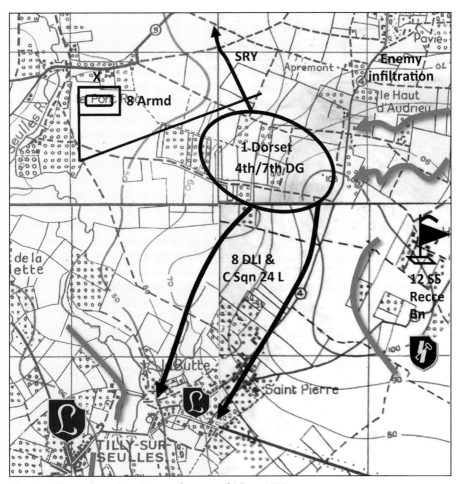

The 8 DLI's attack on Saint-Pierre, afternoon of 9 June 1944.

green Verey lights – the success signal – go up and Major Dunn immediately ordered A and B Companies forward.

The DLI had closed up to the eastern end of the bridge over the Seulles as planned by 1900 hours but had been unable to cross; the German panzer-grenadiers were in strength at the other end. Brigadier Cracroft considered that 'there is no doubt that we were lucky to get into St Pierre so quickly but our luck was in part due to the speed of advance which took the enemy by surprise before he had time to react effectively to the threat of our domination.'

Saint-Pierre had proved to be more heavily defended than had been anticipated and 8 DLI was constantly shelled and mortared, which contributed to a mounting list of casualties, among which the infantry commanders featured heavily. In the dark it proved impossible for the companies to do more than clear their own immediate objectives. Consequently, some Germans infiltrated out of the village, while others it is believed lay up overnight.

From the high ground to the south-east of the village the Germans had a good view over Saint-Pierre and the surrounding country. Consequently, any movement by the DLI while they dug in and prepared the village for defence was engaged by machine-gun or mortar fire. Several of the Lancers' Shermans were hit and set on fire by long-range anti-tank fire from the direction of Fontenay-le-Pesnel. The battalion's anti-tank guns that came down from Point 103 were joined by a troop of guns from 288 Anti-Tank Battery. By the time darkness had fallen, the Durhams held Saint-Pierre securely but, as Captain English confirmed, 'the Germans were far from beaten; on the outskirts of the village they waited patiently for an opportunity to recapture it.'

Two squadrons of the Lancers were called in closer to Point 103 for the night: A Squadron covering the south-east approaches and B the south-west. C Squadron remained in support of 8 DLI covering the Seulles bridge.

The 8 DLI's defensive positions in Saint-Pierre on the night of 9/10 June 1944.

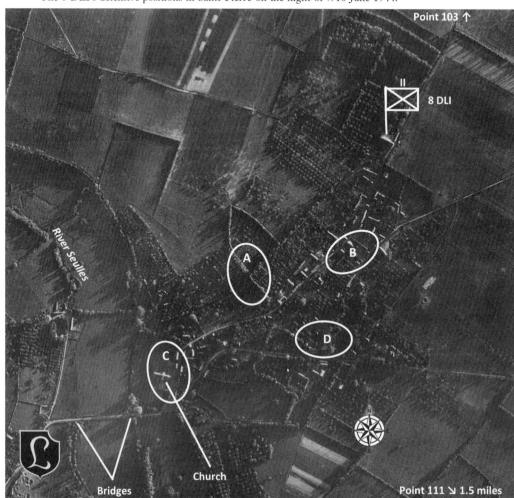

After dark Padre Green accompanied six trucks from A1 Echelon down to Saint-Pierre to replenish C Squadron's tanks. While he was in the village, he visited 8 DLI's Regimental Aid Post (RAP):

> The RAP was in a damaged farmhouse. The wounded lay about the floor all over the place. By the light of a lantern the Doctor, who had been so eager to get to his unit yesterday, worked on his knees, with the wounded groaning all round him, some unconscious, some sleeping fitfully, one or two dead. It seemed quite impossible to evacuate them. I did what I could to help.

With it being clear that there was going to be no advance to Juvigny that evening, it was not until after 1900 hours that Brigadier Cracroft abandoned Route

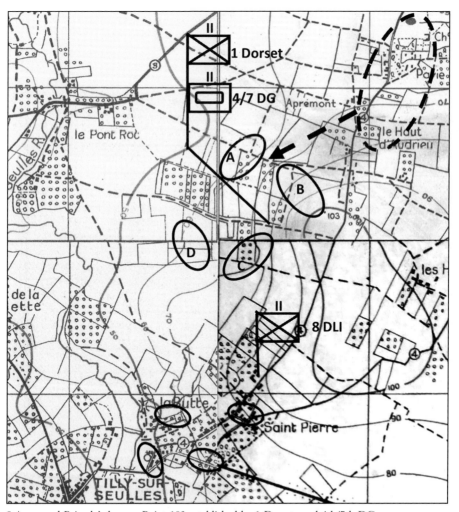

8 Armoured Brigade's box on Point 103 established by 1 Dorsets and 4th/7th DG.

CONGO through Audrieu and ordered the Dorsets onto Point 103 to form a 'defensive box'. Arriving at 2015 hours, they were under fire and time was too short for proper battle procedure to take place; consequently, rough areas were allocated to the company commanders in order to produce the 'defensive box' around the plateau. With no time for liaison, the Dorsets selected positions with little reference to the layout of the armour or indeed other companies. The result of the haste was that the defences on Point 103 lacked coherence on the night of 9/10 June 1944.[11]

Throughout the night the weary Dorsets dug, and across the feature the clink of pick and shovel on the rocky ground of Point 103 could be heard.

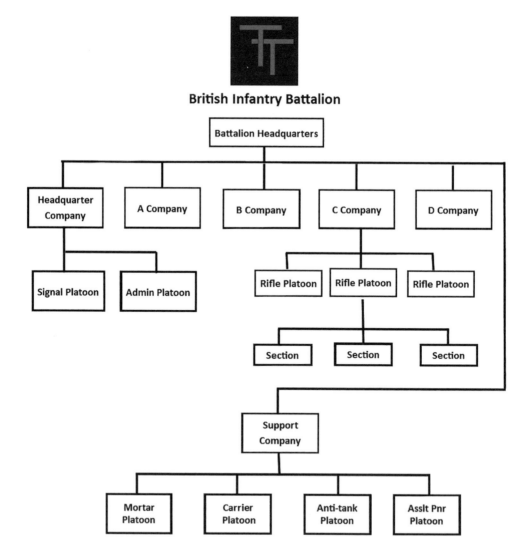

British Infantry Battalion

Chapter Six

Attack and Counter-Attack

On 10 June, with the 7th Armoured Division belatedly assembling in Normandy, General Montgomery's main effort still lay with XXX Corps. The corps' grouping of veteran formations that had delivered him victory in the Mediterranean was expected to do so again, while I Corps held the hinge around Caen. I Corps' role was to fix 12th *Hitlerjugend* Panzer and 21st Panzer divisions with attacks designed to attract German reserves and support XXX Corps in what was clearly a revised plan to capture Caen by envelopment.[1]

Of his plans for 8 Armoured Brigade on 10 June, Brigadier Cracroft wrote:

> I had hoped to be able to continue the advance southward to my next objective, the TESSEL-BRETTEVILLE feature but it soon became apparent that enemy opposition was stronger than I expected. On looking back at it now, in view of the large enemy columns of both tanks and infantry which we had halted the day before, it is not surprising that this opposition was strong.

In Saint-Pierre, after a relatively quiet night, all seemed to bode well and before dawn on 10 June the soldiers of 8 DLI stood to their arms prepared for an attack. After two hours in their trenches, ready and waiting, there was no sign of enemy movement and the Durhams 'stood down' at 0615 hours, then the Germans launched their counter-attack.

I SS Panzer Corps ordered the salient represented by the British at Point 103 and Saint-Pierre reduced by *Panzer Lehr* in order to restore their designated defensive line of Verrières-Tilly-Cristot. Overnight Major Prinz von Schönburg-Waldenburg with the 7th and 8th companies of II Battalion, 130 Panzer Regiment and the infantry of I and II battalions of 901 *Panzergrenadiers* carried out their prepared-for battle. After a sharp artillery and mortar bombardment of Saint-Pierre, they advanced, making good use of the narrow lanes and deeply-hedged orchards, to work their way into the village. Their attack was coordinated with one by elements of the *Hitlerjugend* from the direction of Fontenay, namely the Panthers of the 2nd Company and elements of 12th SS Recce Battalion.

A heavy bombardment of the village was just the prelude to the counter-attack that initially fell on C Company nearest to the Seulles bridge. This company was, of course, already much reduced in numbers by the previous evening's battle. The *panzergrenadiers'* first determined rush quickly overran the company. Meanwhile, A Company in rear of C was under fire as the bombardment crept through the village and they reported 'enemy infantry approaching' and were forced to

The church overlooking the Seulles River and bridges was the centre of C Company's positions.

withdraw towards battalion headquarters. Brigadier Hargest, the liaison officer from the New Zealand army, noted that 'while under heavy fire they panicked and some of them went right back to their previous day's start lines':

> Lieutenant Laws, the Battalion Intelligence Officer, went forward and took command of the remnants of C Company. He quickly reorganised them and the situation was temporarily restored. When the sadly depleted company had to make a further withdrawal Lieut. Laws stayed behind to give them covering fire and used a Bren gun most effectively against the enemy at very short range. He was wounded in the groin and though unable to carry the Bren gun continued to use a rifle. He did not withdraw until C Company was firmly established in its new position.[2]

The tersely-worded entries in 8 DLI's war diary give a flavour of the counter-attack's progress following the overrunning of C Company:

0724: Tanks reported to be on the way. A Company forced to withdraw from positions in village at 0745 hrs as enemy behind them.

0800: D Company report enemy tanks moving along FONTENAY-LE-PESNEL road towards Saint-Pierre. Enemy now only 100 yards from B Company.

0830: Tanks from 24th Lancers move out to protect our left flank.

0845: All companies less D Company now formed round Battalion HQ at 851691. For the next two hours the battalion fought off the enemy in this area – tanks which went into SAINT-PIERRE were shot at by the enemy and destroyed.

The farm on the northern edge of Saint-Pierre which was used by 8 DLI for their battalion HQ and around which the companies took up defensive positions on 10 June 1944.

In more detail, the enemy infantry and panzers from the direction of Fontenay were approaching the village across more open ground, where heavy artillery fire temporarily halted them but, reorganizing quickly, the young SS troops

came on again to drive a wedge between 17 Platoon and the rest of the company. The platoon suffered heavy casualties and was forced to withdraw. This exposed 18 Platoon dangerously on the left, and the company commander, Captain English, was obliged to withdraw the platoon and the anti-tank gun crews to a mutually supporting position with the rest of the company. As D Company took up its new positions more German infantry and tanks worked round to the left of the village to advance towards the B Company sector. [See map on page 89]

During this fight, the depleted C Squadron, with its officer commanding wounded, were driven back up onto Point 103, where they were put into reserve to reorganize. B Squadron was promptly sent down to support 8 DLI. Also in support were the eight 5.25in guns of HMS *Argonaut*[3] and the artillery, whose forward observer parties lost heavily but brought down Mike concentrations at crucial moments. *Obergefreiter* Petrov, a Latvian volunteer in 7 Company, II/901 *Panzergrenadiers*, took part in the attack and was later taken prisoner. His diary entry for 10 June was translated by the 50th Division's Intelligence Section and it described the impact of the Allied defensive fire:

Early this morning we put in our attack. We had three self-propelled guns under command. We attacked a village. That was some show and some shooting. We shot up six tanks. Bullets were whistling overhead. As soon as we got beyond the village the artillery opened up, and I'll say there was confusion. Oh, that was certainly no fun. Nearly became a prisoner of war. Three of our vehicles gone ...

Meanwhile, the panzers advancing from the west partially overran B Company. One section was engaged particularly heavily by panzer and machine-gun fire, and all but one man was either killed or wounded:

> Pte Protano refused to withdraw, although other sections started to pull back, and remained at his post shooting at the tanks with a Bren gun he had taken from a wounded man. When eventually the enemy tanks were driven off the men of B Company who moved forward to re-occupy their positions found Protano still at his post, busy dressing the wounded men of his section. He was awarded the Military Medal.

The Shermans of B Squadron quickly joined the action in the village, but the first tank to enter Saint-Pierre was knocked out and burned fiercely in the narrowest point of the village street, blocking the road. Other tanks that entered the village were knocked out at short range. Consequently, most of the Lancers' tanks deployed to the north of Saint-Pierre, from where they worked their way around to the west into more open country. Here they came under anti-tank gunfire from Tilly and a pair of Shermans were quickly knocked out. The remainder withdrew under cover of smoke to the cover of the orchards around the village:

> In St Pierre the noise of battle was deafening as the fighting reached its climax; the crash of the bursting shells and mortar bombs mingled with the staccato rattle of machine guns and Sten guns. The fierce German artillery and mortar fire was exacting a heavy toll on the men of the 8th and wounded were coming into the Regimental Aid Post faster than they could be dealt with.

A Company and Battalion Headquarters were also under attack. It was one of those occasions when cooks, clerks and signallers found themselves as combat infantrymen when the German infantry supported by three panzers broke into their part of the village. The adjutant climbed onto a Sherman parked up near headquarters and directed its machine-gun fire. Lance Sergeant Wallbanks was instrumental in stopping the panzers:

> While this fight was in progress three enemy tanks advanced in single file down one of the narrow streets of the village, driving some cows before them. L/Sgt[4] S.P. Wallbanks of 17 Platoon of D Company rapidly restored the situation. The No. 1 on the PIAT gun was killed but in spite of the heavy German machine-gun fire and bursting shrapnel from the enemy artillery and mortars, Wallbanks threw himself down behind the PIAT and fired three shots in quick succession. One bomb skidded between the startled

An *Unterscharführer* of the 12th SS Panzer Division inspects a knocked-out Sherman hit in the rear, probably by a *Panzerfaust*.

The spring-propelled Projector Infantry Anti-Tank (PIAT) and the shaped-charge PIAT bomb.

cows and under the tracks of the leading tank. This put a stop to the German advance. The sergeant had saved a critical situation.

Sergeant Wallbanks received the Military Medal.

During the final stages of the battle the Durhams were able to drive the Germans out of some of their gains. *Obergefreiter* Petrov continued his account:

> Then came a counter-attack by the English ... They shot up several tanks and captured dozens of prisoners. After a long search we found the vehicles, but the enemy planes had found us, and the artillery fire came down on us again. Some are wounded, L is killed. We proceed in short bounds to regimental headquarters and await further orders.

By midday the attack by *Panzer Lehr* and the *Hitlerjugend* had been held, at least for the time being. With many casualties in both officers and men, the 8 DLI had been forced out of C and D companies' forward positions around the church and astride the Fontenay road. Major Dunn reorganized the battalion's defences and led patrols and attacks to improve the defences in the northern part of the village that the battalion still held. He and his men were 'confident of staying there' until relieved. As recorded in the Lancers' war diary, the tanks were deployed around the village with 'A Squadron on the right covering the bridge crossing the River Seulles to the east of TILLY-SUR-SEULLES and B Squadron on the left overlooking FONTENAY-LE-PESNEL.' During this period Lieutenant Colonel Anderson was wounded and evacuated.

An account of Lieutenant Colonel W.A.C. Anderson in command that morning is provided by Captain Kenneth Gill, the Regimental Intelligence Officer, who recalled that W.A.C. was 'sometimes unpredictable and always disconcerting!':

> We were in a field of corn, our tanks about 20 feet apart when there was the *whooosh* of a shell right between us and it exploded about 100 yards behind us in some trees. This was the moment when W.A.C. chose to get out of his tank and study some papers, but not before he called to me, 'Come here, 19 ("19" was my radio call-sign) and help me with this bumph.' In a totally terrified state, I shakily dismounted and went over to him. For what seemed an age we discussed some matter and then returned to our tanks. All this time stuff was hurtling about all over the place. To this day I'm sure W.A.C. was not the slightest bit concerned about the possible dangers, to the point of foolhardiness. I believe it was what made him a really powerful leader you would have followed anywhere.

Padre Green, who had spent the night at 8 DLI's RAP in Saint-Pierre, had eventually managed to get away from the village:

> I managed to acquire a 3-tonner, into which we loaded as many of these chaps as we could. Then we set off with it towards the Advance Dressing Station. We got back as far as Point 103 safely but as usual on this infernal spot a battle seemed to be raging. The path back to the Bayeux main road was not made any more inviting by the fact that tracer bullets were whizzing across it from each side. Just then, as I was surveying the scene doubtfully, I met the Brigadier (Cracroft). He was very scornful of the fact that we seemed to be held up by a few bullets and told us to crack on. 'You'll be all right,' he said, 'just push on.' At this moment the young medical Lance Corporal whom I had brought with me said 'You know, Sir, I think we ought to get on. Some of these chaps in the back of the truck aren't too good. If we don't get them treated soon they won't last long.' Feeling much ashamed of myself, I at once told the driver to go as fast as he could without jolting the 3-tonner too much and, just as the Brigadier had forecast, we got through perfectly well though the pandemonium going on all round was not reassuring.

He made it back to the division's Advanced Dressing Station (ADS) in a château at Martigny.

The 7th Armoured Division's Advance South

It had always been a part of Second Army's plan that the 7th Armoured Division would advance to 8 Armoured Brigade's patrol base on the high ground north of Villers-Bocage to create a strong offensive presence to the south of the lodgement. This was to have been achieved by D+3/D+4 but, as with other formations, delays in landing had multiplied and their tanks and artillery had been drawn away to support 56 and 69 brigades in securing the beachhead north and west of

A Cromwell cruiser tank, the main fighting vehicle of the 'Desert Rats'.

Bayeux. Now on D+4, still without 131 (Queen's) Brigade, their lorried infantry brigade, Brigadier 'Loony' Hinde's 22 Armoured Brigade was to begin the attack south through the 50th Division. The part to be played by the division in Operation WILD OATS[5] (see sketch page 186) was revised. Having broken through *Panzer Lehr*'s defence, they would head for Villers-Bocage as originally intended, but from there they would swing east to objectives on the high ground at Évrecy and on Hill 112.

En route, XXX Corps' orders specified the immediate objectives: 'to seize the high ground in the area of Hottot . . . and the high ground east of Juvigny [Tessel-Bretteville].' To help them, the three battalions of 56 Brigade were to come under command of the 7th Armoured Division, as would 8 Armoured Brigade which had been ordered to continue their advance south.

7th Armoured Division's vehicle insignia.

As Hitler, contrary to the wishes of his generals, had insisted on roping off the beachhead within range of the navy's guns, he condemned his soldiers to fighting under the crushing weight of naval artillery. An example of this fire is the support available to the 7th Armoured Division on 10 June during which, in preparation for the attack, the 6in guns of the cruiser HMS *Orion* fired 186 rounds into the village of Lingèvres alone. Throughout the day, *Orion* fired more than 1,000 rounds at key points ahead of the advance using a relay of seven air observation aircraft

The light *Leander*-class cruiser HMS *Orion*, mounting eight 6in guns.

to correct the fall of shot. Other ships in support included HMS *Nelson*'s 16in guns, which shelled Hottot at a range of 33,100 yards, and the Dutch gunboat *Flores*, which increased her range by 'listing ship' to elevate her guns beyond their normal capability.

Based on their experience in the deserts of North Africa, the 7th Armoured Division advanced on two axes, headed in the absence of the 8th Hussars, who were still de-waterproofing their Cromwell tanks, by the recce troops of the armoured regiments. The 8 mile advance to the first objective began at 0630 hours, followed by the Cromwell tanks[6] of two of 22 Armoured Brigade's regiments. Each armoured regiment had a company of the motor battalion, the 1st Rifle Brigade (1 RB), its sole infantry.[7] The three battalions of 56 Brigade would follow on foot, securing gains, with the 2nd South Wales Borderers (2 SWB) and 1 RTR being responsible for covering the four bridges over the Aure with anti-tank guns as the advance progressed south.

As they would be advancing from a start line in the narrow constraints of the ground between the rivers Seulles and Aure, 22 Armoured Brigade's advance was to be led initially by the 4th County of London Yeomanry (the 'Sharpshooters', 4 CLY) followed by the 5th Royal Tank Regiment (5 RTR). Once they had completed their passage of lines through 151 Brigade and the ground opened out, they were to divide into two columns: on the left 4 CLY headed for Tilly with the main road as its axis, and on the right 5 RTR's axis was Ellon-Verrières. 1 RTR followed in reserve, providing Cromwells to support 2 Essex. Artillery support in addition to the naval gunfire already mentioned was provided from

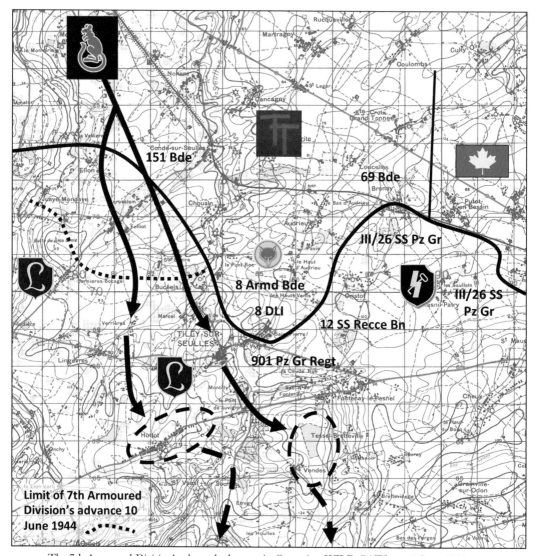

151 Bde

69 Bde

III/26 SS Pz Gr

8 Armd Bde

8 DLI

12 SS Recce Bn

III/26 SS Pz Gr

901 Pz Gr Regt

Limit of 7th Armoured
Division's advance 10
June 1944

The 7th Armoured Division's planned advances in Operation WILD OATS on 10 June 1944.

0545 hours by three field regiments and a medium regiment. As the operation began, 1 RB's three rifle companies mounted in half-tracks and carriers were rushed to join the armoured regiments, their landing having been delayed. The regimental chronicle recorded '... when the advance did start on D+4, A Company and I Company, each with an anti-tank platoon[8] under command were ready to join 4 CLY and 5 RTR, the two armoured regiments with which they normally worked.'

General Bayerlein remarked that 'It was a typical British attack. It started, as always, with a concentrated and heavy artillery preparation but relatively little air support.'

The fire was, however, effective and in I Battalion, 902 *Panzergrenadiers*' sector astride the Bayeux road, the 1st and 3rd companies sited on a particularly rocky hillside south of Jerusalem crossroads had been unable to dig in properly and suffered heavily. The 3rd Company broke and ran and had to be brought back by *Oberleutnant* Ritter. *Panzer Lehr* veterans of the Eastern Front commented that they had never experienced a bombardment like it.

Having conducted the passage of line through 151 Brigade, the first contact with German defences was made as the tanks of 4 CLY approached the Jerusalem crossroads, where one of their Cromwells was knocked out. They had run into the outposts of I Battalion, 901 *Panzergrenadiers*, reinforced by remnants of an *ost* battalion[9] belonging to the 352nd Division, which lay hidden in the hedgerows and brought the advance to a halt until companies of 1 RB could be brought forward into action (see map on page 106).

Instrumental in halting 4 CLY on 10 June was *Obergefreiter* Brasche, who was already a Knight's Cross holder. He earned further laurels on 10 June when he was serving as a section commander in 2 Platoon in *Oberleutnant* Monz's 1st Company, I Battalion, 901 *Panzergrenadier* Regiment. They were deployed near the Bayeux-Tilly road 100 yards from a sunken lane that led to the main road. Among the weaponry available was a *Panzerschreck*.

When British tanks were seen advancing down the sunken lane towards the company's left flank, Brasche took the *Panzerschreck*, dashed forward to the lane, fired at the leading tank and hit it. There was a prompt internal explosion as the shaped charge's self-forging fragment of molten metal bored through the armour and ignited the ammunition. The explosion dislodged the turret, which crashed onto the second tank. Both tanks were on fire. Brasche went after the third tank, leaving his two comrades who had accompanied him to engage the infantry of 1 RB, which had now arrived. Identifying the last tank's location further down the sunken lane by the sound of its main armament firing, Brasche

A Cromwell tank followed by its troop's Firefly.

Some *Geballte Ladung* (concentrated) hand grenades were simply bundled together, but they were so effective that there were also manufactured *Geballte Ladung* as pictured here.

stalked through the bushes to a point where he was able to place his *Geballte Ladung* on the engine deck at the base. The resulting explosion disabled the tank.

Brasche returned to his section and, using the *Panzerschreck* and his section's small arms, halted the British advance. Over the following two days *Obergefreiter* Brasche is credited with knocking out five tanks and damaging a further two.

Being attacked by infantry at close quarters was an unnerving experience for the desert veterans. Despite pre-D-Day intelligence summaries that accurately

Obergefreiter Brasche and the Knight's Cross of the Iron Cross.

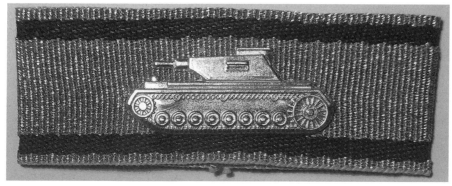

Brasche qualified for the Gold tank destruction badge.

described the bocage, the desert veterans of the 7th Armoured Division, who had retrained in early 1944 on the open Brecklands of Norfolk, were no more prepared for the thick bocage country than 8 Armoured Brigade. The *Official History* summarizes the essence of the problem in the hedge-bound

> bocage country [which] was new to the 'Desert Rats' and the enemy's small infantry detachments, each with a tank or anti-tank gun or two and a couple of 'eighty-eights' lurking in the background, were able to cause considerable delays by skilfully exploiting the close country. Some, hidden in the hedgerows, tried to lob grenades into the tanks' turrets or to fix 'sticky' bombs on them as they moved through the deep lanes.[10] Fortunately ... their bombs were not lethal enough to cause major damage, but it was clear that our tanks must have infantry to work with them.

The nature of the fighting in hedgerows of the western part of the Normandy battlefield was a surprise to British and American soldiers alike. For the 7th Armoured Division whose style of fighting had been learned in the desert where engagements had averaged at 800 yards, the bocage with engagements from 50 to 300 yards was a nasty surprise, not at all what the veterans were used to![11] One junior officer of 5 RTR commented that commanders seemed to have forgotten the lessons of Italy: in close country, tanks and infantry must work together.

Progress towards Tilly and Hottot was, consequently, painfully slow; not what the army expected from an armoured division, especially the Desert Rats. Not only were they facing panzers, but German records show that platoons of *Jagdpanzer* IV belonging to the newly-arrived and equipped 130th *Panzerjäger* Battalion were in action with their high-velocity 75mm guns.

It wasn't just the terrain that inhibited the advance, as explained by a veteran tank gunner of 4 CLY Trooper, Leslie Dinning:

> Poke your nose round corners where sitting a few yards up the road was a bloody big Tiger, Panther or a self-propelled gun, literally waiting for you and BANG! You had no chance. It only needed one shot from an enemy tank

or SP, whereas we had to put multiple shots in the side or the rear of the Tigers or Panthers. We hadn't a hope in hell of penetrating the front of a Tiger with a [lowish-velocity] 75mm gun.

I do know that there was a demonstration soon after we landed where they put a captured Panther in a field and a Firefly 17-pounder fired three armour-piercing shots at close range at the sloping front of the Panther. The first shot bounced off, the second cracked the front plate and bounced off, and the third went through. By that time, in action, the Panther would have finished off several tanks. They only needed one shot. The German gunners were excellent, no question about that.

Despite the quality of German weapons and the often exaggerated perception of their effectiveness among the Allies, for the defender there were problems as well. The Panzer IV's Kwk 40-L/40 gun was long, and the tall hedges severely restricted the traverse of the turret and in narrow winding lanes even movement was constrained. For the Panther with its still longer gun, the bocage was even more problematic. One panzer commander concluded: 'I did not believe we could do anything with panzers; therefore, we simply used them as armoured anti-tank guns or armoured machine guns.' The difficulties of fighting in the bocage, along with Allied material superiority and firepower, sapped *Panzer Lehr*'s offensive spirit.

Initially the infantry did not find the bocage much better. Londoner Rifleman O'Rourke recalled:

> We'd break cover from a hedgerow, which we'd bashed our way through avoiding gates if the enemy were around as they'd probably be mined or booby-trapped, and out into the next small field. We hardly ever saw a German and hoped they were not waiting in the hedge only 100 yards away. Sometimes they would shoot as we broke through the hedges and we'd go back into cover but normally they waited until we were out in the middle and then opened fire with their Spandaus. The NCOs had smoke grenades [white phosphorus] which made an instant cloud and we would drag our casualties back and thank our lucky stars we had survived.

A platoon's 2in mortar firing HE at muzzle flashes that had been spotted was all the platoon could do. If the enemy were not just fighting a delaying action, artillery and/or tank support was needed. However, as observed by 147 Field Regiment, artillery support was not always possible: 'When the enemy was finally located, more often than not, he was so close to or intermixed with our own troops that any form of close artillery support was out of the question.' Arranging and planning support naturally took time and that made fighting in the bocage a very slow business, which was not always recognized by headquarters further up the chain of command. O'Rourke continued:

> Unlike Jerry mortars, when the 25-pounders came down at least we knew they were coming and could get down ready. We were constantly digging

A Panther belonging to *Panzer Lehr*.

small holes to shelter in. As soon as the shells finished a section would blast away at the enemy hedgerow and we would be on our way as fast as our trotters could go to the cover of the opposite hedge, where, if we were unlucky, stick grenades waited for us!

It would take some days before the British would even begin to come to grips with the bocage and develop tactics that worked in the hedgerow country.

While 4 CLY were fighting on the road to Tilly, a mile to the north-west 5 RTR advanced on Ellon with C Squadron leading. 'Progress was very slow' and they were halted by 'roadblocks' covered by panzers or anti-tank guns and infantry with machine guns. Any attempt in the space available to manoeuvre around resistance inevitably resulted in the tanks running into yet another such enemy outpost.

Having left 4 CLY C Squadron behind to mask the Jerusalem crossroads, the rest of the regiment and its supporting infantry advanced to some more open country. A Squadron on the left came under fire; the CLY's war diary records: 'Two Cromwells A Sqn KO'd by friends area 830720.' They had been engaged by the Shermans of 8 Armoured Brigade from the north-west corner of Point 103 firing across the Seulles River. A lack of briefing, the presence of enemy armour and the angular nature of the Cromwell's turret, which had similarities to the panzer's, especially when camouflaged, had led to the loss of two tanks. 22 Armoured Brigade conceded in their report that they should have exchanged liaison officers. Even so, fratricide was all too common.

56 Brigade crossed its start lines south of Bayeux at 0830 hours as ordered. Consequently, it was mid-morning by the time the leading battalions, 2 SWB and 2 Essex, had marched from Bayeux into action. 2 Essex eventually reached Ellon, but joining 5 RTR in the bocage proved difficult in the narrow hedged lanes. Sergeant Benford commanded one of the Essex's anti-tank platoon's carriers when he '... came around a bend and I spotted a tank. I stopped my

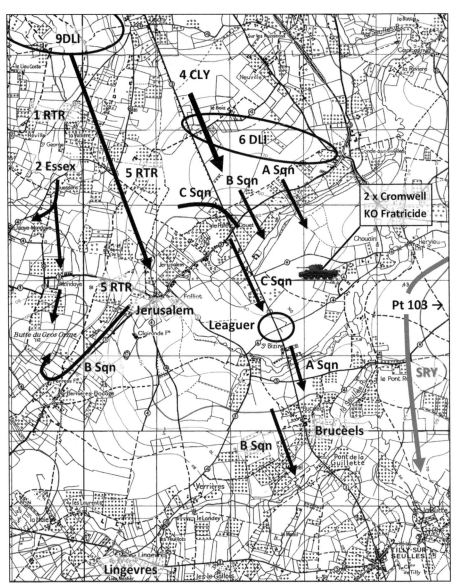

4 CLY's action on 10 June 1944.

147 Essex Yeomanry Field Regiment RA demonstrate loading a 25-pounder aboard their Sexton.

driver immediately and shouted to him to "Back up! Back up!" We got down from the carrier and crossed the road. I took my PIAT Gunner with me.'[12]

Stalking carefully along the hedge, they reached the junction and peering around, Benford saw that the panzer was in fact a knocked-out British tank! His relief was short-lived as they heard another tank approaching from the village and they prepared to take it on with the PIAT:

To behold a tank appeared over the brow of the hill, I got my PIAT gunner down behind the hedge and I said to him 'You have got one shot, get his track and he's disabled.' But it was yet another British tank with a 'Johnny-go-lightly chap' with his beret on sticking out of the turret.

Holding up his bright orange fluorescent recognition panel to get it to stop, Sergeant Benford climbed onto the tank:

The tank commander said, 'Who the hell are you?' I said vanguard of a battalion and he replied, 'Well get the hell out of it; I'm in the middle of a tank battle!' An Essex officer was fetched on the Don R's [dispatch rider's]

A 6-pounder anti-tank gun, its crew and carrier on a typical bocage road.

bike and agreed to get the carriers to turn round. We couldn't do this in the road, as it was too narrow, so we drove through a five-barred gate into an orchard and out the other end. The farmer was there and doing his nut!

Moving south through the bocage, Lieutenant Haywood's troop of 5 RTR surprised an enemy tank bivouac near Folliot, just to the west of the Jerusalem crossroads. He scattered the Germans and knocked out a Panzer IV before having to withdraw. As progress was only being made hedgerow by hedgerow on the regiment's right, an attempt was made by B Squadron to outflank and envelop the enemy to the west via Bernières-Bocage but this was unsuccessful, running into the fire of a Panther in the village. Two Cromwells were eventually knocked out in this incident, which brought 5 RTR's advance to a halt. The regiment spent most of the day fighting here and around Jerusalem village to the west of the crossroads.

While the tanks were advancing, the infantry of 56 Brigade were clearing in detail the area behind them in which there were plenty of Germans variously ambushing the unwary or running into British infantry patrols during attempts to regain their own lines. The result was numerous small actions with, for instance, 2 SWB spending the entire day around Ellon and the 2 Gloucesters clearing woods around the Jerusalem crossroads, more than a mile behind the CLY's tanks. Private Clark of the Gloucesters' B Company recalled that C Squadron,

4 CLY fired 'scores of HE and AP [armour-piercing] shells into every likely-looking building. The place was a shambles.' By the end of the day, B Company was up with the tanks approaching Bucéels. Corporal Partridge recalled:

> We had some tanks come past and I said, 'I should look out. There are German tanks down there. I would keep your eyes open down there mate!' It was a busy place. Lots of firing, bursts of machine-gun fire and shells and mortars and lots of prisoners were passing through as well. One of the sergeants in C Company knocked a tank out with a PIAT.

During the late afternoon on the far right of 22 Brigade's advance, 2 Essex was ordered to attack the large farm and monastery of Juaye-Mondaye and beyond the Butte du Gros Orme (Point 112) and Bernières-Bocage.[13] For the advance on Juaye, the battalion's FOO organized a 'considerable fire plan' to support D Company's attack, which was followed up by A Company. When they went into action at 1800 hours, the objective for Corporal Mansi's section was a part of the monastery:

> We were told that the Germans were using the monastery as an observation post. There was a high brick wall surrounding part of the monastery and also, the entrance to the monastery was like a long driveway with a high wall on the right-hand side and a short wall on the left, and then it opened out to

The Juaye-Mondaye Abbey and farm complex.

This photograph was taken at 1600 hours on 10 June near Juaye-Mondaye and shows officers and NCOs of the Panther and recce battalions.

where the monastery was. What we did was set the Bren-gunner up at the entrance to cover us as we went to the monastery.

The battalion's post-operational report stated that

as we advanced in extended line, the enemy ran for the shelter of the woods to his rear and only a few snipers remained to worry us together with cross-fire from Spandaus in the woods. The monastery area was quickly cleared but the Boche made some pretence of standing in these woods and there was little future in putting one's head above the level of banks or ditches. Again, quite a sizeable piece of ground had been won at the cost of only a few casualties.

Corporal Mansi continued:

As we got closer to the monastery, we could hear voices in the cellar, it had windows open to give light and we were hearing French people down there for protection. But there were snipers up in the roof, so we went forward and some of the chaps behind us went into the monastery, which they cleared. I don't know whether they captured or killed them. Then I remember we stopped in a deep hollow. There were shells screaming overhead.

By 1930 hours the monastery, farm and Butte were reported as being in the hands of the Essex and at the same time General Bayerlein authorized a withdrawal to Bernières-Bocage, but by then the British advance on that village had been halted.

Over on the left flank 4 CLY ended the day having reached the village of Bucéels, which the 2 Gloucesters had largely cleared, and B Squadron had reached a stream south of the village, west of le Pont de la Guillette, which they could not cross. As dusk settled, the CLY pulled back a mile to a leaguer, centred on a crossroads north of St Bazire. This was behind the Gloucesters, who remained forward and dug in around St Bazire. Unlike 8 Armoured Brigade, which had maintained a squadron of the 24th Lancers in Saint-Pierre the previous evening and deployed the whole regiment there on the night of the 10th, the tanks of the 7th Armoured Division resorted to the normal practice of leaguering to the rear. With Bucéels unoccupied, during the night the enemy infiltrated back into the village. The result was that with Bucéels unoccupied the *panzergrenadiers* reoccupied it and 7th Armoured would have to clear it again the following day!

By the evening of 10 June, the division had advanced about a third of the way to its initial objectives around Hottot and Tessel-Bretteville. The main problem was the bocage and insufficient infantry forward with the tanks. The adjutant of 1 RB summed up the day

in country with banks and thick hedges every hundred yards or so. You could not imagine closer country and it was difficult, if not impossible, to spot enemy anti-tank guns, Spandau positions or even tanks themselves if they chose to lie up and keep still. It was hopeless country for an armoured division and our hopes of a rapid 'swan-through' faded rapidly. Company I found themselves clearing one small set of houses no less than three times in the day since small parties of Germans kept filtering back ... A Company were plugging along with the leading armoured regiment and finding it necessary to watch every approach along which enemy infantry might try to stalk the tanks ... All this seemed far removed from the rapid dash some 20 miles inland for which we had been briefed, with its first objective Villers-Bocage.

It is worthy of note that tank losses were minimal: for instance, 5 RTR's war diary recorded the loss of just two Cromwells, five killed and two wounded. This led to the first questions in the chain of command as to the determination and effectiveness of 7th Armoured Division. The *Official History* in its usual style commented that 'Major General Erskine ... recognized that progress had been slow; yet he reported that he "never felt serious difficulty in beating down enemy resistance".'

The *Hitlerjugend* Counter-Attack

Meanwhile, with the counter-attack on Saint-Pierre held, fighting at close quarters went on in the village as both sides sought to improve their positions. Up on Point 103, however, it was their turn to be counter-attacked. Following the previous night's experience of probing by the enemy, Colonel Norrie was given command of the defences, with the forward Dorset companies having under command a squadron of 4th/7th DG.

This redeployment was, however, only just under way when at 1020 hours the enemy followed up their attack on 8 DLI with a counter-attack on Point 103 by fire. This was directed mainly against 1 Dorsets' D Company position, and several casualties were suffered including the company commander, Major Hayes, who was wounded. Major Bredin, the second-in-command, recalled that 'It was quite obvious by now that our penetration into hostile territory was not at all popular with the Germans, and they favoured us with ever-increasing attention.' This came largely from the *Hitlerjugend*, who launched a counter-attack with *panzergrenadiers* and tanks at 1142 hours from a wooded area between Point 103 and Cristot. The Dorsets' B Company bore the brunt of this attack, but beat it off with the assistance of their squadron of 4th/7th DG and 147 Field Regiment.

There was also a potential attack, loosely coordinated with that from the east, across the Seulles from where the 7th Armoured Division were advancing. Brigadier Cracroft wrote:

During the morning I also got reports of bodies of enemy infantry moving in towards 103 from the west, i.e. from the area BUCÉELS and STE BAZIRE. I dealt with this by ordering the SRY to move up from BRÉCY and by clearing the area south of the railway and up to the river NW of 103.

Young *Hitlerjugend panzergrenadiers* waiting in cover armed with K98 rifles and an MG42.

It was probably during the time that the SRY, a squadron of which had been ordered forward from reserve at Brécy, engaged and knocked out two of 4 CLY's Cromwells. Error realized, the squadron patrolled on south and eventually made contact with 24 Lancers around Saint-Pierre before being recalled to Brécy.

The 147 Field Regiment's war diary records that about this time '431 Battery position came under enemy machine-gun fire – enemy driven off.' The regiment's Sextons were of course still within the Dorsets' defensive box and significantly helped them. The gunner's diary goes on to report that 'CRISTOT strongly held by enemy. Several Regimental [Mike] targets fired on CRISTOT – some in conjunction with 86th Field Regiment.'

Brigadier Cracroft wrote that

By the afternoon all counter-attacks had been driven off, with an estimated loss to the enemy of 2 Tigers, 4 Mark IVs and 3 75mm self-propelled guns, and most of ST. PIERRE was again in our hands. I realised, however, that the situation on Point 103 was going to be rather uncomfortable and I was anxious to avoid, if possible, the heavy mortaring to which we had been subjected the night before. The only way in which it seemed possible to achieve this was to send out patrols to try and drive the enemy further away from us out of mortar range.

The 8th Durham Light Infantry were fully committed in ST. PIERRE and 1 Dorsets who had had very heavy fighting ever since landing were committed to holding the vital Point 103 feature. With all of my infantry committed I only had tanks available for patrols. I accordingly ordered the SRY to send out squadron patrols in the east and south-east direction and gave them the support of 147 Field Regiment. These patrols soon made contact with the enemy and succeeded in inflicting quite a lot of casualties as well as finding good targets for the artillery. I think they paid a handsome dividend.

In the evening I ordered the SRY to relieve 4th/7th DG in support of 1 Dorsets and to relieve 24th Lancers on Point 103. I moved 4th/7th DG back to the area of BRÉCY to rest and re-fit. I moved the whole of 24th Lancers into ST. PIERRE as the 8 DLI who had had heavy casualties needed strong support and I was anxious not to lose the village again.

Sherwood Rangers Yeomanry cap badge.

Of the move from Brécy where they had been in reserve north of the N13, the SRY's historian wrote:

> We stayed on the alert as we were expecting an enemy counter-attack at any moment. At dusk, A and C Squadrons moved down from Point 103 to an orchard behind St. Pierre. The noise of the move attracted a good deal of shelling, and one tank had its track blown off. The shelling went on all night and there was no sleep.

There were alarms and excursions up on Point 103 as well, as recorded in the Dorsets' war diary: 'B. [Company] call for fire and 3″ mortar DF[14] tasks to break up suspected enemy counter-attack from the east. Enemy found dead in farm identified as *panzergrenadiers*.' Cracroft commented that 'In spite of our patrols we had another uncomfortable night from enemy mortar fire. It was heavy and went on nearly all night.'

While the fighting had been going on in Saint-Pierre and up on Point 103, the considerable routine problem of delivering 'the life blood of an armoured formation' – combat supplies – had to be maintained. Brigadier Cracroft continued:

> After the fighting we had been through it was obviously necessary to bring up ammunition and petrol; food, of course, was also necessary. I had had assembled during the morning a column of some sixty lorries in the area of ST. LÉGER, ready to move forward whenever a favourable opportunity occurred. This column was moved forward in the early afternoon after the Sherwood Rangers Yeomanry had cleared up the area north-west of Point 103. As it moved up under tank escort, it was subjected to some small-arms fire from the AUDRIEU area into which the enemy had again infiltrated. There were no serious casualties, however. Supplies were delivered and the column returned again under tank escort, taking back wounded, amongst whom was my Brigade Major.

When the supply column arrived, an American officer came with it in a jeep. He said he was a liaison officer from the American 155mm Battalion,[15] and he asked if I would like any heavy artillery support. As can be imagined, I was delighted to see him and gave him a number of targets which were out of range of my own 147 Field Regiment.

Attack on Headquarters Panzer Group West

General Geyr von Schweppenburg's Headquarters of Panzer Group West had come forward to exercise command of the planned counter-attack on the Allied lodgement by the massed panzer divisions. It had been set up in a château at La Caine 12 miles south of Caen and was about to share the same experience of Allied air power as his panzer divisions had on their march to the invasion area. His staff had set up the headquarters in the building, but had left four large communication trucks, several office caravans and sundry tents in the open with little effort to conceal them.

The location of the headquarters had been tentatively identified by Bletchley Park, but pinpointed by a British high-frequency radio direction-finding station when they transmitted to the 17 SS *Panzergrenadier* Division, which was

General Geyr von Schweppenburg.

marching to Normandy. SHAEF immediately ordered a major attack by the 2nd Tactical Air Force (2 TAF): some ten squadrons, all still flying from southern England, consisting of forty-two Typhoon fighter bombers and seventy-two B-25 Mitchell medium bombers.

The attack was delayed by poor weather, but when the force struck the staff officers were just sitting down to dinner in the château. When the air-raid sirens sounded, they went outside to see the Allied air forces that they had heard so much about over the previous days. Joined by General Geyr, who had just returned to the headquarters, little did the assembled group of officers think that they were the target!

The aircraft came over in waves between 2000 and 2115 hours, dropping 552 500lb bombs and firing approximately 340 60lb rockets. Seventeen of the eighteen staff officers of Panzer Group West were known to have been killed in the raid, including the Chief of Staff General von Dawans, and General Geyr was seriously wounded. Casualties were equally high among signallers, clerks and drivers. The château was not badly hit, but the nearby orchard was thoroughly bombed and the HQ vehicles and communications equipment were destroyed. Panzer Group West was comprehensively taken out of the chain of command and it was some twelve hours before Headquarters Seventh Army found out about the disaster. The German counter-attack that the headquarters had been planning was first postponed and then cancelled.

Royal Air Force B-25 Mitchell bombers.

21 ARMY **GROUP**

PERSONAL MESSAGE
FROM THE C-IN-C

(To be read out to all Troops)

1. After four days of fighting the Allied Armies have secured a good and firm lodgment area on the mainland of France.

2. First, we must thank Almighty God for the success we have achieved and for giving us a good beginning towards the full completion of our task.

3. Second, we must pay a tribute to the Allied Navies and Air Forces for their magnificent co-operation and support; without it, we soldiers could have achieved nothing.

4. Third, I want personally to congratulate every officer and man in the Allied Armies on the splendid results of the last four days.
   British, Canadian and American soldiers, fighting gallantly side by side, have achieved a great success, and have placed themselves in a good position from which to exploit this success.

5. To every officer and man, whatever may be his rank or employment, I send my grateful thanks and my best wishes for the future.
   Much yet remains to be done; but together, you and I, we will do it, and we will see the thing through to the end.

6. Good luck to you all.

B. L. Montgomery

General
C.-in-C.,
21 Army Group

France, 10 June 1944.

General Montgomery's message to the Army Group, 10 June 1944.

The burnt out office bus where von Schwepenburg and Rommel had been having a meeting at the original time of the raid.

The air attack on Geyr's headquarters prompted General Bayerlein to take extra precautions with his own headquarters then at Sermentot, 3 miles south of Tilly. He had, of course, been on the receiving end of growing Allied air power in the Mediterranean, which had been reinforced by his division's experience of fighter-bombers during the march to the front. He ordered a 500-metre exclusion zone around the actual headquarters, with radio antennas remoted to a distance of 2,000 to 3,000 yards, vehicles banned from coming close during daylight and constant attention to camouflage.

Chapter Seven

'Tiger Hill': 11 June 1944

(see note on Tigers in the Introduction)

Major General Graham came forward to Point 103 during the night of 10/11 June to review the situation with Brigadier Cracroft, and he 'decided that in view of the strength of the enemy against us it was quite useless at the present to try and push out further South. He therefore instructed me to hold the 103 feature and ST PIERRE if possible.' With the *Hitlerjugend*'s recce battalion active on the left flank, General Graham directed that '69 Bde were to hold on my left from Pt 103 north-east to a wood between BRONAY and the BAYEUX-CAEN road, (892731) and 1 Dorsets were to be relieved in the evening by 5th East Yorkshires.' This relief in place was due to be conducted after dark that evening.

To start the process of securing the left flank, the Sherwood Rangers Yeomanry, which had been holding Point 103 overnight on 10/11 June with the Dorsets, were probing forward 'From first light [when] the brigade began offensive patrolling with the object of dominating the area south and east of the road ST. PIERRE to FONTENAY-LE-PESNEL.' At the same time, they

> moved over to cover the area between Point 103 and LE PARC DE BOIS LONDE (8768). South of the road ST. PIERRE to FONTENAY the enemy had put out a strong screen of anti-tank and self-propelled guns. The Sherwood Rangers located three Tiger tanks in the wood at 868691 but these could not be brought to battle. The Sherwood Rangers also overran two company localities south of Point 103 and inflicted heavy casualties.[1]

In addition, to relieve pressure on Point 103 General Graham ordered 69 Brigade to capture Cristot and Point 102, which controlled a large area to the east. It would be synchronized with other attacks on the *Hitlerjugend* by 69 Brigade, the Canadians and British Commandos. Brigadier Cracroft wrote:

> In the morning in preparation for this attack, I ordered 4th/7th DG to carry out a reconnaissance in force. B Sqn and the CO reached the village and saw a great many infantry about but met no organised resistance. The probability is that they disorganised an enemy counter-attack as it was forming up; but also that the enemy were thereby forewarned of the impending attack in the evening.

During the course of the day the SRY replaced the 24th Lancers in Saint-Pierre. It was here that they lost their second commanding officer since D-Day. The CO, adjutant, intelligence and signals officers were conferring in a farmyard when a shell landed alongside them, killing all four officers. Major Christopherson wrote:

> At midday in response to an urgent call on the air ... I returned to Regimental Headquarters and was told that 'Robin Hood', the CO's tank, had received a direct hit from a heavy shell which instantly killed Major Michael Laycock (who had been acting Colonel since Colonel Anderson was wounded on D-Day) ... Three [of the regiment's] senior officers had been killed and one officer and one sergeant wounded by the same shell, and all from Regimental Headquarters. This was indeed a shattering blow.

Other than the shelling and mortaring that continued to cause casualties, it was 'relatively' quiet on Point 103. The Dorsets' war diary stated: 'Nothing to record during day until late afternoon.'

The Attack on Cristot and Point 102

With 1 Dorsets committed to holding Point 103, Brigadier Cracroft had been allocated the 6 Green Howards from 69 Brigade for the attack on the village of Cristot, which was still held by the *Hitlerjugend*'s SS Recce Battalion. This

'Robin Hood' was repaired and put back into use as the CO's tank. A representation of 'Robin Hood', albeit the wrong version, is on display outside the Vrijheidsmuseum in Groesbeek, near Nijmegen.

Lieutenant Colonel Hastings.

The Green Howards'
cap badge.

unit had mounted an aggressive defence and had been threatening 8 Armoured Brigade's hold on Point 103 since its first capture, not to say making life both dangerous and uncomfortable for its defenders. Major Christopherson, now commanding the SRY, described the situation as '... still fluid and unhealthy, the country was extremely difficult and unpleasant for tanks, and the enemy with tanks and infantry were infiltrating back.'

Lieutenant Colonel Hastings of 6 Green Howards described in his report the preparations for the attack in country which he described as 'exceptionally thick with high hedges on banks, deep ditches, belts of trees and standing corn':[2]

During the [late] morning I was sent for to meet the Brigade Commander and to go to HQ 8 Armoured Brigade. 69 Brigade were to cross the railway and secure the left flank of the armour while linking up with tired Canadians at PUTOT-en BESSIN. Armoured patrols, a squadron of Shermans at a time, had pushed forward into the thick country towards CRISTOT meeting much small-arms fire and some determined men with sticky bombs. It was not known how strong the enemy were; but they appeared to be in strength including amour at FONTENAY on the road CAEN-TILLY. 6 Green Howards were to occupy a position in the CRISTOT area.

The colonel of the 4th/7th Dragoon Guards, who had been out on the recce in that area, was more than helpful on his return. His regiment were to support the Bn in their attack with artillery support from the Essex Yeomanry and two batteries of 90 Fd. B Company 2 Cheshires were available if they could be used. 4th/7th Dragoon Guards did not underrate the opposition; but they could naturally not give sufficient information of enemy locations to make out a complete artillery support programme. After a hurried recce and conference in country where you could hardly see a field, the plan was made for an attack on a two-company front with one squadron in support of the leading companies, one squadron moving with the reserve companies and the remaining squadron ready to escort up the support weapons of the Bn to their objective. The guns were to fire on known enemy targets and one hedge ahead of the advance. In this thick country a lane passing through a farm called Les Hauts Vents was chosen as the Bn axis.

6 Green Howards started their move from the St Léger area at 1400 hours, while orders were being given to the company commanders on Point 103. The abiding impression among the battalion was that this was to be 'a relatively simple operation to take some high ground [Point 102]' and based on the 4th/7th DGs' recce that morning, it was expected to be 'against little opposition'. Another impression held by the veterans of the desert and Sicily was that 'It was all rather hurried.'

At 1700 hours as 6 Green Howards and 4th/7th DG advanced on Cristot and Point 102, battle also erupted to the east and west. On the right, 2 Gloucesters were attacking Tilly under command of the 7th Armoured Division, while to the left of Point 103, on a frontage of just over 4 miles, extending as far east as Rots, three other battalion-sized attacks were launched. The whole idea was to dissipate the already thinly-spread reserves of I SS Panzer Corps.

With the preliminary fire plan under way and 6 Green Howards ready in their FUP, to their north 7 Green Howards were ready to launch their attack under the command of 69 Brigade. Their objective was the woods and château south of Brouay, where the headquarters of III/26 SS *Panzergrenadiers* was located. The attack began north of the Caen-Bayeux railway line, with the left company under fire from the *panzergrenadiers'* 11th Company in the southern part of Brouay before they had even reached the lines. The sound of battle redoubled when the right Green Howards' assault company crossed into the arcs of the *panzer-grenadiers'* 10th Company. On the more open ground between Brouay and le Bas d'Audrieu, the Germans halted the Green Howards before either company had

Allied attacks, afternoon of 11 June 1944.

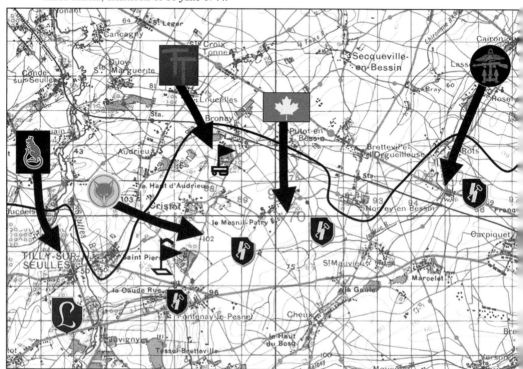

advanced 100 yards. The Yorkshiremen had run into the *Hitlerjugend*'s armoured battalion, which had a significant weight of firepower available to them, beyond that of a normal *panzergrenadier* battalion.[3] 7 Green Howards promptly fell back across the railway and the whole battalion withdrew after dark. They had lost sixty-seven men in total (twenty-seven killed, thirty wounded and ten missing).

Returning to 6 Green Howards, they passed through the Dorsets' defensive positions at 1700 hours and, forming up quickly, began their advance at 1720 hours. They had, however, already been seen by the enemy moving up through Audrieu. *Sturmbannführer* Hubert Meyer[4] recorded that

> *Unterscharführer* Kretschmer of 4th Company of the Reconnaissance Battalion was ordered in the afternoon of 11 June to establish contact with the battle outposts of *Untersturmführer* Karl-Walter Becker of 2nd Company. Even before they were reached, Kretschmer spotted a large tank assembly west of Les Hauts Vents. It was reported to his company and the two anti-tank guns still fit for action were alerted.

With the already depleted squadrons of tanks leading, immediately they crossed the Audrieu-Saint-Pierre road they were into the bocage and both Shermans and infantry had to force their way over and through the embanked hedges, but all at

An Sd.Kfz.251/9 Stummel mounting a 75mm gun. Six of these were in III/26 *Panzergrenadiers*.

this stage was going well. That is until the British and Germans ran into each other, literally. *Standartenoberjunker* (officer cadet) Dienemann described what happened:

> My platoon of five Panthers was assigned to *Sturmbannführer* Bremer [commander] of the recce battalion. Ahead of us we had open terrain of approximately 100m. Beyond that were thick rows of bushes and trees which obstructed our vision, with a village behind them. A ten-man recce patrol of

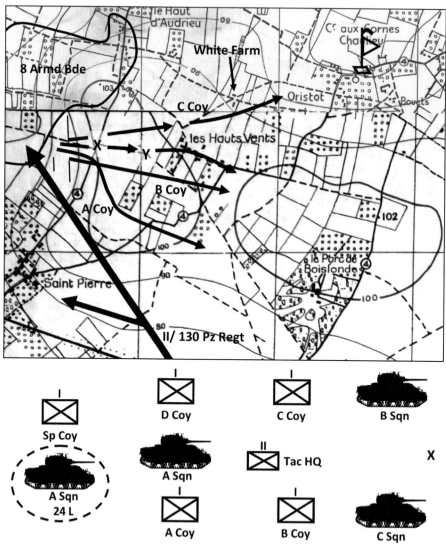

Diagram of the formation of 4th/7th DG and 6 Green Howards as they passed the road/track crossroads marked '**X**' on the map and air photograph.

the recce battalion under the command of an *Oberscharführer* was sent out at approximately 1700 hours to determine the enemy location and intentions. One of my Panthers, commanded by *Unterscharführer* Helmle, drove on the left flank to provide cover and protection. After approximately 150m, the recce patrol came under rifle fire. The commander dropped to the ground, hit in the stomach. The Panther continued to advance in order to get out of a hollow. At a bend in the path, the Panther's gun became entangled with that of a Sherman tank. Neither tank could knock out the other. The English tank commander left his tank and was bending over the badly-wounded recce patrol commander, dressing the wound. He said, in German: 'You're all right now; you'll be going home to hospital. For you, this bloody war is over.'

The Englishman climbed back into his tank and waved at *Unterscharführer* Helmle to indicate there would be no shooting. Both tanks pulled back. The wounded *Oberscharführer* was laid on the panzer. On its return, the patrol reported: 'contact with the enemy after 150m'.

Elsewhere, the farce and humanity of this incident was not replicated. For the majority, it was a bitter uncompromising fight. The German outposts let the advancing tanks through to be dealt with by the anti-tank guns, the Panthers and armoured cars waiting in depth. Colonel Hastings reported that they opened fire on B Company on the right:

This company had fairly heavy casualties, but largely owing to the efforts of the Coy Comd, who walked about the fields in full view of the enemy with total disregard for his own safety, they pushed on until the company commander, 2 i/c and several NCOs were casualties.

C Company on the left was also halted by machine-gun fire, with a disproportionate number of casualties among officers and senior NCOs. *Sturmbannführer* Meyer wrote that

The outposts of the Recce Battalion and the crews of the widely scattered strongpoints in the hedges opened fire on the accompanying infantry with rifles and machine guns. The English tanks and their guns were quite ineffective since the terrain was quite broken and made it impossible to spot the enemy [us].

Brigadier Cracroft's observation on the German positions reads:

Certainly the enemy were not deeply entrenched, but were using the natural cover and protection of hedgerow and ditch. In this thick leafy country, the advantage is with the defenders, who can stay still and hold their fire until the last moment. Tanks are blind in this country.

Colonel Hastings moving along the track from the crossroads recast his plan: B and C were to fix the enemy, while A Company was to attempt to outflank the enemy to the right and D Company was to punch through the centre towards Les

A Panther of I Battalion, SS Panzer Regiment 12.

Hauts Vents. Major Lofthouse, commanding D Company, ordered 16 Platoon, led by the redoubtable WO2 Stan Hollis,[5] with a tank following in support was to clear the line of the track, while 17 and 18 platoons were to advance on the right. WO2 Hollis told his story:[6]

> We moved carefully forward with the sound of firing to our front – left, right and centre. I was leading 16 Platoon along the lane in file, keeping up with 17 Platoon in the field to our right and I was mighty grateful for the banks on either side that gave cover from the bullets that were flying all around.
>
> We had advanced from the crossroads to this spot [about 400 yards] when a burst of Spandau fire ripped down the lane. We dived onto the ground and the enemy could not see us [because of a slight convexity in the gently rising track]. I crawled forward until I could just see over the rise and then a slight movement at the base of that oak tree on the bank [marked Y on the map]. I was still watching when two helmeted heads popped up and fired a burst down the track, not at me, straight down the track. This happened several times, methodically regulation German-style.
>
> I decided that the next burst would be their last but when I went into my [ammunition] pouch all that came out was a pair of socks and my shaving brush – bad battle preps! One of my soldiers threw me a grenade and I waited for the next burst, stood up and threw the grenade; it landed just in front of the bank. The Germans ducked down but as I threw it I realised that I hadn't pulled the pin – my second error in so many minutes!
>
> I just dashed forward with my Sten gun and then found the two Germans crouching down waiting for the grenade to go off and let them have a burst.

With firing going on all around and the fields littered with casualties and burning tanks, as reported by Colonel Hastings:

> D company forced their way up the axis supported by tanks, took 25–30 prisoners of war in Les Hauts Vents and joined up with A Company. This helped C Company to get on [and capture the 'White Farm']. The position was now that the Bn was together one field short of its objective with heavy MG and anti-tank gunfire in front.

The tanks of B Squadron got into Cristot. The regimental historian records that

> Alone by themselves in the orchards, B Squadron pushed forward towards their objective and one by one their tanks were knocked out by guns which, for the most part, they never saw. The crews who bailed out were either shot or captured by the German infantry nearby.

The problem was that the Green Howards' C Company had been halted on the outskirts of the village by the *Hitlerjugend* in well-sited and prepared positions. Consequently, without support, the Shermans, as reported by *Sturmbannführer* Meyer, were knocked out by an anti-tank gun firing down the village street from a position near the recce battalion's headquarters.

Meanwhile, on the right flank, by 2000 hours, A and B companies and the surviving tanks of C Squadron had fought their way towards Point 102 but had culminated and were virtually surrounded by a counter-attack by II Battalion, 130 Panzer Regiment. Colonel Hastings recorded that:

> In the meantime, an attack by Mark IV tanks had developed behind us on the position of 8 Armoured Brigade. These tanks were almost across our axis. I ordered the Bn to reorganise where it was and sent for the supporting weapons to come up. But losses in officers and NCOs had been heavy; there was considerable sniping; 4th/7th were losing tanks. The Brigade Commander told me that I could use my discretion about withdrawal. I ordered the Bn to withdraw and sent word to the 2 i/c to recce positions further back in consultation with the Brigade Commander and CO 5 East Yorks.[7]

The Bren gun was the section machine gun of the British infantry.

Strained expressions on the faces of young *Hitlerjugend panzergrenadiers*. They are wearing oak-leaf-pattern camouflage.

6 Green Howards fell back in good order to the north-west and regrouped around Château d'Audrieu and counted the cost. Losses had been heavy, with B Squadron alone losing seven of its nine operational Shermans, while 6 Green Howards lost a total of approximately 250 killed, wounded and missing. The Germans certainly didn't have it all their own way, with the Recce Battalion losing forty-seven men.

Even though the Green Howards' withdrawal was a success, 4th/7th DGs' war diary records a commendable service to them:

4th/7th Royal Dragoon Guards' cap badge.

> CO of Green Howards asked if we could try to help wounded to get out from fwd positions and also others who were pinned down. 2 i/c was unable to get wireless touch for covering fire so took Blenheim [the second-in-command's tank] back alone to where wounded were. As he got there three Germans fired from about 50 yds range, and he used his Sten from the turret, accounting for one of them. He and his gunner then dismounted and loaded wounded on to tank, the dead body of CO of 5 E Yorks and also some unwounded men who had not been able to move until the arrival of the tank, being pinned down. As he got back into the turret two more Germans raised themselves on the bank as if to fire. A quick burst of Sten was put down and subsequently kept up as the tank withdrew. (The turret could not be traversed on account of the wounded on the outside.) All the men aboard were brought safely back and this action also enabled another fifteen men to get away who would otherwise not have been able to move.

Of the impact of the attack on Cristot, Brigadier Cracroft wrote:

> Though the attack had failed to capture its objective, my main object had been to relieve the pressure on Pt 103 and drive the enemy further away. This we had achieved, and it is possible that the attempt broke up an enemy infantry attack designed to coincide with their armoured attack on Pt 103 ... Even if we had captured CRISTOT, I doubt if we should have been able with the forces available to have held it as I could not afford to risk losing the vital 103 feature.

Meanwhile, of the attack as a whole, the 4th/7th DGs' historian considered the lessons learned during 11 June 1944:

> This was the first time that we had made an attack with infantry on an objective, planned according to the book, and as such it was a dismal failure. The theory which had been preached for combined tank and infantry attack was that the attack should go in waves, with tanks followed by infantry, followed by more tanks. Experience soon showed that to have the tanks leading at all was a mistake; that in close country they must go side by side

with the infantry, and in more open country they could best give support from a position slightly in rear and to a flank.

After a frustrating day the brigadier's final comment summarized the state of the battle in Normandy as a whole: 'It occurred at a time when the Army's initial advance was losing impetus and the contact battle was merging into static warfare; the enemy was recovering from his first shock and was fighting to the death.'

'Tiger Hill'

The first reports of the German counter-attack from the Parc de Boislonde area (see map on page 124) that cut across the rear of 6 Green Howards came from the SRY squadrons patrolling south and south-east. The tank patrols were driven back by the advancing panzers. *Oberst* Scholze, commander of 901 *Panzergrenadiers*, requested panzer support to deal with the British patrols and the attack, which if it secured Point 102 would dominate his positions out towards Fontenay. For him time was of the essence. *Hauptmann* Ritgen, a company commander in II Battalion, 130 Panzer Regiment, wrote that there was some dissention: 'Major Prinz von Schönburg-Waldenburg's objections to such a poorly-prepared and insufficiently-supported panzer attack in unfavourable terrain conditions against a prepared enemy who had tanks and anti-tank weapons fell on deaf ears.'

Oberst Scholze's preliminary bombardment of Point 103 and Saint-Pierre was, however, particularly effective, as recorded by Major Bredin, who was at battalion headquarters, where virtually all the orderly room staff became casualties: 'The enemy's 88mm shells were bursting in the treetops, and this had a shrapnel-like effect on those in trenches or ditches immediately below – we were to learn more of this during the course of apprenticeship in the bocage country.'

Following the bombardment, the panzers, a mix of Panthers and Panzer IVs, advanced into action from the high ground between Fontenay and Saint-Pierre at around 2000 hours. Initially they duelled with the SRY patrols and engaged

Oberst Scholze.

Major Prinz von Schönburg-Waldenburg and the family coat of arms painted on his panzer.

longer-range targets up on Point 103. 8 DLI in Saint-Pierre were able to watch the attack develop:

> About 7pm a second attack was launched against the 8th Battalion in St. Pierre, this time mainly by tanks. Again, artillery and mortar fire swept the village and continued as the German armour – Tigers, Panthers and Mark IVs – approached from the east and south-east, some bypassing the village to make for Point 103 and thus for a time completely surrounding the 8th in St. Pierre. It so happened that the CO was away at a conference at HQ 8 Armoured Brigade when the attack started and was unable to get back until it was nearly dark.
>
> The tanks of the Sherwood Rangers took a severe hammering from the Tigers and Mark IVs which, with superior gun-power, were able to lie back out of range and pick off British tanks one by one. After a while they advanced beyond the disabled and burning British tanks to close in on St Pierre down the road from Cristot. They were soon able to enfilade B Company in its positions along the hedgerows, and immediately swept the B Company platoons with murderous bursts of machine-gun fire at close range.

On their main axis, the panzers steadily worked their way forward, but as dusk fell and the Green Howards and the Shermans of 4th/7th DG fell back, they advanced on Point 103. Brigadier Cracroft, who had been back to divisional headquarters to receive orders for the following day, recalled:

> I arrived on 103 to find a very heavy German infantry and tank attack was coming in from the direction of FONTENAY-LE-PESNEL. It was the only German attack of its sort that I ever saw and was in the approved style of infantry and tanks coming in together. Our tanks were severely handicapped because the Germans were supported by a number of 88mm tanks which were standing off and shelling us with great effect from rather long ranges – the shells burst in the treetops and created a shrapnel effect on those below. The only tanks which we had that could penetrate them were a very few 17-pdr Shermans. Most of the five of these that we had per Regt were already knocked out.

One casualty as the panzers pressed forward onto the high ground was Major Prinz von Schönburg-Waldenburg. His Panzer IV was engaged by one of 102 Anti-Tank Regiment's guns whose shell sliced through the turret, killing the Prince and his radio-operator.[8] The remainder of the crew drove the panzer back and after repairs it resumed its career as Major Ritgen's tank, he having taken over command of II Battalion.

4th/7th DGs' war diary records that

> For a time, the situation was extremely tense. The tanks on the forward edge opened fire and then had to withdraw slightly under cover of smoke. The flashes of their guns mingled with the tracer of enemy shells which were

flying everywhere. An ammunition truck and an SP gun were hit and caught fire. About four Tigers actually reached the position and for a short while pandemonium reigned, but at length they were driven off and we remained in position.

The Dorsets' adjutant noted '2030: A determined enemy counter-attack was launched by their armour against C Company and battalion headquarters' and at

2100: C and D companies and, to a lesser extent, battalion headquarters under heavy fire from Tiger tanks. Our own supporting armour assist companies – to the best of their ability – to repel attack. The two companies hold firm, chiefly due to C Company commander Major Nicoll and the commanding officer. The Battalion orderly sergeant, Sergeant Knight, was wounded, and the intelligence sergeant, Sergeant Park, was killed by airburst [shells] fired by 88mm tank guns.

During this attack battalion headquarters, tucked alongside a hedgerow, and the Regimental Aid Post, a short distance down the same hedgerow, came under repeated artillery and machine-gun fire. One of the two citations for the Military Medal awarded to the Dorsets that night reads as follows:

Pte Goddard was acting as a stretcher-bearer in the RAP at Bn HQ ... A shell exploded between the command post and the intelligence section, wounding some of the staff of both, including the intelligence Sgt. Another shell fell killing the Sgt and wounding Pte Goddard. With completed disregard for his own personal safety and taking no notice whatsoever of his own wound, he continued treating casualties, owing to his great devotion to duty many lives were saved. It was not until some two hours after he had received his wound that he reported for dressing.

8 Armd Bde recorded that up on Point 103 'Visibility was extremely poor and for some time the situation was a little confused.' A Dorset soldier of C Company, Private Town, described the situation:

With Tigers up on the forward edge of Point 103 and in our positions, it was frightening to say the least – far worse than the beach on D-Day. Shermans and SPs [M10 tank destroyers and Sextons] manoeuvring, multi-coloured tracer and detonating shells and mortars made it doubly confusing. It took all my nerve to get my head out of the bottom of our trench and fire when Corporal Thompson shouted at us.

Major Christopherson wrote an anecdote about Padre Skinner of the SRY up on Point 103:

I shall always remember the opening words of the first service which he found time to conduct ... He said: 'There are no atheists in a slit trench.' He continued by telling us that the day before he was compelled to dive very smartly into a slit trench during an unpleasant spell of shelling and found

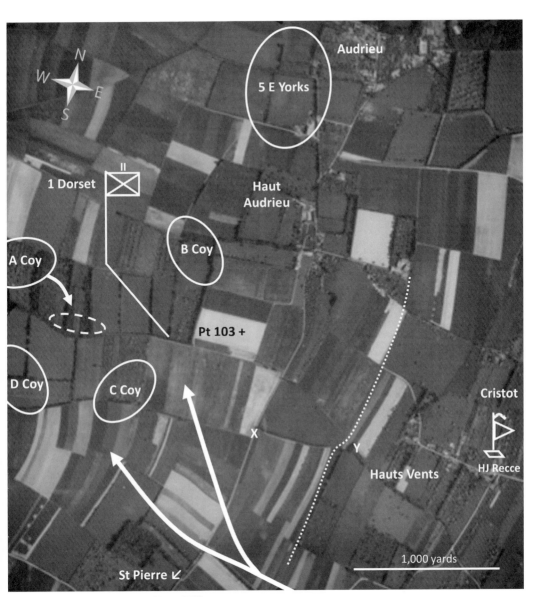

The German attack on 'Tiger Hill'.

himself with four others, all endeavouring to make themselves extremely small. Some of the shells fell uncomfortably close and when he looked for the reaction on the part of his companions he saw only too clearly that each one was praying silently and fervently to some god, obviously for deliverance from their temporary and exceedingly unhealthy predicament.

The brunt of the attack fell on C Company and they were soon running low on ammunition. The second MM was awarded to

L/Cpl Hockley of the provost, seeing that C Coy was running short of ammunition – although it was in no way his duty to do so – for four hours

One of 8 Armoured Brigade's padres undertaking the grim task of preparation of the dead for burial.

gave assistance in carrying ammunition and messages under very heavy fire from a number of tanks. L/Cpl Hockley gave no heed to his own safety.

With the attack coming from the south-east, Colonel Norrie, as recorded in the war diary, redeployed one of his sub-units at '2140: A Company is moved round behind C and D companies to give depth to our position there.' Using the banks and hedges, the company was reasonably well protected from the front but exposed to shell and mortar rounds falling behind them.

The view across the open eastern part of 'Tiger Hill' across which the panzers attacked to the hedges where the Dorsets were dug in.

With the enemy at close quarters, Private Cawley of D Company earned his Military Medal:

After the fighting had been going on for almost an hour it was found that the crew of an anti-tank gun had not reached their position. The German tank threat was serious, and it was essential to man the gun. Pte Cawley led the crew forward, crawling over ground which was continually being swept by bursts of fire from the tank machine guns. The small party eventually reached the position where Cawley then helped to fire the gun at the German tanks, only 250 yards away. Crouched behind the gun shield, the crew were unable to see the tanks so Cawley stood up in full view of the enemy and directed the fire of the gun. The Germans were kept at bay but had the gun not been manned it would have been a very different story.

The war diary of 24 Lancers recorded that at one point 'Tigers' penetrated the positions on Point 103. They appeared to be all round, and worked their way up to Brigade HQ. Lieutenant Wareham recorded the scene:

Six of our tanks were knocked out in as many seconds. We withdrew to the west of the hill. Hidden in the trees and orchards we sighted our guns onto the advancing monster Tigers and Panthers. The order came to fire. The Shermans shook with the recoil of their guns; the commanders, glasses in position, watched their shots. Most of our armour-piercing shells were bouncing harmlessly off the enemy. This was serious. Quickly the few remaining tanks were called up, those that mounted the new enormous 17-pdr anti-tank gun. An ear-splitting crack, a vivid flash – and *whoosh* – the leading Tiger stopped, smoked and then burst into flames. The others caught in the open began to withdraw to cover. Meanwhile the German infantry were working their way up the left flank of the hill. Everyone fired everything they had. I could hear the bullets pattering on the outside of my tank. I was glad I was inside. The infantry could hardly lift their heads from the ground without being shot. Tank crews whose tanks had been hit joined the infantry on the ground. A Troop Leader I knew waved up to me; apparently all his three tanks had been knocked out. There seemed to be some panic in the rear among the soft-skinned vulnerable lorries. The firing became intense. The critical moment had come. We held.

The Lancers' medical officer Captain Aitken kept a diary which reveals the terrible nature of warfare and makes the military historian's comments on casualties sound glib:

I have the wireless on and can hear everything that is going on. The voices 'on the air' are getting tense and high-pitched; one tank commander has lost his nerve and his operator eventually rings up with this information. What a pity that things like this are heard by everyone. For a long time, it appears only too certain that the enemy are getting the better of us – there's a certain

Tanks knocked out in an obvious position tended to be hit and claimed more than once!

lack of information and what does come in troubles one – there seem to be Tigers everywhere. Our particular necessary defensive actions have lost us a number of tanks. It is in a situation like this that the true worth of any men shows up. Norman Bourne commanding A Squadron stands out a mile. He is commanding his tanks well; very calm and collected on the air.

It's getting dark. Suddenly three very fast-travelling rounds come through the other end of the orchard – they must have come from an enemy tank.

Royal Army Medical Corps' cap badge.

Only one explodes; must have been two armour-piercing and one HE. There is a call for stretcher-bearers, but I have none and send off the nearest people with stretchers. Five casualties come in – three fairly light and one man with the whole of his lower jaw blown away, and the other with one leg badly injured; none of them are ours and no vehicle has been hit. I look at the man with no jaw; it is very ugly and I see no hope for him. I give him a very large dose of morphia – an assurance of a peaceful death ... A stream of bullets passes over my head and one chips the tree above me; how fortunate I was kneeling. I say to myself that whoever fired them is unlikely to fire in exactly the same direction again and we all go on working. We have fifteen cases waiting to go; all but three are stretchers and I daren't send them. If any more come I don't know what to do; I can't hold any more. If we have to retire – but we *won't* retire, whatever the pressure. The noise is terrific and gradually mortar explosions become more prevalent than tank guns as it is getting dark. Darkness will save the situation which is already improving immensely. I don't know how many Tigers we have hit; a number I know.

Thirteen more infantry come in – a mortar landing in the middle of them and two have their legs off below the knee – there is one with both off and one with one off and the other hanging by a bit of skin and muscle. Some of the others are serious, too. We sort them out and Sinclair and I get down to

At the height of the battle casualties were evacuated by carrier from Point 103 to an ambulance exchange point to the rear.

the job in the dimmed light of a torch. This is so dim that it is hardly worth using but it's all we dare use. We are constantly losing scissors and things when we lay them down. I remember noting never to use anything but white bandages and triangulars at night. I talk to Sinclair about blood transfusion, but we agree to risk leaving it at the moment; it may only open up the main arteries that we cannot find in all the mess of blood and flesh.

Meanwhile, things were far from quiet down in Saint-Pierre:

2015: Two enemy tanks 600 yards away at 865685.
2030: Enemy tanks and infantry attack B Company – enemy tanks fire down into trenches occupied by our infantry and overrun B Company. More enemy infantry observed at 865685.
2045: Adjutant calls for artillery to disperse enemy infantry.

What happened is that as the panzers advanced on Point 103, 901 *Panzer-grenadiers* worked their way into positions from where they were

able to enfilade B Company in its positions along the hedgerows, and immediately swept the B Company positions with murderous bursts of machine-gun fire at close range ... Meanwhile other tanks were shelling St Pierre, including the barn where the Regimental Aid Post was established. This made the work of the doctor and medical orderlies almost impossible.

Back up on Point 103, as darkness fell, Lieutenant Wareham of the 24th Lancers recalled:

The enemy withdrew. A self-propelled gun in the rear was on fire. Its exploding ammunition lit up the hill and made us a perfect target for the enemy artillery. But the shelling didn't matter much; it was unpleasant, but we didn't mind. Point 103 was still ours.

By 2300 hours the enemy attacks had died down and, according to Major 'Speedy' Bredin 'the situation was in hand' and he went on to say that as a result of the attack on Point 103 'it became known to all those who fought there as "Tiger Hill".'

At about the same time the enemy broke off the attack on 8 DLI in Saint-Pierre:

In spite of the determined and ferocious German attack the 8th Battalion refused to give way. Stubbornly the companies held their positions, and when darkness fell the Germans withdrew from the battered village, leaving the tired defenders confident in the knowledge that they had smashed another German attack. On his return from Brigade, Lieut Colonel Lidwill moved A Company into B Company's positions to strengthen the left flank, and pulled back D Company into the old A Company area. Apart from intermittent enemy shelling the night passed quietly, and at dawn next morning the expected enemy attack did not develop. It seemed that the Germans had, for the time being at any rate, given up the fight for the village and withdrawn.

Even though 'Tiger Hill' remained in British hands, it proved to be a nervous night for all. Corporal Noble of A Company, which had returned to its trenches, ambushed an enemy patrol killing or capturing most of them. Both B and D companies had alarms during the night when attacks seemed imminent. Meanwhile, the SRY's war diary recorded that 'The DLI were holding ST PIERRE and that night we formed a circular compact leaguer round what remained of the Inf.'

One knock-on effect of *Panzer Lehr*'s attack was that the relief in place of the Dorsets was called off. The battalion war diary recorded: 'Relief of battalion – scheduled to be carried out by 5th Battalion, the East Yorkshire Regiment – could not take place, but 5th East Yorks took up positions covering our left flank, at about 857708.'

The 5 East Yorks had been approaching Point 103 via Haut d'Audrieu when the German attack began. Private Craddock recalled:

Our platoon was instructed 'dig in' in the midst of a large cornfield. Having started the digging, Jerry, who was concealed in positions in woods on each side of the field, commenced firing with Spandau machine guns and almost immediately my officer (Lieutenant Sykes) was caught in the chest and died.

A typical bocage lane. This one, on Point 103, is where the Dorsets and the armoured regiment had their headquarters.

His last words to me were to get the PIAT into action against a Tiger Tank which was coming up from the bottom of the field. In twisting round for the PIAT, I was caught with a bullet in the side which bounced off a rib, went through a lung and came out. I coughed up some blood, but otherwise was not too bad.

It was by now getting dark and I was able to crawl under the tracer bullets, which lit up in the dark, and were criss-crossing just above the corn. I managed to reach a nearby First Aid Station. They bandaged me up and onto a hospital ship back to Dover (Jerry bombed the ship but fortunately missed) and I arrived back in 'Blighty' on Wednesday, June 14. As it subsequently transpired this was the extent of my active service (just eight days).

With 6 Green Howards having withdrawn to Audrieu and 5th East Yorks digging in on the reverse slope of Point 103, 69 Brigade had effectively secured the hold on the vital feature.

A section of a German military map covering the Point 103 area.

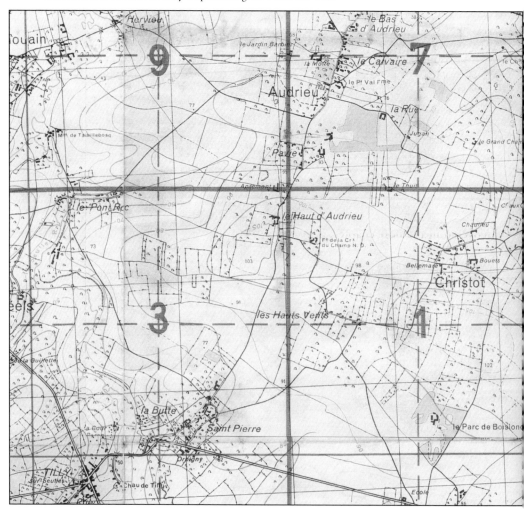

Chapter Eight

Tilly-sur-Seulles and Essex Wood

Since the link-up with US V Corps north of Port-en-Bessin the main effort of 50th Division and 7th Armoured Division had been to the south-east of Bayeux at Point 103 and down the Tilly-sur-Seulles-Bayeux road. With resistance hardening here with the arrival of firstly the 12th *Hitlerjugend* SS Panzer Division and latterly *Panzer Lehr*, the battle started extending west to where it was becoming apparent that there was a 'soft spot' in the German defences. It was into this area that elements of both 50th Division and 7th Armoured Division, led by their respective reconnaissance units, extended during 11 June but during that day the main effort was still directed towards Villers-Bocage via Tilly and Juvigny.

The 'soft spot' was caused by the collapse of the German 352nd Infantry Division, which had been originally been holding the coastline inclusive of part of Gold and Omaha beaches and had been fighting inland since D-Day. Shattered and exhausted, now they and 30 *Schnell* Brigade were falling back to St Lô in front of the 1st US Infantry Division's advance south. On the evening of the 11th the Americans had reached a point south of Balleroy and by 12 June this area would become the 'Caumont Gap' covered only by advanced elements of the 2nd Panzer Division and *Panzer Lehr*'s reconnaissance battalion, with that of the 17th SS *Panzergrenadiers* being rushed forward.

On 50th Division's right flank 231 Brigade, having handed over Bayeux, were marching south from the city to enlarge the bridgehead. The objectives of 1 Hampshires and 2 Devons were on the Tilly-Balleroy road, being respectively Saint-Paul-du-Vernay and la Belle Épine. These operations on 11 June are covered in the next chapter.

The 352nd Infantry Division's badge.

The late-war tactical markings for vehicles of the 2nd (Vienna) Panzer Division.

7th Armoured Division's Advance Renewed

The lesson of the previous day, 10 June, when tanks had led into the bocage, each with just a single company of 1 RB infantry, had been learned. The operation resumed at first light with 2 Gloucesters advancing on Bucéels which by late morning they reported as secure. To reach Tilly-sur-Seulles, just over a mile to the south, they had to cross a stream at the Pont de la Guillette bridge and a second at Marcel. As noted in the CLY's war diary, recce identified that the 'Bridges [were] not held by enemy but kept under observation.'

Meanwhile, on the right 5 RTR had resumed their advance with the initial objective of cutting the important lateral route, the Tilly-Balleroy road, around

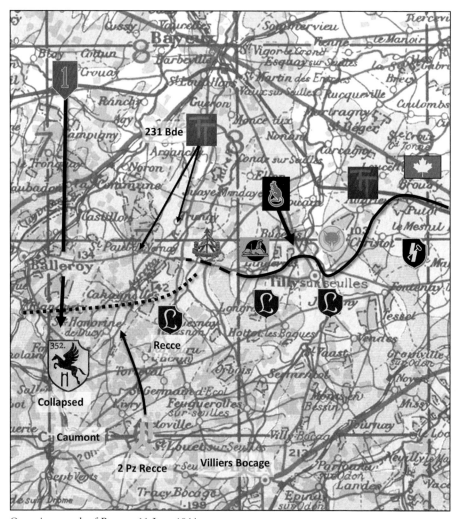

Operations south of Bayeux, 11 June 1944.

Lingèvres. South of Jerusalem the going was more favourable and, having shaken themselves free of the thick country where they had been bogged down for most of the previous day, progress south was more rapid. The attached tanks of an 8th Hussar's reconnaissance squadron pushed on a mile beyond Jerusalem, with the Cromwells of A Squadron 5 RTR and I Company 1 RB in their half-tracks following, where fresh resistance was encountered. The 5 RTR's war diary explains that

> The large open space between FOLLIOT and LINGÈVRES was crossed by A Sqn. On reaching the woods near LINGÈVRES enemy tks opened up and two CROMWELLS and a FIREFLY were KO'd. A Sqn in cooperation with a Pl of I Coy 1 RB was ordered to proceed south through the woods to LINGÈVRES. Good progress was made up ... Rifle Secs who had got too far ahead of Tk support were ambushed and suffered a few casualties.

The 1 RB's war diary records a different view. They complained about the 'slow progress' of the tanks into the close country north of Lingèvres where a section was overwhelmed by a rush of some forty enemy infantry. They also highlight the Cromwell's lack of success in hunting down a 'Tiger' in the woods which 'our own tanks were unable to locate and dislodge; in fact he [the Tiger] rather saw them off, and so they had to pull back a bit bringing our people with them.' 5 RTR concluded that 'It was impossible to get through the wood. Lieutenant

A US Lend-Lease M5 International Harvester half-track vehicle provided the motor battalions with mobility and protection from small-arms fire.

HEYNES was on the right flank of A Sqn close to the wood and was suddenly hit by a presumed Mk V [Panther] Tk, which had crept up along a sunken road unobserved.'

On 5 RTR's right flank, the village of Bernières-Bocage which had been reported by recce as being clear was still occupied by the enemy. Panzers stalked tanks and vice versa, while the platoons of 2 Essex combed the hedgerows and houses.

Despite revised command arrangements, this was as far as 5 RTR progressed and it is further recorded that '1 RTR made a limited advance'. It was still early in the day and 2 Essex were warned to attack the woods and orchards. However, recalling them and then going into battle procedure would take some time to complete.

By midday it was more than apparent that the frontage on which 22 Brigade was advancing was too great for Brigadier Hinde and his slim brigade staff to control. Consequently, commander of 56 Brigade, Brigadier Pepper, took responsibility for the division's left axis directed on Tilly, with the Gloucesters and the SWB under command, with the CLY being his armour. Brigadier Hinde

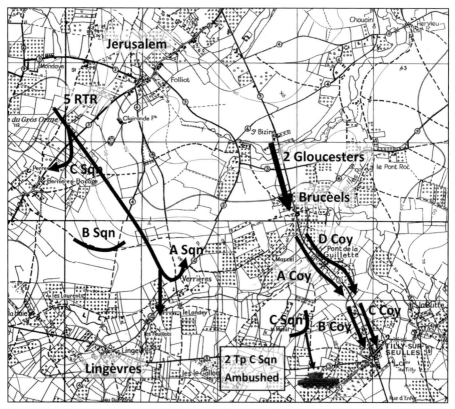

22 Armoured Brigade's advance on Tilly-sur-Seulles, pm 11 June 1944.

commanded the two RTR regiments with the infantry of 1 RB and 2 Essex under his command. The latter had spent the morning clearing the Butte du Gros Orme and rounding up following its capture. They handed Juaye-Mondaye and the Butte to B Squadron, 8th Hussars which was tasked to patrol the right flank of the advance.

Tilly-sur-Seulles

Oberst Gerhart, commander of the recently-arrived 130 *Panzer Lehr* Regiment, led the *Kampfgruppe* defending Tilly. He had under his command most of his Panther battalion, 902 *Panzergrenadier* Regiment, four companies of which were the immediate garrison, the division's panzer pioneer[1] battalion and two battalions of artillery plus the infantry regiment's gun company (9th Company).

Having reorganized in Bucéels, 2 Gloucesters were by 1300 hours ready to mount a battalion attack on Tilly astride the Bayeux road. Vital time was, however, allowed to slip through the Gloucesters' fingers by preparing a formal attack on Pont de la Guillette before establishing if such a likely point was held. This additional time, with an attack so obvious, enabled the Germans to reinforce with Panthers and additional infantry. Two companies led through the orchards with C Squadron, 4 CLY in support to their right.

Captain Kiln, a forward observation officer from 86 Field Regiment, was sent to support the attack in an OP Sherman:[2]

> I am briefed on the plan, which is that the Gloucesters are to be deployed on the east side of the road, to advance and capture Pont de la Guillette. The tanks are to advance to support on the right. I am given the job of shelling the hamlet on the far side of the bridge as the attack goes in. In the morning sunlight the whole thing seems unreal.
>
> I leave my tank well-hidden and crawl on foot down the ditch by the road until I have a perfect observation post over Pont de la Guillette and the hill on the other side. We do a little excavation, just in case someone fires along the ditch, and settle down to register our target.

At this point he spotted an armoured vehicle moving in what was to be his target area, but it turned out to be one of his regiment's carriers laying line back to the guns from another OP forward and to the right:

> On enquiry, the bombardier says that Pont de la Guillette is deserted except for some nuns with a party of children sheltering in the hamlet's barns – my very target. The nuns report no Germans there; there have been, but they have moved south at dawn, so I pluck up my courage and walk down the ditch into the village. No Germans, only nuns, children and one farmer, and all is very quiet, so post-haste back to the column commander to report, so that the attack can be called off. Not a bit of it, he refuses point-blank, and we wait another two hours until all is deployed and ready, then the set-piece attack goes into an empty hamlet.

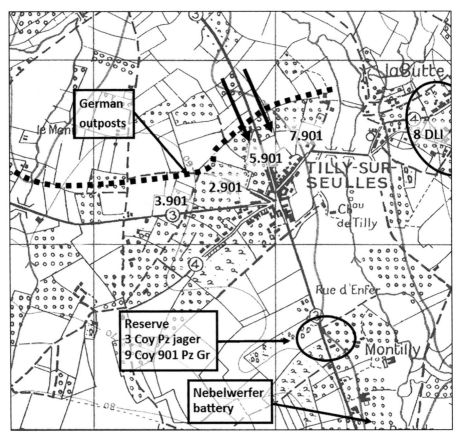

The German defences of Tilly, 11 June 1944.

As noted by the CLY, the first phase was a 'success':

> Attack by two Coys Gloucester Regt on left-hand bridge [Pont de la Guillette]; one Coy Gloucester Regt with C Sqn in attack right-hand bridge [Marcel]. Both attacks successful and the first objective, the road parallel to river at 834695, gained. A & B Sqns remain in reserve area BUCÉELS.

Having secured Pont de la Guillette, two of 8th Hussars' armoured recce patrols passed through the Gloucesters and the companies continued to advance. Private Gordon Duffin, a Bren-gunner in A Company, later recalled:

> We were advancing through this orchard, thick banks topped by hedges, hiding a sunken lane. It's peaceful, it's quiet. The sun is shining. We get so far and then there is a forward slope. I think, 'I don't like the look of this', because at the bottom is another thick hedge, hiding no doubt a sunken lane with a thick hedge on the other side. So, we get halfway down this forward slope and a Spandau opens up from the middle of this hedgerow. So down

The bocage, or hedgerow country.

we all dive in the grass about a foot and a half high. This Spandau keeps spraying the field we are in.[3]

A tank was called up to deal with the enemy and, having endured the usual mortaring and advanced to a dip some 1,000 yards short of Tilly, the next two companies took over the lead. Out in front, however, the Hussars were halted at *Oberst* Gerhart's outpost line by a pair of Panthers and a 75mm anti-tank gun, sited at the Montilly hamlet, some 500 yards short of Tilly. Warned of their presence, C Squadron and the Gloucesters came forward:

> 2 Tp C Sqn go round to left and destroy disabled Panther; infantry with PIAT destroy other. C Sqn advance to short of village TILLY-SUR-SEULLES in support of Gloucester Regt, who entered TILLY (8468). C Sqn withdraw to outflank town to right; close country encountered and one troop is ambushed area 832690 (3 Cromwells, 1 Firefly under Lt T.S. Vine).

Captain Kiln was remounted in his OP tank:

> As we advance over the brow of the hill, the ground flattens; suddenly there are reports of German tanks ahead. A hasty conference and I am asked with the other gunner to bring down fire on them. I drive my Sherman tank very gingerly up the road. Round the second bend and hell! 250 yards ahead in the centre of the road, two German tanks! We back very hastily and squash the Company Sergeant Major's bicycle, luckily missing the Sergeant Major

himself. So into the ditch again, and very gingerly forward until I can see the German tanks quite clearly.

Anyway, for the next twenty minutes or so I fire a precision shoot, using one gun only and ranging carefully as our forward troops are within 200 yards of the tanks. I use cap on high-explosive shells on these two tanks, as leaving the cap on the shell delays the fuse, and the shell should penetrate the tank armour more effectively. It is a lovely little pinpoint shoot and I register quite a number of hits and near misses.

At the same time the infantry advance along ditches, and one sergeant with a PIAT hits the tanks too. We both claim them as our kill, no time to argue, as we soon pass them. I think we must have caught the German crews when they had dismounted to repair the second tank.

We advance. The Germans are there this time. Still, we make the wood and the edge of Tilly under heavy fire; Ted Hall and Dick Greig are on foot with the infantry, and I am going up the road behind them in my Sherman feeling very isolated in a lone tank.

As the road enters the orchards, we come over a slight rise and I can see, from the top of the tank, clear down the road south through the village of Tilly, past the crossroads and down a long wooded avenue towards Juvigny. As I watch, I can see German reinforcements, vehicles, half-tracks, tanks and guns coming up the road into Tilly from the south.

A British Sherman and infantry with a heavily shelled village and trees in the background.

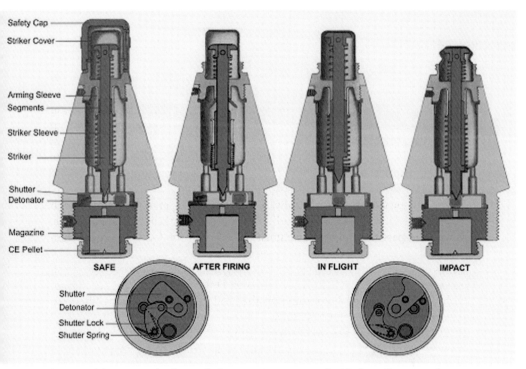

Safety Cap
Striker Cover

Arming Sleeve
Segments

Striker Sleeve

Striker

Shutter
Detonator

Magazine

CE Pellet

SAFE   AFTER FIRING   IN FLIGHT   IMPACT

Shutter
Detonator
Shutter Lock
Shutter Spring

A diagram of the 25-pounder fuse with the protective cap on and with the striker exposed.

Not only was the enemy reinforcing, but a part of the support plan was not going entirely to plan: the Armoured Vehicle Royal Engineers (AVRE) attached from an assault regiment of the 79th Armoured Division were in difficulty. Captain Holgate recalled:

> The AVREs which should have supported the two leading companies had found the country too difficult for them. Only one managed to get up with B Company and with C Company. They did some useful work with their block-busters, but all eventually became stuck or lost their tracks, leaving no alternative to the crews but to fire them and join the rifle companies.

C Squadron helped shoot the infantry in from the flank, but panzers were both in the village and its surroundings, so their support was limited by the need to fight their own duels with the enemy. The AVREs accompanied the infantry through the orchards until disabled. Corporal Enticott of D Company wrote in an account of the battle:

> I was almost relieved to get my section into the village but all we did was exchange one danger for another; instead of mortaring and Spandaus we had grenades and sniping. Clearing the wreck of houses and other buildings one by one was a slow and deadly business.

Private Rossier was one of those searching for the enemy:

> Most firing is on distant targets, but on my own, I came upon a young, tall, blond German soldier. I can still remember his face today. His weapon

The AVRE was a conversion of a standard-gun Churchill, which could be fitted with a variety of engineering equipment. Its armament was the 290mm Petard gun/mortar which replaced the standard 6-pounder/75mm gun.

dangled by his side, mine was in my hands. My weapon cut him in half. I sat on the floor and cried. I had killed a human being.

Corporal Enticott continued '... and then the Germans down the other end of the village counter-attacked with tanks and infantry. We were soon fighting for all we were worth.'

The Gloucesters had reached the junction at the centre of the village and were clearing the houses when, as recalled by Captain Holgate, an enemy counter-attack erupted into the village:

The Gloucestershire Regiment's cap badge.

> Corporal Braid, of No. 13 platoon, hearing amidst the din a heavy rumbling on the road outside, looked out of a window ready to welcome a 7th Armoured tank. Instead, he saw, and they saw him, a German Mk IV with a section on it armed with *Schmeissers*. The Boches piled off the tank in quick time and No. 13 platoon left the house equally quickly, leaving behind their small packs and shovels which they had discarded during the house-searching. They had no answer to the pounding this tank shortly gave the houses in which they had been.

This was the first immediate counter-attack by the *panzergrenadiers* of 5 Company at a point when C and D companies were still fighting through and had not reorganized for defence. Enticott continued:

> The leading tank was firing at a C Company platoon on the other side of the road with its machine guns. The boys fired back uselessly but the tank kept going and stuck its barrel through a window and fired. The building was a mass of dust and smoke. 'Oh my god, I thought.' And then the beggar started to turn across the wide street and come towards us. I didn't need to

be told what was going to happen and I shouted to the section to 'Get out' and barged into the platoon commander bringing up the PIAT – too late for that!

The PIAT was the only anti-tank weapon forward with the assault companies and brave attempts were made to use them. Lieutenant Evans of 13 Platoon, C Company went out into the open to take on a panzer. The citation for Lance Corporal Rhodes' Military Medal tells the story:

> This NCO, whilst his unit was clearing TILLY-SUR-SEULLES on 10 June 44 [*sic*], led his section in the last block of houses to be cleared. Seeing the PIAT man knocked down, he rushed forward and picked the PIAT up just as an armoured car was coming towards him. Showing great presence of mind, he ducked till the car was passed and then fired two shots into it and stopped it. He was spraying the car with his Sten gun when it fired its anti-tank gun at him, wounding him in the leg and also fatally wounding his Pl Comd. Not until he had silenced the car did he allow his wound to be dressed.

The Gloucesters held the first German counter-attack, but with only the northern part of the village in their hands they remained in close contact with the

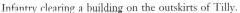
Infantry clearing a building on the outskirts of Tilly.

enemy. In a period of over three hours, *Oberst* Gerhart ordered increasing numbers of troops and artillery into the area to regain the village. *Feldwebel* Hoffman, a crewman on a 75mm infantry gun, told of his day in battle:

> On Sunday 11 June, an attack of great scope was repeated in all sectors and lasted all day. The six guns of 9th Company fired thirty-eight shells each. According to reports from our forward observer, enemy tanks were burnt. The attack crumbled and the position was held.

Captain Kiln concluded:

> Now it is late, the sun has gone in, and a sense of foreboding sets in. The tanks of the 7th Armoured are conspicuous by their absence; the Gloucesters are in almost their first battle … My report of the reinforcements that I have observed has not helped morale much. Anyway, the optimism of a swan of the morning changes dramatically, and we start to experience the extraordinary feeling of fear spreading. Rumours circulate that we are surrounded: 'The Germans are coming up the valleys on either side of us.' The fear is triggered by the officer commanding one of the Gloucesters' forward companies who seems to have had some sort of breakdown.
>
> His company starts to stream back down the road. His company sergeant major does his best, but once the contagious fear spreads, it's difficult to stop. I am grabbed by the second-in-command of the Gloucesters, who says 'You and I are going to walk up and down this road smoking our pipes to show these bastards that there is nothing to fear.'

However, with mortar fire steadily increased and growing numbers of Germans pushing forward personally led by *Oberst* Scholze, as dusk fell pressure grew and the positions of the remaining Gloucesters in the village were unsustainable. Consequently, the order was given for them to withdraw to positions between the dip and Pont de la Guillette, where the troops rallied by the second-in-command were already digging in. They needed no encouragement to dig as they were being deluged with mortar fire.

According to 4 CLY's war diary:

> C Sqn and Recce withdrew to battle positions north side of river (830695) [the dip] to support Gloucester Regt who were being counter-attacked. Leaguer north of BUCÉELS 830705.
> Casualties: Lt T.S. Vine missing, 17 ORs missing, 2 ORs wounded.

The 50th Division's war diary concluded:

> The general impression gained from the day's fighting is that the enemy is trying to delay our penetration southwards for as long as possible, in particular along the axis of the two roads leading from BAYEUX to VILLERS-BOCAGE. He is doing this by adopting offensive tactics and taking every opportunity to infiltrate forward with infantry and tanks.[4]

Essex Wood

It was still early when Lieutenant Colonel Higson returned from brigade head-quarters with Brigadier Hinde's orders for 2 Essex to mount a full-scale attack to capture 'the orchard-type woods' approximately 500 yards to the north of Lingèvres and just west of the hamlet of Verrières. Major Elliott wrote:[5]

> The Battalion Orders Group[6] drove hurriedly in jeeps to the higher ground just outside Folliot, but the view was not worth the drive: the tops of all woods and orchards look alike in this country at a distance of a mile, and in this particular case the line of orchards to our south were on a slight reverse slope: we could only see, in fact, the terrain to the south and east of Bernières-Bocage which we were about to attack [across] was comparatively open, and consists of cornfields and other low crops: the only comparatively open country for many miles around.

The Essex Regiment's cap badge.

Colonel Higson reflected on his task:

> This was a formidable task, because 1,500 yards of flat open country which lay between the Battalion and its objective provided the enemy with an ideal killing ground and was, moreover, especially suit-able for the enemy tanks which had been observed in Verrières Wood. It was therefore necessary to arrange for the maximum fire support to cover the Battalion over this long advance, and to include artillery in sufficient weight to dislodge the enemy tanks. In these respects, the Battalion was well served, and it was decided to subject the objective to a concentration of medium artillery and to support the advancing infantry with a moving barrage of 25-pounders.

Despite the level of artillery support, members of 2 Essex were critical of the lack of armour to help them break into the belt of orchards, as Major Elliott wrote. However:

> It was understood that tanks would follow us up as soon as we had cleared the orchards of the enemy infantry. I am unable to recall what orders were given to our own anti-tank guns and mortars, but there was some initial and natural reluctance to move those vehicles close behind the infantry across the open country and under the enemy's observation until the situation in front had been cleared up.[7]

2 Essex moved forward through Bernières-Bocage, which was eventually cleared, into some thick bocage where forming-up proved to be difficult astride various hedgerows, despite tapes laid out by the Recce Platoon. The attack was to be led

Operations of 2 Essex, 10 and 11 June.

by C Company on the right and A Company on the left, with D Company following on the right and B on the left. Colonel Higson's tactical headquarters was forward between the two leading companies, with the second-in-command following between the rear companies. The regimental historian records that 'the country was so confusing that leading companies were forced to advance on a compass bearing.'

The Essex crossed the start line at 1800 hours after the artillery fire plan had blasted the orchards and moved forward through the standing corn at a rate of advance of 100 yards in two minutes. The leading companies followed the

25-pounder's creeping barrage. Major Elliott recalled that they advanced to 'The accompaniment of the continuous whine and explosion of our own shells as they pounded the enemy.' It was only when the leading platoons were within 500 yards of the objective that the *panzergrenadiers* opened fire with artillery, mortars and small arms.

With the main German supply depots east of the Seine and Normandy all but isolated by Allied air power, the German defenders were perennially short of ammunition. Artilleryman *Gefreiter* Becker recalled during the battle of Tilly that

> The stack of shells ready by our guns got smaller as the battle went on. Almost immediately we arrived at the invasion front, it was obvious that supplies arriving at the battery were not keeping up with the rate of fire. The numbers of shell we fired soon reduced to emergencies as a result.

To the Germans, however, even the Eastern Front veterans, it was plain that the Allies suffered no such disadvantage.

A medium 5.5in gun of the 5th AGRA firing in support of the 7th Armoured Division.

A 25-pounder of the type issued to the 50th Division's three field regiments.

Despite suffering casualties, A and C companies kept moving forward steadily until keeping close to the barrage, with only 100 yards to go, German small-arms fire joined the battle as the barrage lifted. The Essex found that the enemy had cut fields of fire or 'tracks' through the tall corn, down which they fired with machine guns on fixed lines. These enfilade shoots effectively created walls of lead from left and right through which the Essex had to pass to advance on the objectives: 'Men could be seen going down.'

Charging through the last few yards of standing crops, the leading companies reached the hedges and they swept through the orchards and quickly cleared the objective. The battalion was soon digging in in a square defensive box based on the north side of the Verrières orchards. The left of the position was being raked by Spandau fire from the direction of Verrières. Consequently, D Company was ordered out to the left to clear the opposition, but as orders were being given, mortar fire struck the company headquarters and one of the platoons, which suffered casualties, both killed and wounded.

Before the Essex had dug more than a few inches, I/902 *Panzergrenadiers* counter-attacked with infantry supported by panzers and B Company forward on the left was quickly overrun by the *panzergrenadiers*. At this crucial moment there was no sign of either 5 RTR or the battalion's anti-tank guns and most of the radios had been damaged during the fighting or when crashing through hedges. 'In this critical situation,' Major Elliott wrote, 'particularly on the left flank ... by nightfall the sole means of reliable communication was through the artillery forward observation officer.'

Dismounted radio communication based on fragile valve technology was notoriously poor up until the 1970s. The adage was that 'If you were moving, you weren't communicating.' A particularly harsh note from an armoured regiment sums up the situation in 1944:

Bad Infantry Communications: These are without exception deplorable. There is the general defeatist attitude amongst infantry that their communications are bound to fail once the battle starts. The attitude is justified as they always do. The result is that the plan has to be too rigid, and once

A photo taken on 11 June 1944 of a No. 18 radio in use with 6 DLI.

troops are committed it is impossible for them to adjust themselves to the enemy's reactions. The whole system of infantry communications seems to require a complete overhaul.[8]

Without communications and little chance of 5 RTR's Cromwells finding their way forward, matters for 2 Essex worsened. The commanding officer later wrote:

> Despite gallant efforts with the PIAT, the situation soon became critical. The enemy tanks, working in pairs, blasted the section positions at point-blank range, and very heavy casualties were sustained, including two platoons of B Company which were rounded up and taken prisoner. Nevertheless, the battalion held its ground and, as night began to fall, the enemy tanks withdrew.

For the Essex, the night was, however, by no means a quiet one. Soon after midnight a sudden infantry counter-attack supported by flame-throwers was launched by the enemy: 'By using this rather terrifying weapon the enemy made serious penetration into the Battalion position, the flame-throwers being operated from armoured half-track vehicles.' The attack was halted in the centre of the battalion's position at the headquarters, mainly by Lieutenant Price using a combination of a 2in mortar and a PIAT. A half-track was burned out, and the enemy withdrew from the illuminated area. The regimental historian wrote:

> So serious was the general position that the Commanding Officer decided to call for artillery fire on to the Battalion location, on the assumption that our

Sd.Kfz.251-16 flame-thrower of the type issued to *Panzer Lehr*.

A PIAT loaded and ready to fire.

own troops would be relatively immune in their slit trenches. This critical action was successful, and the artillery concentration which followed proved too much for the enemy, who withdrew.

The Essex were still completely out of radio communication with 22 Armoured Brigade and with their rear link at the battalion main headquarters in Bernières-Bocage.

The situation was grave and the outlook for the morning gloomy. At about 1.00 am on 12 June Lieutenant Colonel Higginson instructed Major Elliott to make his way across country to the Armoured Brigade Headquarters and to request some tank or SP anti-tank support by first light. Unfortunately, that headquarters had moved from their reported location at Jerusalem and Major Elliott, after contacting the battalion rear link at Bernières-Bocage, went next to Headquarters 56 Infantry Brigade. Before leaving rear headquarters Captain Townrow told him the battalion anti-tank guns were on their way up to the forward area and had, in fact, started immediately after dark.

Presumably, the Essex's support element had been unable to find the battalion in the dark. Major Elliott's visit to 56 Infantry Brigade's headquarters and briefing of Brigadier Pepper in his caravan to explain the situation prompted a middle-of-the-night call to the divisional commander requesting that either the tanks or self-propelled anti-tank guns needed be sent forward to his battalion 'by first light as a matter of urgency. This was done and thereafter matters improved.'

The support, or perceived lack of support, to 2 Essex by 5 RTR and 22 Armoured Brigade was questioned at the time and has been the subject of continuing comment up to this day. This is, however, to ignore the parlous state of communications to the rear and the practical difficulties, as witnessed by the Essex's own anti-tank platoon, in finding the battalion in the dark in difficult country. The abiding feeling is, however, that more could have been done.

The Essex's anti-tank guns and the tanks of 5 RTR duly arrived and the defensive box was reorganized into a more conventional deployment, and the wounded were evacuated from the overflowing RAP by the Carrier Platoon. As the regimental historian concluded: 'So ended a memorable battle. The casualties had been severe, but Verrières Wood (better known as Essex Wood) remained firmly in the hands of the 2nd Essex.' The cost of the grim battle to capture and hold Essex Wood from *Panzer Lehr* had been high, with around 450 killed, wounded and missing.

The day of 11 June, despite some hard and costly fighting by 22 Armoured and 56 Brigade, had been another disappointing day for the 7th Armoured Division, spent battering against General Bayerlein's *Panzer Lehr*.

The memorial in Essex Wood.

Chapter Nine

La Belle Épine and Bernières-Bocage

The 61st Recce Regiment was one of the regiments deployed on the left flank of the Second Army and early in the morning was reporting that they had been halted by opposition in the area of La Senaudière and la Belle Épine but further to the west they reported a gap covered only by enemy patrols. The gap had been created by the collapse of the remnants of the 352nd Division in the face of an attack by the 1st and 2nd US infantry divisions. The enemy patrols they encountered were from the recce battalions of panzer divisions that were strung out on the route of march north to the invasion front. This was all the Germans had available to fill the 'Caumont Gap'.

To the west of Tilly and Verrières, shortly after first light, 231 Brigade resumed its 5-mile advance south to the Tilly-Balleroy road. 2 Devons were to start off from overnight positions at Trungy south of Bayeux and advance south to the crossroads of la Belle Épine. 1 Hampshires had reached Saint-Paul-du-Vernay the previous day, and once relieved by 8th Hussars, were to come around to the left flank and advance from the area of Bernières-Bocage and advance on La Senaudière. Capture of these places would deny an important lateral route to *Panzer Lehr*.

The Devons began their advance at 0610 hours against light opposition with their carrier platoon deployed ahead of them in the recce role. The battalion's main body was led by B Company, while C Company moved behind them as a flank guard with patrols out to the west. The battalion duly signalled that la Belle Épine was in their hands at 0832 hours without enemy interference. The regimental history commented that 'This was so good as to be almost fishy.'

Meanwhile, A Company, moving to the left rear of the battalion, had also secured its objective: a bridge over the River Aure. The 50th Division noted that '295 Fd Coy RE. Tac HQ moved to ST AMATOR. Coy placed under comd 2 Devon as inf (not to be used as aslt tps).' It was, however, intended that the Royal Engineers would dig in and secure the bridge, releasing A Company for other tasks.

The Devonshire Regiment's cap badge.

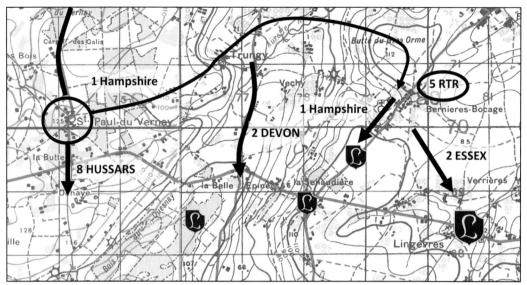

231 Brigade's operations, 11 June 1944.

With a lack of defenders at la Belle Épine, the Devons' commanding officer, Lieutenant Colonel 'Cosmo' Nevill, ordered B Company to probe south. Accordingly, Lieutenant David Holdsworth, a platoon commander with B Company, led his men down from the crossroads. He wrote:

> We were formed up, strung out by platoons and sections on either side of the road. Nervously, we negotiated the crossroads. Nobody fired at us. About a mile further south there was a sudden nasty clatter of a German Spandau. Down we went on our faces.
>
> This is one of those occasions when platoon commanders hope that someone higher up the chain of command knows his battle tactics. Someone did; we withdrew.

B Company had run into one of *Panzer Lehr*'s armoured patrols and with D Company reporting the presence of three panzers to their east at La Senaudière, the commanding officer pulled B Company back to the crossroads.

The battalion was at least 2 miles forward of any other British unit in the area and was very much on its own. The commanding officer, with the Hampshires behind him and to the right and his left flank open, ordered the B, C and D companies to dig in. It, however, soon became apparent that they were not alone, but saw an increasing amount of enemy movement less than 1,000 yards to the east across the Aure. 231 Brigade's historian commented that 'The enemy at La Senaudière obviously intended to dispute any farther advance.' Indeed they did; they were a part of 130 *Lehr* Reconnaissance Battalion, reinforced by a platoon of four Panzer IVs which were deployed on higher ground east of the river around La Senaudière from where they could overlook la Belle Épine. The regimental historian wrote that 'These tanks were immediately made the subject of a gesture by all the mortar fire available, which sent them back under cover. But digging in was done warily, with one eye cocked for trouble.'

Lieutenant Colonel 'Cosmo' Nevill.   Lieutenant David Holdsworth in 1943.

Over the next two hours the Devons' companies dug in around the crossroads, with the battalion's anti-tank guns echeloned in depth, covering the approaches, especially from the east. Importantly, the Assault Pioneer Platoon surface-laid mines on the road south from the crossroads. Lieutenant Holdsworth continued:

> We re-formed the battalion so that all approach roads to la Belle Épine were blocked to the enemy. My platoon dug itself in along a hedge giving rather restricted vision over a thickly wooded area about 300 yards away. On our left was one of the roads running towards la Belle Épine. On the far side of this road was another platoon. Some way behind us was the anti-tank platoon. For a long time, nothing happened.

An entry in the battalion's war diary at 1327 hours records that D Company, forward on the left reinforced by a platoon of C Company, reported that an attack was developing in the valley of the Aure to the east and at 1350 that they were being attacked by tanks. Unbeknown to the Devons, British armour, probably the recce Cromwells of B Squadron, 8th Hussars, were working their way south down the valley. A thirty-minute battle resulted before it was discovered that they were British! The regimental history, however, records that just after 1500 hours '… the heavy mortaring which broke out against the whole battalion position hardly came as a surprise. Nor was its accuracy a surprise since the enemy had perfect observation from La Senaudière Hill.'

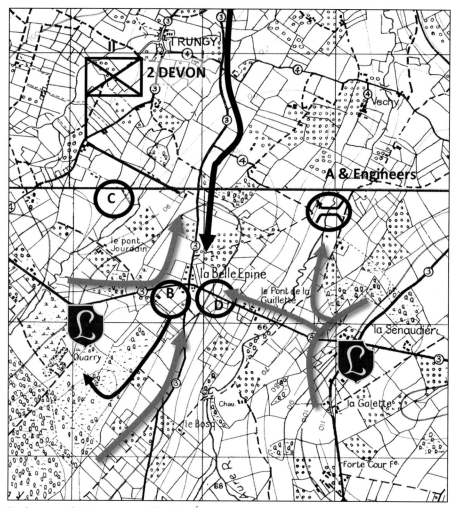

Deployment of 2 Devons around la Belle Épine.

When the Germans attacked at 1730 hours, Lieutenant Holdsworth was patrolling the wood to B Company's front with two of his sections when he heard tank and motorcycle engines starting up:

> By now the engine noise had begun to move away to our left, presumably towards the road, and so to attack la Belle Épine. Although we could only guess at the time, my platoon and the German tanks and motor-cyclists were advancing on parallel but opposite courses. They were going hell for leather towards the crossroads.

The leading Panzer IVs approached B Company with a friendly arm waving from the turret. This ruse worked, as the earlier 'engagement' with British tanks led to unquestioning caution. Consequently, 'the "friendly" tank's wave was followed up by three rounds of rapid fire, which killed the crew of an anti-tank gun.' The second of the section's 6-pounder guns hit the panzer on its turret but failed to knock it out. At least two more panzers broke cover around B Company's defensive position. Behind the panzers came the German infantry.

The German attack on B Company was led by 130 *Lehr* Reconnaissance Battalion, with a mix of half-tracks, armoured cars, its attached panzers and

Panzer Lehr soldiers prepare for battle.

probably reinforcements from 130 *Lehr* panzer pioneers. Due to the difficulty of armour crossing the Aure from the east and a lack of cover, the Germans knew from previous experience that the attack would inevitably be broken up by Allied artillery. Consequently, the attack was launched from the south and south-west where there was far more cover.

Meanwhile, without a working radio there was little Lieutenant Holdsworth could do but carefully retrace his steps. When he reached B Company's position, he found his reserve section gone with all their equipment. The battalion's war diary recorded that

> B Coy had been caught quite unprepared by the tanks and had no trenches or positions to man. The Coy became disorganised and their carrier was knocked out by a direct hit. By this time, it appeared that there were between six and eight tanks operating in B Coy area. The Commanding Officer rushed all available anti-tank guns up to hold the crossroads.

In the initial stages, parts of B Company's position had been overrun thanks to a combination of the *ruse de guerre*, the speed of the attack and because the company was still at the early stages of digging in, thanks to their probe south. Some, such as Holdsworth's reserve section, had extricated themselves with difficulty and had fallen back towards the battalion headquarters.

During the battle D Company initially held on against an attack by *panzergrenadiers*, but when the enemy changed tactics to infiltrating around and into their positions, by early evening they were eventually forced to withdraw as well. Meanwhile, the enemy also worked their way around the battalion's flanks to threaten A Company. With the time taken for word of events to climb the chain of command, an entry in the 50th Division's war diary was timed '1900 – Enemy with tks start working between 2 Devons posns from West.'

Member of the battalion headquarters' intelligence section Private Powis had just left the large farmhouse or 'château' where he had been digging in when the attack began:

> As I climbed over the wall into the field where our partially-dug slit trenches were, I could see the 3in mortarmen setting up and some boxes of mortar bombs being carried from a stack to the mortars. At this point I heard small-arms fire in the direction of the front line, but a skirmish now and then was not unusual whenever we stopped and 'dug in'. This time it was not just a skirmish as the firing was rapidly increasing and was getting closer and closer with the added sound of hand grenades exploding. I spotted German soldiers entering the far end of the field in large numbers, realising immediately that the enemy had counter-attacked and broken through one of the two forward companies. I immediately picked up my rifle and ran to the 3ft-high boundary wall of the château, vaulted over it and shouted to the mortarmen and to those inside the château to warn them of a breakthrough. Then I got down behind the wall and fired a number of shots towards the many

A 3in mortar in action.

Germans approaching us across the field and out rushed several Battalion HQ men to the wall and began firing.

The Germans immediately split up, to the left and to the right, and it seemed clear from the move that they had already planned to surround the château. The 3in Mortar Section were soon sending HE bombs towards the other end of the field as fast as they could, whilst one of their men struggled to drag heavy boxes of bombs from the stack to the mortar. I could see that the man dragging the boxes would not keep up with the speed of firing, so as the Germans were now out of sight, I jumped over the wall and helped drag the boxes.

After a while the mortar Sergeant looked at the boxes we were bringing and those left on the stack and said, 'Blast! We can't fire any more, we're

Château la Londe, the site of the Devons' battalion headquarters. The country immediately around the complex is more open than it was and the farm's orchards have been removed.

out of HE!' I said, 'What's wrong with these?' He said, 'They're no good; they're all smoke.' I replied, 'Put smoke down then; they'll think we're going to counter-attack them!' His description of me for making such a suggestion was far from flattering! I got back over the wall and carried on firing my rifle at any enemy movements that I could see.

Behind me in the château I could hear the pandemonium as the rest of Battalion Headquarters and the Intelligence Section realised that we were all being surrounded by the enemy. I heard the Intelligence Officer shout over the other loud voices, 'Corporal! Stand by to burn the War Diary!'

The Battalion Commanding Officer arrived and shouted, 'What's going on here!?' I quickly explained to him that the Germans had counter-attacked, had broken through the forward Company and were now surrounding the château. The CO immediately bellowed to the Sergeant, 'Why isn't the mortar firing?' He replied, 'We've run out of HE sir, we've only got smoke now!' The CO angrily shouted back, 'Then put that down man.' I jumped back over the wall again and helped with the boxes of ammunition to the mortar as before. The whole of the château area was very quickly enveloped in thick smoke. The enemy small-arms firing ceased almost immediately except for single shots, a burst of sub-machine gunfire, plus hand grenade explosions now and then.

A crucial factor at this stage was that the panzers, having seen the mines laid on the road south of the crossroads, cautiously held back. Colonel Nevill later opined that 'the mines saved what might have been a disaster.' The *panzergrenadiers* fought over 500 yards into the Devons' positions, latterly without support by the panzers. They began to run out of steam and were unwilling to engage at close

A heavily-laden infantryman carrying bandoliers of additional ammunition, his rifle and PIAT.

quarters in the area around battalion headquarters where the commanding officer had formed a defensive strongpoint with the headquarters company and the remnants of B and D companies. Powis continued his account:

> As the smoke was thinning, I saw the enemy making a rapid withdrawal and got glimpses of three Germans beyond my slit trench. Two of them were running whilst supporting one of their men between them who had one knee bent as if unable to put his foot to the ground, but I couldn't bring myself to fire at them and focused my attention on others spread out across the field.

Colonel Nevill and the second-in-command Major Browne had run back to bring the A and C companies forward. A Company down in the river valley was not in radio contact and were engaged in their own battle and had to give up their bridge, while C Company was similarly out of touch with battalion headquarters, was unaware of what was going on and eventually joined the fighting.

Meanwhile, Captain Mike Holdsworth, Lieutenant David Holdsworth's brother, and Captain Cox, while attempting to find and reorganize B Company ran into some *panzergrenadiers* at close quarters: 'Cox's Sten gun jammed but a grenade thrown by Holdsworth dispersed the enemy.' Powis continued:

> I followed in pursuit of the Germans, stopping at intervals to fire a few shots at them from the shoulder whilst adopting a slightly stooped standing firing position. Some of them turned to fire back without taking careful aim.
>
> One of the companies very soon passed either side of the château and went in pursuit of the enemy. The Commanding Officer gave orders for the whole Battalion to move forward into an attack, which meant us having to rapidly attach our packs and entrenching tools to our equipment, abruptly ending the rest period we had anticipated having.

The Devons were very much on their own as they had advanced beyond the range of their radios in rolling country and were out of touch with brigade headquarters. The first 231 Brigade knew about the attack on the Devons was when Captain Mike Holdsworth ran 3 miles back to report what was going on. At the time, however, Brigadier Stanier was forward on a visit to the Hampshires' battalion headquarters to discuss their patrol programme for that night. Corporal

Captain Mike Holdsworth
MC.

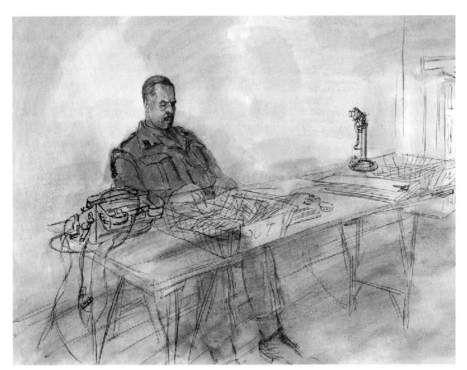

A war artist's depiction of Brigadier Stanier at work during the campaign.

Richards, a signaller in Headquarters 231 Brigade, was the brigadier's driver and radio-operator:

> While at the Hampshires' headquarters, which was under mortar fire, we picked up a message intended for Brigade HQ from the Devons, stating that the Germans had counter-attacked and cut the road behind them. We stopped when we saw one of our tanks and the Brigadier spoke to the officer in charge, whilst I stayed in the Jeep listening to the radio. The Brigadier decided that we should return to Brigade HQ but I said that I could hear the Devons, but Brigade HQ couldn't.
>
> As we drove back some soldiers of the Devonshire Regiment came up and told us that the Devons' Battalion Headquarters had been wiped out, the Colonel was dead, and the Second-in-Command had been killed. I explained to them that they were mistaken, as I just had been speaking to those persons on the radio. The soldiers said that they were out of ammunition but, having plenty, I supplied them, and Lt Montgomery got them together and called on the tanks to help the Devons out.

These tanks were the seven of the surviving Crabs of the Westminster Dragoons' B and C squadrons.[1] They had been placed under the command of 231 Brigade and were holding the Butte du Gros Orme (Point 112) along with AVREs of

81 Assault Squadron, plus a mixed bag of Cheshire machine guns and Royal Engineers. Despite their specialist role as flail tanks, they were, however, the only armour available, as 5 RTR was supposedly committed to supporting 2 Essex in their battle at Verrières at that time. The Westminster Dragoons' history records that

> This composite Sqn was ordered to the assistance of the 2 DEVONS who, having fought continuously since D-Day, had been repulsed from LA BELLE ÉPINE, and the task of the composite Sqn was to support the 2 DEVONS back into the village. The Sqn arrived in the forming-up area just before dusk and in the failing light it was impossible to distinguish any definite enemy points as the information was also scanty. It was therefore decided as the objective was only some 300 to 400 yards from the start line that the flails, used as ordinary tanks, should bring maximum fire to bear on the village, all the hedges and likely enemy-held positions. In the dusk it was a terrific sight. Tracer streaked through the gloom, and fires caused by the 75mm shells from the tank's guns lit the scene with a red glare. The attack was successful, and no casualties were incurred by either B or C Sqns.

Also taking part were some Churchill Crocodiles of 141 Regiment RAC, again in a conventional armoured role. Their war diary records that 'In the evening jettisoned [flame fuel] trailers and participated in counter-attack on LA BELLE ÉPINE firing 75mm and BESA into the buildings.'[2] Two batteries of 102 Anti-Tank Regiment were sent to thicken up the defence against panzers, particularly infiltration up the Aure valley.

The German counter-attack had first been halted and held for some hours by the Devons before help finally arrived. The day culminated at 2200 hours just before dark with a determined counter-attack by A Company supported by the Westminster Dragoons in which la Belle Épine crossroads was recaptured within thirty minutes and B Company's positions restored. Ten men were listed as wounded including the commanding officer, whose injury was not serious enough to warrant evacuation and he remained on duty with the battalion.

A factor that could have helped the Devons is that the attacks by the Essex's on the orchards around Verrières and the Gloucesters on Tilly were both taking place that same evening. That was the epicentre of the fighting south of Bayeux and was clearly a greater threat, which precluded German resources being sent to la Belle Épine.

As a demonstration of effective liaison between the British and 1st US Infantry Division, during the evening the 26th Regimental Combat Team dispatched across the army boundary a 'small force to cover the crossroads'. In the event they were not needed.

By 2300 hours word reached the headquarters of 50th Division that '2 Devons restore sit with coy counter-attack, tho' enemy penetrate and hold woods at 7869.' There were still enough veterans in the Devons' ranks for the sudden

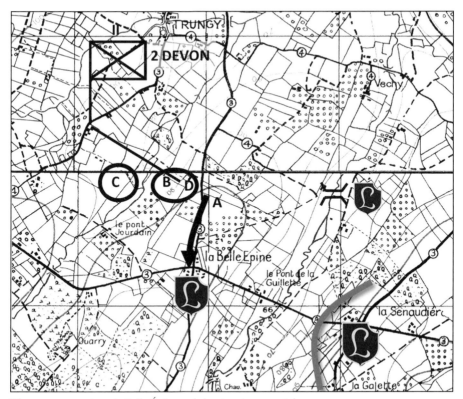

The counter-attack on la Belle Épine and the situation overnight.

eruption of German armour into their midst not to be met with panic and a collapse of the battalion. The considered opinion was that

> This had been a minor action, but a sudden and testing one. When the 2nd Devons had leisure to breathe again and take stock, there were several outstanding deeds of gallantry for the records. Among them was that of Corporal Ratnage who, firing his Bren from the hip, had dashed along the road to knock out an enemy Spandau.

The following morning, 12 June, A Company with the support of AVREs were back in possession of the bridge they gave up to the enemy the previous evening. The rest of the day was quieter, despite fears of a renewed counter-attack, although the Devons were regularly mortared and Germans infiltrated into sniping positions in the battalion's area 'which made life uncomfortable'.

1 Hampshires at Bernières-Bocage

During 11 June the 7th Armoured Division, while attacking Tilly-sur-Seulles, had little work for their Recce Regiment; consequently it joined 61st Recce Regiment and XXX Corps' recce to the west. With the arrival of the 8th Hussars (see Chapter 11), Lieutenant Colonel Howie was ordered to take 1 Hampshires back east to the Bernières-Bocage area, where there was a 'persistently trouble-some pocket of enemy that needed mopping up' on their way to La Senau-dière (see map on page 162). 2 Essex had spent the night of 10/11 June and the following morning in the area, which contained what was rather more than a 'pocket'; it was the tip of a broad salient that stretched south to La Senaudière. As the Essex were under orders to launch their attack on the orchards around Verrières (Essex Wood; see previous chapter) during the late afternoon, the Hampshires were to mop up the pocket. The battalion's war diary records that

> Arriving at the start-line NW of the village of BERNIÈRES-BOCAGE the bn launched an attack on the enemy pocket of resistance SW of the village where our supporting tanks were held up by a well-camouflaged 88mm gun firing point-blank at the sharp bend 500 yards south of the village.

This was the first time that the Hampshiremen had come up against stiff resistance in the bocage country and they joined virtually every other unit in bemoaning in their war diary the difficulties of dealing with a 'well-sited position with all approaches and tracks covered by Spandaus':

> The enemy mortars from the security of their natural concealment bombarded the village, the road, the tracks and the fields via which our mopping-up coys had to advance. In spite of these natural advantages, our rifle coys gained ground and dug in in a defensive area SW of the village.

A German 80mm mortar in action.

The 'mopping-up' had, in fact, only been partly completed and what is more, the Hampshires had to fight to hold their gains when the Germans mounted 'a fierce counter-attack' which they beat off with 'substantial casualties being inflicted on the enemy'. The Germans who withdrew towards La Senaudière overnight continued to drop mortar bombs with unerring accuracy on the company locations until it was realized that they had OPs in some of the taller trees.

The battalion's renewed mopping-up operations on the following day, 12 June, fared little better, with the modest number of flails and Churchill AVREs which had successfully supported the Devons the previous evening now under command of the Hampshires. They did not get far before they ran into the same determined resistance; their war diary only requires a modicum of interpretation to appreciate the level of the failure:

> Bn with sp arms tried to mop up enemy resistance at Pt 110 [south of La Senaudière]. The start-line forward of the village was dominated by ridges from the enemy side. The sp arms consisting of flails and AVREs moved too far forward of the infantry, got knocked out and provided little help to the battalion.

Following a counter-attack, which the Hampshires again beat off, they retired back to their overnight position south-west of Bernières-Bocage, complaining that 'The artillery missed an important ridge to the left from which considerable opposition came.' This was the Lingèvres feature that was the scene of bitter fighting on 16 June.

231 Brigade would continue attempts to advance south over coming days (see Chapter 13).

A Sherman Crab flail tank.

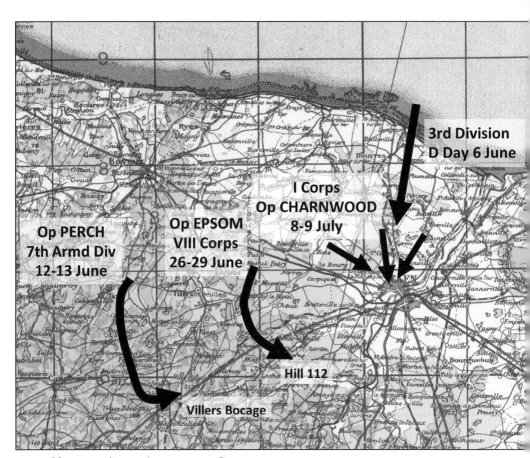

**3rd Division
D Day 6 June**

**I Corps
Op CHARNWOOD
8-9 July**

**Op EPSOM
VIII Corps
26-29 June**

**Op PERCH
7th Armd Div
12-13 June**

Hill 112

Villers Bocage

Montgomery's operations to capture Caen.

Chapter Ten

A Change of Tack: 12 June 1944

12 June, D+6, was when British commanders finally accepted that battering their way south through the defences provided by one of the best German panzer divisions and that fighting in country favourable to the enemy was only ever likely to make slow progress at the cost of unforeseen levels of casualties.[1] At the same time, the opportunity of exploiting the Caumont Gap where the 1st US Infantry Division was making progress south against little serious opposition was realized, but initially it was to be another day fighting south with Villers-Bocage still the objective.

Hauptmann Ritgen, who was now commanding the Panzer IVs of II Battalion, 130 Panzer Regiment, recalled that at

> 0800 hours the battalion was divided into two 'fire brigades', preparing for counter-attacks behind the *panzergrenadiers*, who were being hard-pressed by either the Tommies, artillery and mortar fire or air-strikes ... For the most part we were degraded by being turned into *panzeräger* or bunkers.

Brigadier Cracroft's account outlines what 8 Armoured Brigade intended to achieve on 12 June:

> ... our attack [6 Green Howards on Cristot the previous evening] had achieved some success as the enemy mortaring was less intense and more inaccurate than previously. The night before I had issued Warning Orders for the attack on the TESSEL-BRETTEVILLE feature [a point on the original Route CONGO south to Villers-Bocage]. A further conference was held, and detailed orders of the attack were issued. The attack was to start from ST PIERRE with the first objective the high ground overlooking la Caude Rus. The second objective the road JUVIGNY-FONTENAY-LE-PESNEL. The attack was to be carried out by 24th Lancers and SRY with elements from 8th DLI.

The plan to resume the offensive was delayed by a renewed German attack; one of a quite different nature to the previous evening's all-out assault. At first light the surviving tanks of 24th Lancers were deployed forward observing eastwards, but near regimental headquarters on Point 103, enemy helmets were spotted moving in an abandoned trench in the centre of the position. The Germans were flushed out and a dozen of them were taken prisoner, revealing that they were a part of an infiltration attack by the *panzergrenadiers*. 24th Lancers' historian wrote that 'From them we learnt that a whole company of *Panzergrenadier* Regiment 901 (*Lehr*) were sited in ditches surrounding our position, armed with the *Panzerfaust*, sticky bombs[2] and other anti-tank weapons and numerous other automatic weapons.'

Lieutenant Wareham, the regimental headquarters troop commander, mounted in his tank, was among those sent to investigate:

We faced out towards a wood some 600 to 800 yards away where we could see some enemy activity; also some vehicles, probably anti-tank guns, and there was a certain amount of exchange of fire. It was too hot a gap to try to cover without losing more of our now rather scarce Shermans and we had, so far as I knew, no artillery support and there were not many infantry about. It seemed to have become again a holding game. By nine in the morning – it seemed a long time since first light – I had moved up to the apex of the L-shaped hedge and down the other side of it. I could see a German armoured car, probably knocked out. It was often really so difficult to see what was happening when you were enclosed inside a turret. I asked permission to dismount to go and have a closer look ... Asking Cpl Field, an Intelligence Corporal of HQ Troop who was my wireless-operator, to

The *Panzerfaust* 100.

A sketch of aiming, firing and the *Panzerfaust*'s back-blast.

Sherman Firefly with its long 17-pounder gun in the Normandy bocage.

follow me with his Sten gun, we set off down the hedge. After about 100 yards there was, what seemed to me, a terrific burst of automatic fire just behind me and I felt as if someone had hit me with a sledgehammer. I was knocked to the ground ... I lay doggo, wondering what the hell to do. I unbuttoned the top pocket of my denim blouse with my right hand, fished out a [white phosphorous] grenade, and it's true, pulled the tape off with my teeth and tossed it into the hedge. The white phosphorus liquid in fact sprayed back, some of it even over me, but I think it surprised the occupants of the hedge as it gave off quick smoke. I picked up my left arm with my right and did the fastest 100 yards I have ever done.

Despite tank losses to *Panzerfausts*, the Lancers eventually drove the enemy out of the hedgerows and the company of *panzergrenadiers* was engaged with high-explosive and machine-gun fire: 'A few enemy escaped but we estimated that nearly the whole company was wiped out.'

The infiltration dealt with, A Squadron was ordered to begin the planned advance, with the immediate objective of securing the Saint-Pierre-Fontenay road. Sergeant Daws recalled that

> As troop sergeant, I was leading Third Troop, but our particular advance was rather short-lived. No sooner had we crossed the road than we were fired on and the tank knocked out by an 88mm anti-tank gun. It had not been possible to find cover. The crew bailed out and fortunately ended up in the ditch but unfortunately on the southern side of the road – no man's land. The five crew members crawled back along the ditch until we reached a point on the outskirts of St Pierre where we were able to cross into the garden of a cottage from which we were able to see our own infantry positions, to which we made our way. Other tanks were knocked out, but A Squadron reached its objective. The Germans, however, redeployed and with more tanks knocked out it was obvious that there was no prospect of an advance further south.

Brigadier Hargest, the New Zealand army liaison officer to the 21st Army Group, was with the 50th Division and had been a regular visitor to Point 103 for some days and in a report on the superiority of German armour he wrote that a solitary German Tiger tank 'fired for one hour' and then 'drove off unmolested' as 'not one tank went out to engage it'.

The day was the worst the Lancers experienced in their short operational history, suffering the loss of twenty-five casualties and further tanks knocked out, plus the commanding officer was wounded and evacuated. For the SRY it was little better. Major Christopherson recalled that it wasn't only infantry that had infiltrated onto the slopes of Point 103:

> On 12 June, we were given a 'holding role' for our immediate front; at the same time, we protected the left flank of the 7th Armoured Division, which ... was to attack Tilly-sur-Seulles. A Squadron again operated in the neighbourhood of Point 103, with which we had all become so very familiar. We received a nasty shock in finding that some German Tiger and Panther tanks had, during the night, worked their way through a gap in our lines into the thickly-wooded area around Point 102. It was extremely difficult to engage and after a game of hide-and-seek in the woods they slipped away down a sunken lane, but Squadron Sergeant Major Hutchinson had his 17-pounder tank knocked out at very short range; fortunately, he himself escaped injury.[3]

For the infantry up on Point 103, after a tense night, the handover of the defences from 1 Dorsets to 5 East Yorks resumed, following the disruption caused by the German counter-attacks the previous evening. By late morning the Dorsets' companies were beginning to march away to rejoin 231 Brigade to the south-west of Bayeux at Trungy.

British infantry on the march in Normandy.

Meanwhile, to the west of Point 103, Brigadier Cracroft 'could hear and see a part of 7th Armoured Division's attack'

> which appeared to start well but soon came up against very strong opposition in the northern outskirts of TILLY. Our attack from ST PIERRE went in during the morning but [as told above] the leading tanks soon came under very strong fire from enemy tanks.

The Attack on Tilly Resumed

The 7th Armoured Division resumed its attack south at first light with the aim of bypassing Tilly to the west and attacking through the lines of 56 Brigade. Of the preparations for the attack, Lieutenant Colonel Craver commanding 1 RTR wrote a damning report:[4]

> 12 June: 1 OR KIA [Other Ranks Killed in Action], 5 wounded, 3 tanks temporarily damaged. Information about own and enemy troops before op started was almost nil. Never knew 4 CLY were at St Bazire [north of Bucéels], nor did OC 1/6 Queens know the Essex bn were in wood 804692 [Essex Wood].[5] No time spent on Recce. There seemed to be a lack of general inquisitiveness to discover what the opposition was and where it was.

By 12 June, the Desert Rats' much-delayed 131 (Queen's) Brigade (lorried infantry) had finally arrived with the division and was ready for battle. The plan was to advance on two axes: firstly, south from Bucéels to Tilly-sur-Seulles and secondly, on the right towards Hottot via Verrières. The objective remained Villers-Bocage.

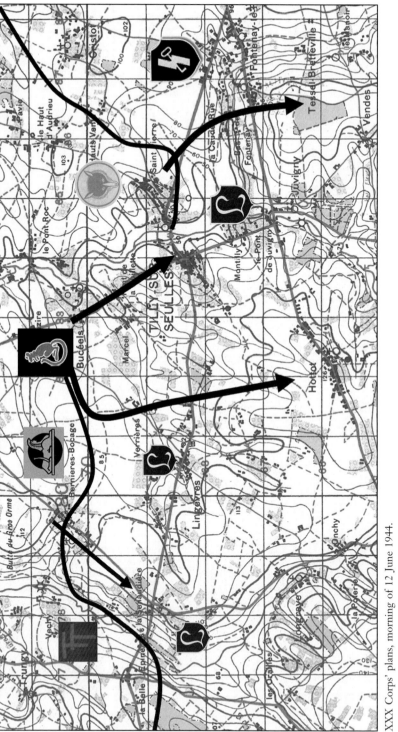

XXX Corps' plans, morning of 12 June 1944.

1/5 Queens, with a squadron of 1 RTR and a battery of the also newly-arrived 3rd Royal Horse Artillery (3 RHA) under command, were to advance on the right south on the Folliot-Verrières road. 1/6 Queens attacked, also with a 1 RTR squadron in support down the Bayeux-Tilly axis. The 4th County of London Yeomanry (4 CLY) and 1/7 Queens were in reserve.

4 CLY's task was to follow south from St Bazire and Bucéels. Their war diary provides a flavour of the day:

> Recce Sqn ordered to advance down CL [Centre Line or Axis of Advance]. Order of march: B Sqn, RHQ, A Sqn, C Sqn. VERRIÈRES (815692) strongly held by enemy. Recce withdrew to high ground to North. B Sqn left in battle positions on ridge 810708-820712 [Bernières-Bocage-St Bazire].
>
> New orders [Operation PERCH] in afternoon – Regt move at 1600 to outflank to right. Orders given verbally.

A Cromwell tank and crew of 4 CLY preparing a meal.

Once again, the effects of the bocage on the desert veterans are highlighted: 'About 20 enemy tks in whole area, not more than 6 seen. Countryside exceptionally favourable to A/Tk defence. Rumour of presence of a few German tanks still puts a brake on any operations and causes excitement quite out of proportion to their potential material effect.'

The divisional history sums up the morning's operations to advance south via Tilly and Verrières as '. . . they made a limited advance in very thick country. There was no opportunity anywhere for a breakthrough by tanks.'

7th Armoured Division Redeployed

Meanwhile, Lieutenant General Bucknall, commander of XXX Corps, in consultation with the army commander, decided to capitalize on the 'soft spot' adjacent to the army boundary with the 1st US Infantry Division reported by the armoured cars of the 11th Hussars, XXX Corps recce regiment. However, this 'gap' was by no means undefended as is commonly supposed and its existence since 9/10 June was only slowly realized by the British. The diary of the GSO1 of the 50th Division makes the point:

> Further WEST, the enemy has obviously not yet been able to bring up sufficient troops to fill in the gap held by the depleted elements of 352 Div and of 30 *Schnelle* Bde, between the River AURE and the main road BAYEUX-ST LÔ; elements of 17 SS Div identified in the area BALLEROY are so far in no great strength and have today been falling back steadily in front of the Americans.

This was, however, already hours behind the reality on the ground and at Headquarters Second Army General Dempsey confided to his diary that 'Provided this [advance] is carried out with real drive and speed there is a chance we will get through before the front congeals.' By the time he wrote this on 12 June, the Germans were rushing units to fill the Caumont Gap. Enemy units that would be encountered to the west included not only 130 *Lehr* Recce Battalion but the Divisional Escort Company and the recce battalion of 17 SS *Panzergrenadier* Division. In orders issued at 1900 hours on 11 June the 2nd Panzer Division had also been ordered to rush its recce battalion into the gap, but as General Fritz Krämer, Chief of Staff I SS Panzer Corps wrote:

> On 13 June advance elements of the 2nd Panzer Division [the recce battalion] arrived in the area of Caumont, and removed much of our anxiety about the gap . . . Thus the gap that might have enabled the enemy to make an easy breakthrough almost without loss was sealed off.[6]

Around midday on 12 June, General Erskine received orders to break off the current battle at Tilly and launch his part in another plan to gain ground and threaten Caen with envelopment. To this end he was to redeploy 22 Armoured Brigade via Jerusalem, the Aure bridges and on west to an assembly area south of Bayeux. From here they would advance south and then swing east towards

General Bucknall and his Chief of Staff Brigadier Pyeman.

Villers-Bocage and secure the high ground of Point 213, 1.5 miles north-east of the town. From there, in line with the concept of Operation WILD OATS, there would be a further advance on Évrecy, all with the aim of providing the western arm of an envelopment of Caen.

Assembly, orders and regrouping were quickly completed in an impressively short time, with A Squadron 8th Hussars, from the division's reconnaissance regiment, redeploying west at 1400 hours. 4 CLY began their drive south against negligible opposition at 1600 hours. The first stage of the route to Villers-Bocage was the 12 miles to Saint-Paul-du-Vernay, which had already been secured by 1 Hampshires. From there it was to be via Saint-Honorine-de-Ducy, Livry and Briquessard on the Villers-Bocage.

General Erskine left 1 RTR and the two Queen's battalions to hand over the Tilly/Verrières front to 56 Brigade, while the remainder of the division set off west following the Hussars and CLY battlegroup. The latter had their usual attached motor company with them: A Company 1 RB and the self-propelled

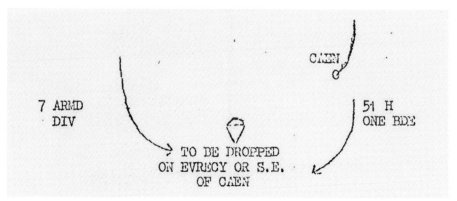

The basic Second Army concept of Operation WILD OATS (from 50th Division's war diary).

Sextons of K Battery, 5th Royal Horse Artillery (5 RHA). 1/7 Queens, 5 RTR, the remainder of 1 RB and 5 RHA, plus the Achilles[7] M10 tank destroyers completed the long column of march. 1 RTR and the two Queen's battalions, their artillery and the 3 RHA would follow in due course.

A Squadron, 8th Hussars of 7th Armoured were operating in country that had hitherto been largely uncontested. Once south of Arganchy and heading to Saint-Paul-du-Vernay, the Hussars' patrols reported that the column would be on narrow roads, but they were suitable for one-way traffic of both tracked and wheeled vehicles. There was, however, little option as to the west they would

General Erskine had commanded 7th Armoured Division since January 1943.

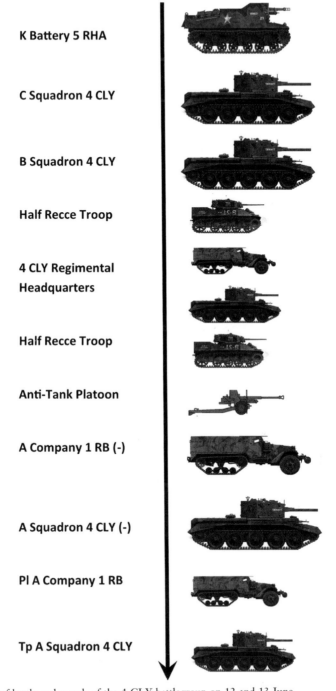

K Battery 5 RHA

C Squadron 4 CLY

B Squadron 4 CLY

Half Recce Troop

4 CLY Regimental
Headquarters

Half Recce Troop

Anti-Tank Platoon

A Company 1 RB (-)

A Squadron 4 CLY (-)

Pl A Company 1 RB

Tp A Squadron 4 CLY

The order of battle and march of the 4 CLY battlegroup on 12 and 13 June.

cross the army boundary into the US sector and any further east they would get entangled with the Devons' battle around la Belle Épine.

The Hussars' commander, Lieutenant Colonel Gouldburn, wrote that 'We were all beginning to think we had obtained a complete breakthrough.' With a 6-mile advance into enemy territory during the early evening of 12 June 1944 he had grounds for optimism but, as his war diary reveals, there were enemy troops about:

> The Regt moved out, A Sqn leading, and good progress was made as far as LIVRY 7361 [1 on map on page 191] where the Tp Ldrs tk of 2 Tp A Sqn was knocked out by an infantryman with a *Raketen Panzerbuchse* 43, the German equivalent of the 'Bazooka'. Two of the crew were killed and the remainder, Lt. D. Rampf included, were wounded.

The area was held by a part of *Panzer Lehr*'s Escort Company being used as an ordinary infantry sub-unit due to the long front being held by the division.

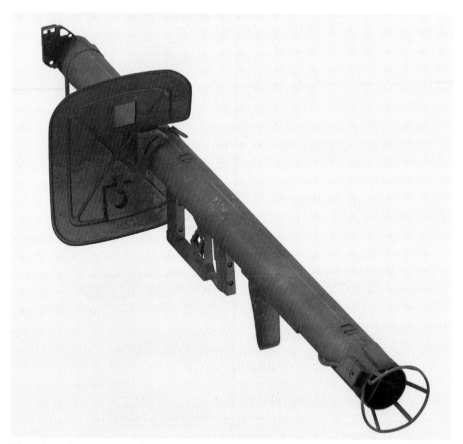

The *Raketen Panzerbuchse* 43, better known as the *Panzerschreck*.

Colonel Gouldburn records what happened:

A direct advance up the road is the only way ... to go for Talbot-Hervey's troop. After 2 or 3 minutes we hear an anti-tank gun fire about three shots. Hervey goes off the air. Shortly afterwards the troop corporal returns in his tank, very shaken and in tears to say that both leading tanks were brewed up.

During the contact the commanding officer of the CLY had closed up and decided to deal with the situation. The Hussars' war diary continued:

At this moment 4 CLY decided to put [a platoon of] his motor coy into LIVRY to clear the village and to take over the lead when they had done so. The motor coy ([A] 1 RB) cleared the village but as it was then getting late, no further advance was made that evening. Meanwhile the Brigadier had ordered 8H to recce down the main CAUMONT-CAEN road as far as the X rds at 767637 [2 on map on page 190].

At 764636 [3] the two leading tanks of 3rd Tp A Sqn were knocked out. Lt. Talbot-Hervey and 6 other Ranks are missing. No further progress was made, and the Regt leaguered in the area 733617 [4] with the remainder of 22 Armd Bde.

It was 2000 hours by the time the riflemen of A Company had cleared Livry and the rest of the brigade was strung out on the narrow roads north. Consequently, Brigadier Hinde decided to leaguer up some distance to the north of Livry on the Caen-St Lô road, centred on La Mulotière. By stopping here his intent was to leave the Germans guessing if the advance was to continue south alongside the 1st US Division or swing to the east and envelop *Panzer Lehr*.

It was almost midnight, however, by the time all the brigade's units were in the leaguer for a few short hours' rest, replenishment and maintenance.[8] In Livry, without too much damage or civilian loss of life, there were reports of some noisy liberation celebrations.

Thanks to casualties in 8th Hussars during the day, Lieutenant Bill Bellamy, who up to this point had run the A1 Echelon of A Squadron, found himself appointed as a replacement troop commander. This was not, however, before he had considerable difficulty in communicating with his No. 19 set in broken country and found himself at one point, while looking for his squadron, driving through a column of marching German infantry, to the great surprise of all concerned. With both 7th Armoured Division's plans and the location of his squadron leaguer having been changed, since he set out during the morning, Bill Bellamy and his trucks continued blundering about in the dark in what was no man's land before eventually finding the regiment.

Point 103 and Saint-Pierre

The transfer of 7th Armoured Division west along with the point of main effort led to the closing down of the battle to advance south from Point 103 and the replacement of 8 Armoured Brigade on the hitherto vital ground. At midday,

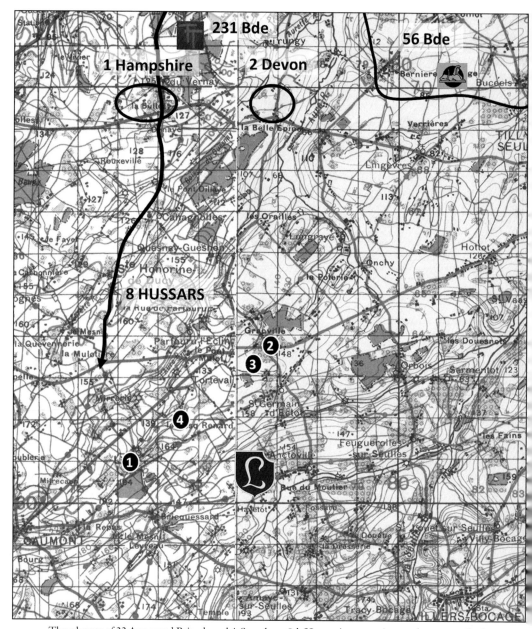

The advance of 22 Armoured Brigade and A Squadron, 8th Hussars' recce action on the western flank.

a dispatch rider delivered fresh instructions to Brigadier Cracroft. He later wrote that

> Following orders that 50 Div were to hold the line from Pt 103-LA BELLE ÉPINE and would contain the enemy on this front, under direct orders from the Commander 50 Div and much to my regret in view of the struggle that ST PIERRE had cost me I ordered 24th Lancers to cover the withdrawal of 8th DLI from the village.

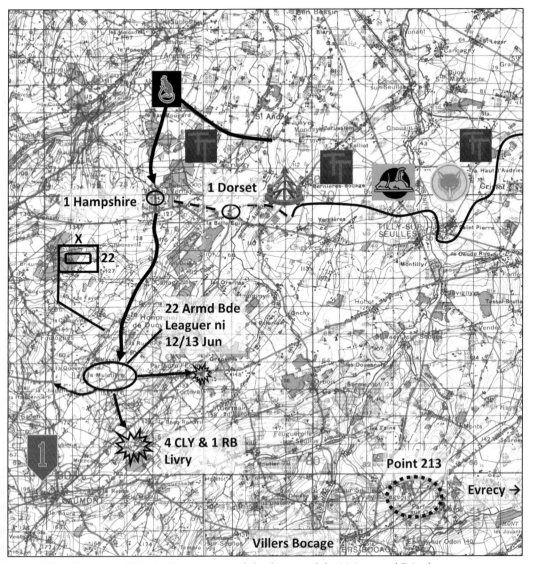

The 7th Armoured Division's move west and the thrust south by 22 Armoured Brigade.

For 8 DLI down in Saint-Pierre, orders to withdraw were bittersweet. Major English explained:

> Everyone was now extremely tired, and the effective strength of the Battalion was only about half of what it had been three days previously when the 8th first entered St. Pierre. The casualties numbered 12 officers and nearly 200 other ranks, so naturally a short rest out of the line sounded very attractive. On the other hand, to give up the village after such a gallant struggle seemed poor recompense for the effort and great sacrifice which had been made in order to hold it.
>
> So it was decided to regroup. The Battalion was to withdraw and, reverting to the command of 151 Brigade, was to move back into Brigade Reserve

in the area of Cachy. Nevertheless, it was a great shame that the village had to be evacuated, for some days later when 10th DLI, part of 70 Brigade of 49 Division, had to attack the village they only captured it after a stiff fight.

At 2315 hours, having regrouped, the battalion began its withdrawal, unmolested by the enemy, from Saint-Pierre. They passed through 5 East Yorks up on Point 103 and in Audrieu the exhausted Durhams were met by the welcome sight of Royal Army Service Corps trucks to take them back to Cachy. So it was, with 8 DLI extricated from the salient at Saint-Pierre and two of his tank regiments out of action, Brigadier Cracroft handed over the command to 69 Brigade and later wrote:

With 69 Bde holding Pt 103 with 5 EYs and the road to LOUCELLES held by 146 Bde [49th Division] who subsequently relieved 69 Bde in that area, the whole scene of the operation of the mobile column was static. There ceased to be a *raison d'être* for its existence and it was disbanded in the

A Sherman Firefly belonging to the 24th Lancers.

evening. I ordered the 4th/7th DG and SRY to move back just South of BAYEUX to rest while I remained in support in the 103 area with Bde HQ, 24th Lancers and 147 Fd Regt. For the first time since we had reached Pt 103 we had a comparatively quiet night.

After seven days in almost continuous action, most of 8 Armoured Brigade leaguered out of immediate contact and was able to have a well-earned rest and carry out maintenance of their Shermans. After the loss of men and tanks, reorganization and replacement were necessary, but at this stage of the in-load across the beaches, there were insufficient replacement Shermans to bring the regiments back to full strength. This contrasts with the availability of tanks in the aftermath of the grievous losses to the three British armoured divisions during Operation GOODWOOD, when little over a month later they were fully reconstituted within days.

69 Brigade would only hold Point 103 for a short time before handing command of the area to 49th (West Riding) Division, which had two brigades ashore by the evening of 13 June.

Winston Churchill and Generals Alanbrooke and Smuts visit Montgomery's headquarters in Normandy on 12 June.

22 Armoured Brigade

Originally a brigade made up of Territorial Force armoured yeomanry regiments, 22 Armoured Brigade went through many changes in its order of battle with, by June 1944, the only original regiment being the 4th County of London Yeomanry. The brigade had been a part of a number of divisions before joining 7th Armoured Division in the Western Desert during 1942 and was permitted to retain its own stag's head brigade sign alongside the division's jerboa badge.

1st Battalion, The Rifle Brigade joined 22 Armoured Brigade in June 1942 as its motor battalion. The role of the three motor companies in the battalion, rather than the four in a normal infantry battalion, was to take and hold ground in detail. Motor companies would normally be detached along with sections of mortars, machine guns and anti-tank guns to the brigade's three armoured regiments. To keep up with the tanks, especially across country, they were mounted in lightly armoured half-track vehicles.

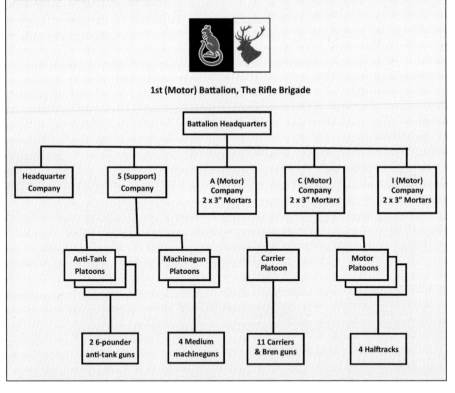

1st (Motor) Battalion, The Rifle Brigade

Chapter Eleven

Operation PERCH: Villers-Bocage

'It takes years to gain a reputation and only moments to lose it!'
[Brigadier A.E.C. Bredin]

The debate as to whether Operation PERCH was a 'disaster', a 'draw' or a 'victory' has been under way since 1944, usually ignoring the much more significant issues for the 7th Armoured Division of Operations GOODWOOD and BLUECOAT. There are, of course, elements of disaster, draw and victory to be found in PERCH, but one thing is certain and that is that the vaunted Desert Rats lost much of their reputation, which took new commanders and months of campaigning to restore.

Operation PERCH, a continuation of the WILD OATS concept for the envelopment of Caen and its defenders, was to exploit a gap around Caumont that was created on 9 June by the forced withdrawal of the 352nd Division towards St Lô in the face of US V Corps' drive south. Despite the all-too-obvious presence of *Panzer Lehr* and its attack of 9 June and stout defence of Tilly on the 10th and 11th, General Bucknall's XXX Corps remained wedded to an attack on Villers-Bocage by the direct route from Tilly. As reports of negligible progress against *Panzer Lehr* arrived in his headquarters during the early morning of 12 June, the general was forced to reconsider and transfer 7th Armoured Division to the west where the 1st US Infantry Division was advancing on Caumont, against little opposition. The redirection of 7th Armoured was achieved quickly and the forward elements of the division leaguered for the night of 12/13 June 6 miles deep in enemy territory. This was a full two and a half hours before nightfall.

An important element of the plan was a continuation of the battle against *Panzer Lehr* by the 50th Division. It was intended that such an attack would, firstly, fix *Panzer Lehr*, preventing General Bayerlein from redeploying against the 7th Armoured and secondly, with the British enveloping *Panzer Lehr*, the 50th Division was to be ready to advance south to Villers-Bocage against reduced resistance or a withdrawal. These operations on 13 and 14 June 1944 are covered in Chapter 13.

During a very short night the trucks carrying the infantry of 131 Brigade and the Cromwells of A Squadron, 8th Hussars had caught up with 7th Armoured, with its leading elements passing La Paumière at 0615 hours on 13 June. Ahead of them, 22 Armoured Brigade was already on the move, led again by 4 CLY.

A column of artillery moving on a bocage road.

After confirmatory orders to his commanding officers before dawn, Brigadier Hinde set 4 CLY on the road south to Livry and Briquessard, from where they would swing south-east towards Villers-Bocage, a distance of 8 miles. The battlegroup deployed from its leaguer at first light in the same order of march as the previous day, but in this case the commanding officer Lieutenant Colonel Viscount Cranley was mounted in his Humber armoured car. This small vehicle allowed him to 'swan' up and down the column to wherever he could influence the march or battle; i.e. sort out hold-ups at choke points or contacts with the enemy.

The two recce regiments were deployed as follows: 8th Hussars; RHQ [Regimental Headquarters] and B Squadron were '...ordered to cover the right flank parallel to the centre line' and the 11th Hussars were to fan out ahead and further out to the flanks.

5 RTR's part in the operation was to secure the high ground south-west of Villers-Bocage with its tanks and attached motor company, while 1/7 Queens were to secure Villers-Bocage itself along with the immediate area. A battery of anti-tank guns from 102 Anti-Tank Regiment was to cover the ground between these two battalions. The remainder of 131 Brigade was to be deployed in the Livry area. Lieutenant Colonel Carver of 1 RTR wrote of his mission on 13 June:

> My orders were to make sure that the village of Briquessard and the two crossroads north of it were securely held. Briquessard was where the minor road, by which we had moved south, joined the main road from Caumont to Villers-Bocage. I sent 1/6 Queen's to Briquessard and looked after the other crossroads myself, sending the reconnaissance troop to make contact with the Americans on our right.

The approach to the area of Livry was cautious, but finding that the Germans had not reoccupied the village, the orders were to 'Push on as quickly as possible.' Even so, moving tactically, leapfrogging by bounds, it took two hours, thirty minutes to cover the next 7 miles. In the taking the decision to move to Point 213

7th Armoured Division's plans, 13 June 1944.

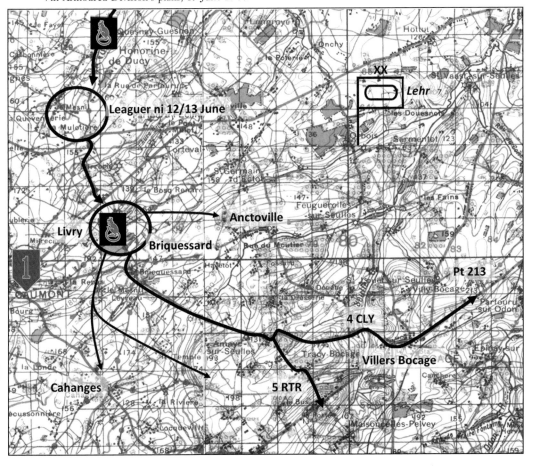

as quickly as possible, the trade-off was denying the Hussars' patrols the opportunity to work as far forward, around the flanks and to pass back information to commanders. One early contact was at Anctoville 2 miles east of Briquessard where a Daimler armoured car of 4 Troop, C Squadron, 11th Hussars was knocked out. Enemy were also reported at Cahagnes, 2 miles south of Briquessard. Consequently, reports that there were Germans about were circulating on recce radio nets, but even if these reports were able to be passed on to the rest of the brigade in a timely manner, the CLY's war diary recorded that there was 'No opposition and A Sqn reach feature East of VILLERS-BOCAGE (area 8358) [Point 213].'

However, one of the CLY's liaison officers, Lieutenant Pearce, mounted in a scout car, recalls seeing

> a German eight-wheel armoured car half-hidden in an orchard on the facing slope 600 yards away. I could clearly see its commander watching our column. I was following behind the second-in-command's tank and shouted a target indication of the enemy vehicle over to him. Unfortunately, his turret was jam-packed with kit and he could not traverse it, and nothing happened. I broke radio silence and spoke to the RHQ troop leader but again nothing happened. A few minutes later the enemy armoured car disappeared into the trees of the orchard.

Clearly contact reports were circulating on the German radio nets, with word of the presence of an armoured force in the rear of *Panzer Lehr* climbing the

A Cromwell tank is the centrepiece of 7th Armoured Division's memorial near Thetford training area in Norfolk, their spring 1944 training ground.

German chain of command. In the meantime, B Squadron, 4 CLY was following behind Regimental Headquarters. Sergeant Allen wrote:

> Progress seemed slow and without a troop leader I managed to follow behind my squadron leader's tank. Other than from the smell of rotting animals, we approached Livry without any signs of destruction, then on to the village of Briquessard where no sign of life was apparent. Slowly we came to Amayé-sur-Seulles and halted for a short while.[1]

What seemed slow for Sergeant Allen was, in retrospect, described as incautiously quick by those leading in A Squadron as they approached Villers-Bocage.

Being on the road south of Tilly-sur-Seulles, Villers-Bocage was on *Panzer Lehr*'s divisional main supply route, but by this point in the campaign most logistic units had learned that concealment in woods and orchards, away from centres of population and their Resistance radios, provided the best place from which to operate. Consequently, the only German units actually in Villers-Bocage on 13 June were two medical companies established in the town's hospital and an ambulance platoon.

A Squadron, without encountering opposition, crested the ridge west of Villers. Lieutenant Cloudsley Thompson, following with the RHQ troop, recalled his impressions: 'Villers-Bocage is a fair-sized town; there was no sign of the enemy so we drove straight along the main street.' Having motored through the town without more ado, A Squadron reached Point 213 between 0800 and 0900 hours. The squadron and A Company, 1 RB, which was going to prepare defensive positions on the key feature, closed up and pulled over on the road from Villers, with the Stuarts of the Recce Troop and RHQ halted in the western part of the town. B Squadron and the rest of the CLY's column were still west of Villers.

The commanding officer was joined by Brigadier Hinde, who told Cranley to drive up to Point 213 to satisfy himself that dispositions were correct, while he returned to the rest of the brigade. Meanwhile, battle procedure had swung into action, with the three infantry platoon commanders being summoned in their half-tracks for orders up on the high ground while, with the prospect of spending the next few hours digging in, their platoons dismounted from their half-tracks and were beginning to make

Brigadier 'Loony' Hinde, renowned as brave but eccentric, had commanded armoured brigades since 1942.

brews. The *Rifle Brigade Chronicle* records that they were 'halted on the road in close column ready to take up dispositions for holding the ground gained. At that moment the front half of the column was attacked by German tanks.'

These tanks were the Tigers of *Obersturmführer* Michael Wittmann's 2nd Company of 101 *Schwere* SS Panzer Battalion.[2] This was I SS Panzer Corps' heavy tank battalion, which had the previous night completed a tortuous journey to the invasion front from Gournay-en-Bray between Amiens and Rouen. The march took five days, beginning on 7 June. En route 1st Company was strafed from the air shortly after starting out, as was the Maintenance Company. 2nd Company was also attacked on the 7th and twice on the 10th. Due to the destruction of the Seine bridges their journey by road took them south-west through the centre of Paris where all three companies drove down the Champs-Élysées! In the Paris area the 3rd Company was repeatedly strafed on 8 June and was forced to move panzers singly from cover to cover to avoid detection. One Tiger commander claims to have shot down a 'Jabo' (fighter-bomber) with his MG 34. From the 9th all movement was ordered to be carried out at night.

As a result of the long move, of the forty-five mechanically unreliable Tigers[3] that set out on the 150-mile road march, only eighteen reached Normandy without needing serious repair. Wittmann's panzer was one of those that broke down and only six out of his fourteen 2nd Company Tigers arrived, but of these

Lieutenant Colonel Viscount Cranley accompanying General Montgomery on his pre-invasion inspection of his regiment.

just three were fully operational at the beginning of the battle on the morning of 13 June.

To the east in position behind the *Hitlerjugend* was a second group of Tigers belonging to *Hauptsturmführer* Möbius' 1st Company, with 3rd Company further back at Falaise. The broken-down Tigers arrived at the front and were repaired over the next ten days, the problem being that both fuel and spare parts were increasingly scarce for the Germans. (See Appendix III for further details on Tiger reliability.)

The two companies of the 101's Tigers were in the process of being deployed by I SS Panzer Corps behind *Panzer Lehr* and the *Hitlerjugend* as a reserve ready to block any breakthrough by the British. Wittmann's Tigers had arrived the previous day and were parked up facing north-east, camouflaged under trees in a hedged lane that ran parallel to and less than 200 yards from the main road from Villers to Point 213. Here they were resting and carrying out maintenance while awaiting the call to battle (see map on page 207).

Wittmann, alerted by the sound of A Squadron passing, could see the Cromwells heading up to Point 213 and quickly mounted Tiger 234[4] but it would not start. Changing tank to another panzer, possibly call sign 231, Wittmann ordered the driver to advance and drove to the crossroads near the Ciderie, where he turned left towards a junction with the main road. Almost in front of him were the two rear tanks of A Squadron. A Cromwell was quickly knocked out and there was a Sherman Firefly just beyond, which with true army black humour was nicknamed 'Ronson' and it, true to its name, was soon burning as well.[5]

Tigers of 101 *Schwere* Panzer Battalion on the march to Normandy.

A well-camouflaged Tiger and its crew carrying out maintenance tasks.

One of Wittmann's first victims at the road junction.

Obersturmführer Wittmann's Action

A Company's peaceful brewing of tea was shattered by the firing and, as Wittmann turned left, he fired at the half-tracks and the anti-tank platoon's carriers. The M9A1 half-tracks had been closed up in anticipation of allowing B Squadron to pass through and take up the lead eastwards. Hence they made easy targets for the Tiger's 88mm gun, with one armour-piercing shot at such close range probably able to slice through several lightly-armoured M9s. With the deafening crack of the Tiger's main armament and the sharper crack of machine-gun bullets cracking around them, the riflemen took cover, scattering into ditches, while oily black smoke poured from their vehicles.

Obersturmführer Michael Wittmann.

The aftermath of Wittmann's passage past the wreckage of A Company 1 RB's carriers and anti-tank platoon.

Meanwhile, the other two operational Tigers were cutting across country from the area of the Ciderie to take on the rest of A Squadron which was strung out over some 500 yards up to Point 213 and whose tanks were attempting to get off the road. Lieutenant Colonel Cranley and Majors Scott and Wright successfully formed a defence on the top of the hill, but not before further palls of smoke marked the scene of the fighting.

Lieutenant Wilson, a troop commander in 5 RTR, expressed his view of the CLY's and RB's stance at Point 213 as 'incredible tactical incompetence'.[6] Having the Recce Troop ahead in the order of march may well have flushed *Obersturmführer* Wittmann and his Tigers out at a much lower cost but this, of course, was not conducive to making best speed. A legacy of desert tactics may also have been at play, where dashes to seize ground of tactical importance were commonly executed with little risk of a lurking enemy.

Having driven down the hill, taking on and scattering A Company 1 RB, as already described, Wittmann approached the town where the leading three Stuart tanks of the Recce Troop were caught and destroyed by Wittmann. Another 200 yards into the town on Rue Clemenceau, the four RHQ tanks and medical officer's and the fitter section's half-tracks were attempting to get out of the way of the rampaging Tiger. Unfortunately, hampered by the lack of warning, few turnings off the road and the slow reverse speed of the Cromwell, only one of the tanks escaped the next bout of 88mm gunfire. Lieutenant Pearce, still in his scout car behind the second-in-command, recorded that

> The Tiger fired and knocked out Major Carr's tank which caught fire. The flash from the 88mm was terrific with a very loud bang, then the Tiger

started forward again coming closer. My driver very calmly turned the scout car round and we started back down the road towards B Squadron. I must say that the Tiger was uncomfortably close when we turned round!

Captain Dyas had managed to back his tank off the road and thus avoided the destruction and after the Tiger passed and a discreet pause, he drove out onto the road and followed the Tiger, hoping to stalk it and get a shot into its less well-protected rear. It is also apparent that the second group of three recce Stuarts escaped.

Meanwhile, Wittmann had rounded the bend onto the long straight Rue Pasteur through the centre of the town, where in front of him were two 5 RHA OP tanks, which lacked main armament. Another Cromwell and a Sherman were quickly added to Wittmann's tally.

Gunner Coombs described the fate of G and K batteries' OP Shermans:

Andy Merrifield who now drove a G Battery OP tank managed to escape with his tank. K Battery CO's Sherman was in the main street of the town when the driver, Jock Rae, saw the Tiger. He alerted the Major who

Initial phase of the Tiger's attack.

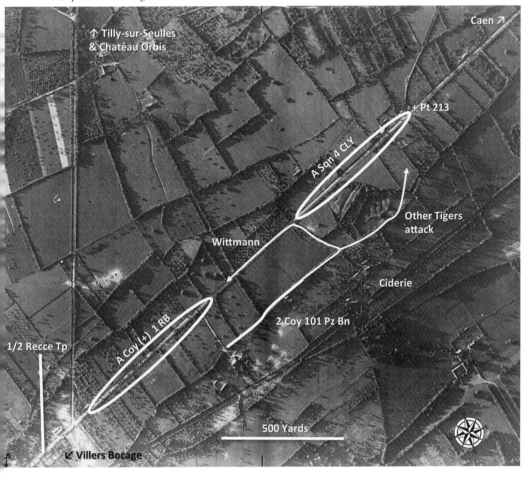

One of the knocked-out RHQ tanks.

Captain Pat Dyas.

escaped through the turret while Jock went through the escape hatch in the floor, as the first 88 round, HE as it happened, blew the track off, and the second, armour-piercing, set the tank ablaze. Like all the command tanks in the regiment this one had a wooden gun. I wonder what the Germans made of that.

At this point the course of the action is far less clear, but a number of events are well-established.[7] The first is that as Wittmann turned the corner and advanced past the knocked-out OP tanks into the long straight Rue Pasteur, he was engaged by Sergeant Lockwood's Sherman Firefly firing from the west at a range of about 200 to 300 yards. Lockwood had been warned of the presence of the Tiger by Lieutenant Pearce as he headed to inform B Squadron headquarters of events east of Villers. Lockwood duly engaged, having seen the 88's flashes further down the road, but such was the smoke, dust and the flash from his 17-pounder, he could not see whether he had hit the Tiger. He did not subsequently claim a kill and Wittmann fired twice in return.

Wittmann's next action in the town was about 50 yards beyond the OP tanks where the leading troop of B Squadron was already in the small Place Richard Lenoir adjacent to the Rue Pasteur. Members of Lieutenant Hedge's 2 Troop

Major Wells' K Battery Sherman OP tank knocked out near the centre of town. Note the broken wooden dummy barrel amid the debris.

remember the long barrel of the Tiger's 88mm gun slowly coming into sight. Wittmann was probably moving cautiously now, aware that he was under fire. As the hull of the tank appeared around the corner of the building one of the Cromwells, commanded by Sergeant Moore, fired its 75mm gun at very close range, hitting the Tiger's frontal armour adjacent to the driver's vision port, but the shot failed to penetrate it. Realizing that his 'Morning drive' was over, Wittmann ordered his driver to reverse and retire from sight. In addition to being

The deployment of 4 CLY's battlegroup at the time of the Tiger's attack.

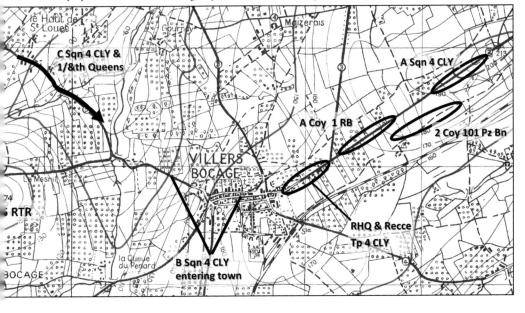

on his own without infantry, Wittmann said in his account that he was 'now out of contact with the rest of his company'.

The Tiger turned and retraced its steps heading out of the town, but as Wittmann approached the bend back into Rue Clemenceau, he was confronted by Captain Dyas' Cromwell coming towards him. The British tank fired twice before the hand-traversed 88mm demolished the Cromwell, killing two members of the crew.[8] Captain Dyas was virtually blown out of his turret, but survived the encounter and regained British lines.

At the outskirts of the town Sergeant Bray of the anti-tank platoon attached to A Company 1 RB had survived Wittmann's earlier destructive passage down the column of vehicles and brought his 6-pounder into action near the junction with the Tilly-sur-Seulles road. As Wittmann approached from the town the riflemen, knowing they had no chance of knocking out the Tiger through its frontal armour, aimed for the tracks and destroyed the Panzer's running gear.[9,10] Fire was returned, under the cover of which Wittmann and his crew abandoned their panzer and set off to walk the 3.5 miles north to Château Orbois, the head-quarters of *Panzer Lehr*, where he would report what was happening in Villers.

In about fifteen minutes, Wittmann had knocked out two Shermans, six Cromwells, nine half-tracks, three Stuart tanks, four carriers and the other 6-pounder in Sergeant Bray's section. For this achievement the *Obersturmführer* was awarded the Swords to his Knight's Cross with Oak Leaves.[11]

Wittmann and his Tigers were presented with an opportunity that they exploited to the full, being luckily in the right place just as the CLY's spearhead paused close to them before deploying tactically on Point 213. Wittmann certainly did not, as we will see, 'singlehandedly stop 7th Armoured Division in its tracks'. There was, as we will see, far more to it than just the actions of a single panzer commander. The continuing notoriety of Wittmann's action on 13 June 1944 is the lingering effect of the SS publicity machinery that saw every *Kriegsberichter* (war correspondent) and PK cameraman rushing to Villers-Bocage to record an SS success. Other factors are the abiding interest in 'aces' and their achievements, military elites, which included both the 101st *Schwere* Panzer Battalion and 7th Armoured Division, and then there is the iconic status of the Tiger tank.[12]

Also on his way to *Panzer Lehr*'s main headquarters was Major Werncke, the division's 1b or senior logistic staff officer. He was travelling from the rear head-quarters via Villers-Bocage to the main HQ at Château Orbois. He had an interesting journey to the main divisional headquarters:

> The noise of combat grew louder and louder. Shortly before reaching the town, I ran into a stream of wounded with bandages on every part of the body. They warned me about continuing, that the enemy had penetrated into the town, that they had overrun the medical company and the main first-aid station. The enemy was now advancing to the east, 'deep into the flanks' of our forces. The wounded had fled through the windows.

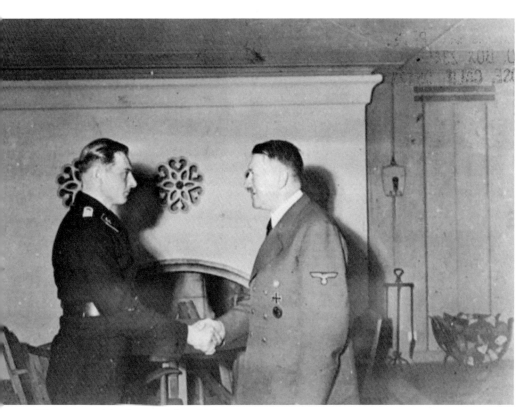

Wittmann receiving his award from Hitler.

The Knight's Cross of the Iron Cross with Oak Leaves and Swords.

What was I to do? I had to get to the command post, which couldn't be that far away. I told my driver to take cover behind a hill and return to the Ib command post in thirty minutes, if I didn't return by then. I fought my way through the bushes on foot in order to get to the main road that led to the east and reconnoitre the situation. When I crawled over a hedgerow, I saw four [A Squadron] Cromwell tanks in a field in front of me. Their crews were gathered around their commander; they were worrying over a map.

The tanks were empty, their motors running. Since, as an old panzer company commander, I was familiar with such vehicles, and it appeared that I could use the armoured protection – this time British – for my trip further through no man's land, I crawled into the nearest Cromwell, hidden by the other vehicles. I grabbed the steering mechanism – which was similar to ours – and drove the tank over the roadside ditch onto the main road, turning to the west.

The situation was curious. I passed burning British tracked vehicles, tanks and trucks. I had to be in the Tommies' rear area. Later I heard that Wittmann had caused this total confusion. My advance continued without incident. After about 2 kilometres I saw a confused-looking infantryman in German uniform in a ditch and waved him over. He was reluctant but he came, and I ordered him onto the turret to wave a white rag if any of our own forces appeared. That was how I reached the division command post.

Major Werncke leaving the driver's hatch of his misappropriated Cromwell.

Since the gate was too narrow, I drove over the iron fence up to the front of the château. When they saw us coming all the staff and sentries dived for cover [one can imagine the scene!]. That was the first time I heard the enemy radio traffic coming from the headsets hanging inside the turret of the tank. I asked a translator to listen to the traffic. He couldn't hear much until the motor was turned off. Ignorant of how to turn off the engine, I stalled it against a large tree.

Major Werncke's arrival at divisional headquarters in a Cromwell may have disconcerted the staff and sentries, but overall the Germans held their nerve, despite enemy armour sitting astride their line of communication. *Panzer Lehr*'s positions were not 'unhinged': there was no withdrawal from the Tilly-sur-Seulles area, let alone the hoped-for collapse of the defences. Luck as to Wittmann's location was clearly on the Germans' side, and at divisional level General Bayerlein was preparing a response. At Headquarters I SS Panzer Corps SS *Brigadeführer* Fritz Krämer ordered the *Hitlerjugend* to send *Hauptsturmführer* Möbius' 1st Company west to help *Panzer Lehr* and leading elements of 2nd Panzer Division were to resume their march north immediately.

Point 213

Meanwhile, the remaining Tigers had advanced on Point 213 but with the sound of gunfire behind them, A Squadron up on Point 213 had more time to react to the developing threat and some tanks were able to deploy off the road and into the fields. Nonetheless, a further three tanks were knocked out in a continuing battle.

Already alerted by various reports of the column's presence to the rear of *Panzer Lehr*, Headquarters I SS Panzer Corps urged 2nd Panzer Division to speed north to intervene in the battle, but they were too far away for a timely intervention at Point 213.[13] However, with the enemy having broken through and his division in danger of being enveloped, General Bayerlein and his 1a (chief of staff/operations officer) Major Kauffmann needed an immediate response. According to Major Ritgen, Kauffmann 'gathered all available soldiers from his staffs and other units in order to cover towards the south. All elements, especially the supply column, were warned to avoid Villers-Bocage.' Ritgen continued:

Before 1100 hours [0900 hours Allied time] I received orders to advance north of Villers with every available panzer – about fifteen – in order to prevent the feared strike into the division's rear.

Driving along the road from Juvigny, I received instructions directly from General Bayerlein in Villers-Bocage. I was ordered to advance along the road to the west, and block all exits from the town at positions north of the stream in order to prevent an attack into the division's rear. When the lead panzer reached the road to Anctoville north-west of the town, it was destroyed by a concealed anti-tank gun and burst into flames [8th Hussars].

Germans scavenging fuel from knocked-out Cromwells and a Firefly on the crest of Point 213 after the battle.

Having reported to *Panzer Lehr*'s command post and summoned his *Schwim-wagen*, Wittmann, in company with Ritgen's panzers for a part of the way before he turned east, went to brief *Hauptsturmführer* Möbius' 1st Company on the situation at Villers-Bocage. By 1030 hours Möbius had been joined by *panzer-grenadiers* of its 4th Light Escort Company and several Panzer IVs that had been in repair in the division's workshop a couple of miles to the north. By 1135 hours reports were coming over 22 Brigade's radio net that five Tigers were trying to encircle the nine remaining tanks of A Squadron up on Point 213. At 1240 hours Cranley reported that he was surrounded up on the feature and at around 1200 hours A Squadron's radios went silent as the men up on 213 surrendered, including seventeen members of 1 RB.

Captain Milner, the second-in-command of A Company, had taken cover when the firing started and had made his way onto Point 213:

> Suddenly there was a rumble of tanks from the east and as I darted round to the front of the cottage I was astonished to find that the tank shooting seemed to have ended and that some tank officers in black berets were standing about talking to one or two of our officers in the middle of the main road. Since there had been no shooting and everyone seemed very friendly I took them to be members of the RTR [*sic*] and stepped out to join in the conversation, only to be frozen in my tracks when I realised they were German tank crews!

Milner was the sole Rifle Brigade officer to escape from that morning's disaster to A Company in which they lost eighty men; nine were killed and seventy-one were prisoners, with the *Regimental Chronicle* adding that 'Of the whole company only one officer and thirty other ranks finally returned during the next few days.'

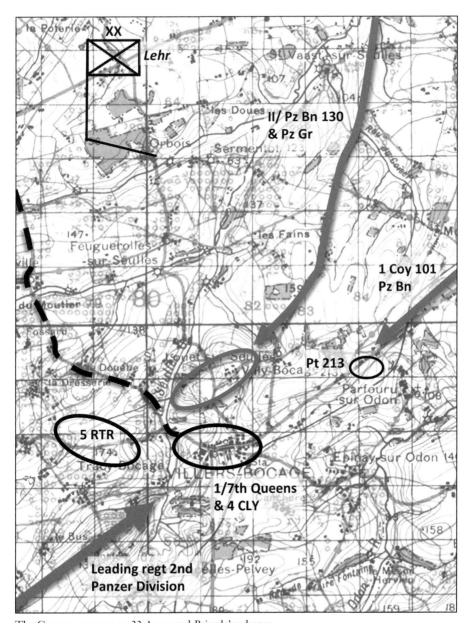

The German response to 22 Armoured Brigade's advance.

Renewed Battle in the Town

While the fighting was under way on Point 213, 1/7 Queens and the tanks of C Squadron were being hurried forward to join B Squadron in Villers-Bocage where they were to deploy to defend the town. Lieutenant Colonel Gordon commanding the battalion wrote in his after-action report:

> ... the Bn had debussed and was preparing to take up a firm base position on the high ground East of the village when orders were issued at once to move into VILLERS-BOCAGE itself and cover its main exits.
>
> The carriers and A/tk guns moved off at once, the leading coy encountered a German Staff Car and two motor-cycle combinations which suddenly appeared from a side-track. The leading platoon suffered some casualties when the car and combinations had been ditched and the crews taken to the fields where they commenced sniping.
>
> These had to be dealt with before the Coy could move on. Three prisoners were taken, and the remainder dispersed. On arrival in the village contact was made with the reserve Sqn of 4 CLY. It appeared that the leading Sqns west of the town were facing serious difficulties by overwhelming numbers of 'Tigers'.

Worryingly, the three captured German staff officers were quickly identified as being an advanced party from the 2nd Panzer Division. A report interpreted as 'enemy in company strength' erroneously climbed the chain of command.

Colonel Gordon and Major Aird, now commanding the CLY, attempted to rescue A Squadron: 'A plan was then made to send up one of our coys with the reserve Sqn to do to their assistance, but it was found impossible to get through to them and the plan had to be abandoned.'

With the sound of battle increasing, Major Aird had already sent Lieutenant Cotton's troop of three Cromwells and a Firefly into Villers-Bocage via a loop south of the town. This route, however, brought him into contact with the enemy, certainly also elements of 2nd Panzer, near the château less than 1,000 yards from Villers. The Germans were not just on the south side of the town but to the north as well. Here Major Ritgen's Panzer IVs had formed a blocking line to contain the British about a mile from Villers where they were engaged by the Hussars and guns of the anti-tank battery. Ritgen wrote that 'During a counter-attack the commander of the 7 Coy, *Panzer Lehr* Regt, *Oberleutnant Freiherr* Marschalck von Brachtenbrock, was killed.'

In Villers itself the Queens were in the process of laying out their defences, but before they could be properly established, *Hauptsturmführer* Möbius' panzers attacked. Having rounded up prisoners, at around 1300 hours they advanced into Villers-Bocage. Private Kingston recalled the moment:

> We were in the town centre, a little square and not much else. There were a few shops open, cafés I think, and we were just standing about waiting for orders when we heard the sound of gunfire coming from the road out of

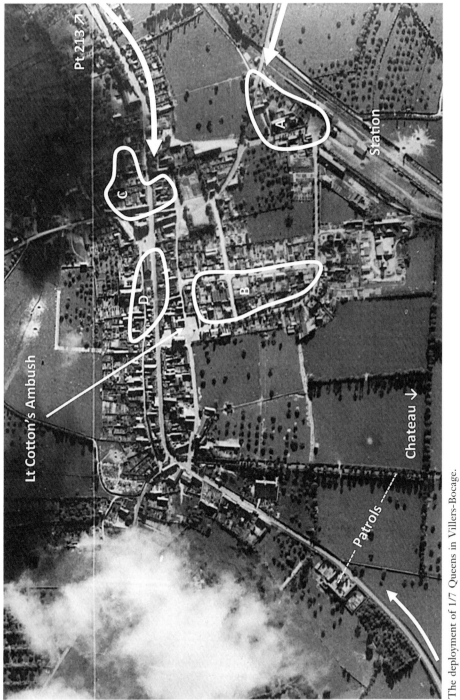

The deployment of 1/7 Queens in Villers-Bocage.

Labels in image:
Pt 213 ↗
Station
Lt Cotton's Ambush
Chateau ↓
Patrols
A
B
C
D

town. There seemed from the noise to be a big battle going on and presently we saw black clouds of smoke in the air. One of our soldiers said they were tanks blowing up. All of a sudden, our anti-tank platoons were ordered into action – to take post. The ammo trucks were driven into side streets and all the rifle sections were told to take up positions in windows of houses on the 'enemy' side of the village.

On the outskirts of the town, Sergeant Bray's 6-pounder knocked out two further enemy tanks, probably Panzer IVs, before his gun was in turn knocked out. Colonel Gordon continued his report:

> ... a Tiger was seen moving down the main street and blew down a house at the corner of the square where the 4 CLY and the leading Coys were gathered. This caused some confusion and the troops were ordered to get into the houses and use their PIATs whilst the Cromwells and our six-pounders covered all approaches into the high street. Further tanks, both Tigers and Mk IVs, appeared in the main street.
>
> A Coy meanwhile had encountered infantry opposition on the further [south east] face of the village and were pinned to the ground while a small armoured battle raged for some time. Bn 6-prs in the area of the station had acquitted themselves well and claimed four tanks, all Mk VI Tigers knocked out and hit two without apparent damage.

Major French, commanding C Company 1/7 Queens, soon found himself in action as a Tiger bore down on his company. His Military Cross citation records:

> Major French immediately ordered his Company to disperse into the houses in the side streets which overlooked the main road and to be prepared to take aggressive action. He then personally took a PIAT and together with a small party armed with sticky bombs, went off further into the town in the direction from which the enemy tanks were approaching. He found four Mk VI tanks and one Mk IV in the main street and approached the leading one from a side street to within 20 yards. He fired two rounds with his PIAT while his party threw their sticky bombs. The results of this attack could not be observed but it caused one tank to move forward where it was driven onto the waiting 6-pdr anti-tank guns and the guns of our waiting tanks [Cotton's Troop 4 CLY] and completely destroyed. During this attack one of the enemy tanks blew down a house near which Major French was standing and he was wounded in the leg, but in spite of this he returned to collect his Company and take them to their allotted positions.

Lance Corporal Kay wrote:

> Spandaus were firing from house windows and there was the clatter of roof slates falling and of breaking glass. The Tigers seemed to be unstoppable and the guns of our Cromwells seemed to have no effect on the giants. This had been a gruelling battle and many of our lads were lost.

Sergeant Brady's 6-pounder knocked out by the Tilly road junction during the German attack.

In addition to the infantry companies, which bravely took on the German panzers with light weapons, the Fireflies and, as Colonel Gordon reported, 1/7 Queens' anti-tank guns provided a serious punch. With increasing sounds of approaching armour, Lieutenant Cotton's Troop of B Squadron had made their way to the square in front of the Hotel du Ville, from where, alongside a Queen's 6-pounder gun, they prepared an ambush. They had a field of fire across the square in which they could engage panzers advancing west along Rue Pasteur.

It was not long before the sound of tank engines and the grind of tracks could be heard. Two Panzer IVs edged their way into the square, having tangled with Major French further down Rue Pasteur. They were both hit in the flank by the 6-pounder; however, a Tiger followed them into the square but at such a short range that Sergeant Bramwell's Firefly's sighting system did not work and its 17-pounder round flew over the top of the Tiger. The Queen's 6-pounder, however, notched up another kill with a quick flank shot into the 56-ton monster.

At this point the remaining Tigers fanned out onto other routes through the town where, in a four-hour battle, they were taken on as described in Major French's citation at close range. Typical of one of the actions by the Queen's men was that of 'Capt Beard and a party from the Carriers in stalking these tanks

Two of the Queen's 6-pounder's targets knocked out alongside each other.

through the side streets and houses and tackling them with PIATs and Sticky Bombs. This period of tank-hunting went on for about two hours.'

Of the seven panzers knocked out during the afternoon's fighting, six were knocked out by the Queen's.[14] 101st *Schwere* Panzer Battalion was learning, as had the *Hitlerjugend* in their first days in action against the Canadians, that the Eastern Front tactic of simply charging and dominating the enemy did not work against British infantry in Normandy.[15] The lack of accompanying infantry in the first attacks cost the Germans dear in Villers-Bocage on the afternoon of 13 June and in his after-action report Colonel Gordon was able to report: 'The myth that the Tiger was invincible has now been exploded.'

Meanwhile, there was a stand-off on Rue Pasteur where a Tiger awaited an incautious move by a CLY tank, but with Lieutenant Cotton out of his tank on his feet he realized that the two tanks were on either side of a corner. Sergeant Bramwell backed up a few yards along his side of the building, traversed his gun and, according to Major Aird, 'eventually finished it off by drilling a hole through the side of a house with the 17pdr HE until he could see it, then administered the coup de grace with AP' into the flank of the lurking Tiger.

Once the tank-hunting parties had restored the situation, Colonel Gordon's companies

> ... were ordered to get into the original dispositions to cover the approach into the village. This was found to be a most difficult task as personnel of Coys had got very scattered throughout the houses in the village. In the meantime, A Coy was sweeping the ground in the further outskirts and was directed on the railway station.

During the afternoon there were reports of panzers approaching from virtually every direction. Colonel Gordon noted that this time it wasn't just panzers:

> By the late afternoon the enemy tank threat had been smashed and the serious problem now was some pockets of infantry attempting to work their way through into the village. A Coy had been driven back from their original positions [near the station] and there was a large gap between the south and north-western edge which was not covered by any of our Coys and there was no Coy available to do it.

Private Kingston makes it plain that with armour-piercing rounds going through the building he was fighting from, the Queen's were in a severe fight:

> There were several loud bangs which were our 6-pounder a-tank guns going off and then one very loud explosion ... a Bren carrier of ammo went up. The firing seemed to spread ... Jerry infantry were working their way into the town. Then there was some more tank gunfire, some machine-gun fire and then dead silence. We waited ... The street was a mess. Bricks and rubble all over the place. A couple of hundred yards up the road was the biggest tank I have ever seen. It looked undamaged. One of our 6-pounders was lying on its side just opposite our house.

The CLY's war diary records that at '1600 – B Sqn reports village still held by us, but [enemy] infantry in area 820575 [south-east corner of Villers]. 1/7 Queen's attack but fail to clear opposition':

> By 1800 hrs small infantry elements had worked their way round to within close proximity of the tanks of 4 CLY. Bn HQ was almost pinned to the

The *Illustrated London News'* depiction of Sergeant Bramwell's engagement. His tank, though, is shown as a Covenanter rather than a Firefly.

Prisoners of the Germans: a mix of yeomen, riflemen and Queen's men.

ground and the road leading into the village from the remainder of the Bde was under quite heavy Arty fire which knocked out a complete detachment of the mortars and 'brewed up' a carrier.

Unable to regain their defensive cohesion following the tank-hunting phase of the battle, pressure mounted on the Queen's over the afternoon hours. The remainder of the brigade was, however, well-dispersed and as the Germans closed in, unable to provide immediate support. Colonel Gordon observed that

A decision had to be made as to whether we could hold the village that night or not; without further infantry Coys it did not appear possible and the Bde Comd issued orders for the Bn and Sqn 4 CLY to withdraw onto the high ground West of the village from where we had started that morning and there join up in a firm base position with the remainder of 22 Armd Bde.

Brigadier Hinde commended his units in Villers-Bocage in his report:

The performance of 1/7 Queen's and two squadrons of 4 Sharpshooters [4 CLY] in holding the town until ordered to withdraw was deserving of high praise and the action of the tanks in covering the withdrawal of the infantry was admirably executed in very difficult circumstances.

It would be almost another two months before the British re-entered Villers-Bocage. By then it would be a bombed out ruin.

On 14 June General Bayerlein issued a special order of the day:

Enemy attacks into the deep flank and rear of the division with armoured formations were defeated in co-operation with elements of II Bn, Pz Lehr Regt and the Tiger Battalion from the 12th SS Panzer Division [*sic*], as well as hastily gathered together forces in the Villers area. About forty tanks and twenty tracked vehicles were destroyed . . . I express my heartfelt thanks to all division elements for their excellent efforts during the recent heavy English attacks. We can be proud of your efforts. In all, 110 enemy tanks have been destroyed by the division.

The decision by Brigadier Hinde to withdraw from Villers has often been criticized as being made in the face of only German reconnaissance troops and with a fresh battalion of his own (1/5 Queen's) in reserve, but they were some 7 miles to the rear. As far as the Germans were concerned, firstly, as was demonstrated by the performance of the *Hitlerjugend*'s recce battalion at Audrieu and Cristot, German recce units had a lot more punch than their Allied equivalents and, secondly, 2nd Panzer Division's *panzergrenadiers* had arrived.[16]

German Operations to the South and West of Villers-Bocage

German records and post-war interviews with US intelligence reveal that in the late afternoon of 13 June 2nd Panzer Division was indeed in action. Both of the division's *panzergrenadier* regiments had started the day resting from a torturous night approach march and were awaiting the concentration of the rest of the divisional road party, including some of the artillery. Out in front of them providing a security screen was the 2nd Panzer Reconnaissance Battalion, with its 2nd Company located at Coulvain. It should be noted that the trains moving the panzer regiment and some of the other tracked vehicles were very badly delayed by Allied air interdiction of the railway system, and their symbols only appeared on operational maps in the Jurques area on 15 June.[17] The advance of 7th Armoured and 1st US divisions, plus contact with patrols of the two British hussar regiments as far south as Cahagnes prompted action. 2 *Panzergrenadier* Regiment (*Kampfgruppe* Brassert) and 304 *Panzergrenadiers* (*Kampfgruppe* Schake), each of two battalions, were ordered to advance on Villers-Bocage and Briquessard respectively. Despite the distance of some 5 miles, they were able to move quickly thanks to all four battalions being mounted in half-tracks.

Allied air power had delayed and broken up 2 Panzer's columns of march to the invasion front, which led to the division's *panzergrenadiers* being committed to battle piecemeal without their full range of supporting arms.

As the *Kampfgruppen* advanced, the majority of the contacts with the British were exchanges of fire with patrols, including with the 11th Hussars at Cahagnes, which were forced back by the weight of German numbers. An increasing number of reports detailed German advances south-west of Villers-Bocage, which at the end of a narrow penetration 10 miles deep into enemy territory were of increasing concern to Brigadier Hinde and his staff at Headquarters 22 Brigade.

Kampfgruppe Brassert advanced, using the main Jurques to Villers road with British reconnaissance falling back in front of it. They had almost reached Villers-Bocage when the advance guard of the right battalion reported 'enemy [i.e. British] tank and anti-tank positions' at the Seulles bridge a mile south-west of the town. According to General Lüttwittz, they 'sealed off and later destroyed this position'. The direct route into Villers-Bocage was blocked, so the advance guard followed the river further north, but behind them the main body of the battalion in response to reports had already turned north and secured Tracy-Bocage, having driven back elements of 5 RTR. G Battery, 5 RHA's war diary records that at 1430 hours:

> Tigers & Mk Vs reported south of us & moving up – our protective squadron of 5 Tks was forced to withdraw & the battery was left with no protection on its right flank. A Troop faced right & prepared to engage tanks at a 400yd field of fire. The attack did not develop, though the troop remained in

An overlay trace of 2nd Panzer Division showing their intent as at 1500 hours German time. The *Kampfgruppen* were at the time beginning their march.

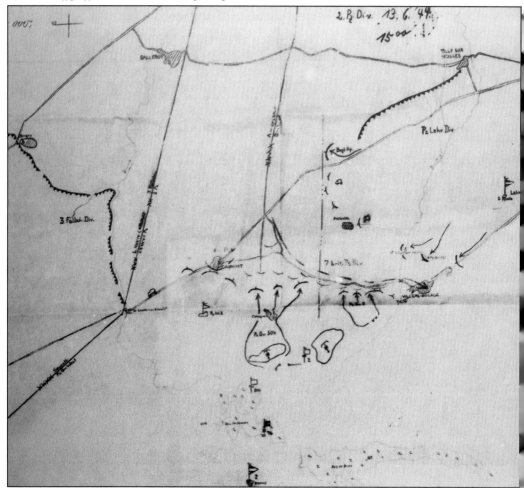

an uncomfortable position all day – snipers were a nuisance & two men per gun had to help flush them out to prevent infiltration through the long grass.

There are indications in German records that three Tigers commanded by *Obersturmführer* Philipsen and some Panzer IVs from *Kampfgruppe* Lex (*Panzer Lehr*) were operating with the 2nd *Panzergrenadiers* in and around Villers-Bocage. General von Lüttwitz later wrote that 'With the concentration of our heavy weapons, the right wing of our main attack succeeded in containing the impetus of the enemy forces and destroyed its best units.'

Kampfgruppe Brassert now held the high ground dominating the Villers-Bocage-Briquessard road and further west the left battalion had taken Point 193 also overlooking the same road. Further west still, *Kampfgruppe* Schake had advanced to successfully contain the 1st US Infantry Division at Caumont. Overlapping the US/British boundary, their advance caused the withdrawal of some British artillery which had been brought under fire by the *panzergrenadiers*.

Even though they occupied the high ground west of Villers the men of *Kampfgruppe* Brassert were exhausted and out on a limb, with their artillery only just beginning to come into range. Consequently, they were unable to take on the vulnerable 22 Armoured Brigade, as the Queen's and CLY withdrew from the town and the brigade formed its defensive box.

One indisputable benefit of Operation PERCH was firstly deflecting the strength of the 2nd Panzer Division from 1st US Infantry Division to

Operations of 2nd Panzer Division on 13 June 1944 based on a post-war interview with General von Lüttwitz.

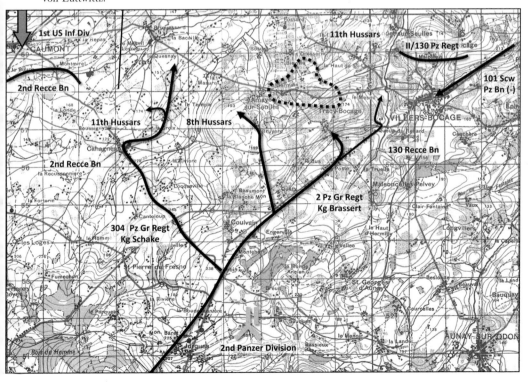

General von Lüttwitz,
commander of
2nd Panzer Division.

7th Armoured Division, which allowed the Americans to consolidate their positions at Caumont. Secondly, in accordance with Montgomery's overall design, PERCH drew the panzer divisions onto the Second Army's front.

On the evening of 13 June, the British were allowed to occupy the 'Box' or Island Position largely unmolested.

Chapter Twelve

The Island Position

At 1800 hours on 13 June plans to consolidate positions in and around Villers-Bocage were abruptly cancelled and Brigadier Hinde issued orders for the formation of a defensive box or 'Island Position' somewhat over a mile west of Villers (see map on page 226). Brigadier Hinde reported:

> In consultation with Comd 131 Bde, I now organised a defensive perimeter for the night with 1/5 Queen's astride the road east of Amayé-sur-Seulles and including St-Germain, 1/7 Queen's completing the 'box' east of 1/5 Queen's, also astride the road; one motor company of 1 RB was also used to fill a gap between 1/5 and 1/7 Queen's south of the road. At last light the armour and anti-tank guns were all drawn within the infantry dispositions. During the evening, enemy infantry mainly south of the road, confined their activities to patrolling and sniping; enemy shelling was negligible. I much appreciate the help of Brig Ekins [Commander 131 Queen's Brigade] in arranging the dispositions of his two battalions. [See map on page 226]

Of the withdrawal Major Aird, acting commanding officer of the CLY, wrote:

> A few hours before dark the order came to withdraw from the town to the village of Amayé-sur-Seulles, some 4,000 yards to the west along the main axis, where Tac Brigade had been for most of the day. This was not easy, as part of the road was exposed to anti-tank and machine-gun fire, while the sunken portions of the road were too narrow to allow a Cromwell to turn. Eventually, under a heavy barrage of smoke and HE by the American 155mms and British 25pdrs laid just before dark, the Queen's infantry and the two surviving Squadrons were extricated to leaguer in the village of Amayé. Tanks of the 8th Hussars were there, helping to remove an uncomfortable feeling of loneliness.

With the loss of not only A Squadron but more importantly regimental headquarters as well, there was much work for Major Aird and the adjutant overnight in Amayé, where the CLY were nominated as the brigade reserve.

G Battery, whose position was overlooked by the Germans on the high ground, recorded in their war diary that '1/5 Queens came up before dark & formed a perimeter though they required encouragement to make it in front & not behind the guns.' What the battery captain did not record was that the battery had already been forced to detail gunners to act as infantrymen to keep the enemy at a respectable distance from the guns.

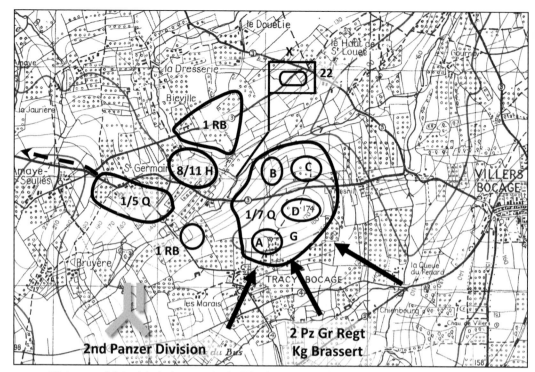

22 Armoured Brigade's deployment in the Island Position and the main German attacks. 5 RTR's squadrons were deployed in support of the infantry.

The box was just over a mile long by under a mile wide, a very small area for the vehicles of two vehicle heavy brigades but a long frontage for just three battalions to hold. 1 RTR 1/6 Queens and 3 RHA, who would form their own box further north at Granville, were tasked to keep the route north to Livry and beyond open.

A situation report from 7th Armoured to XXX Corps timed at 1945 hours reads as follows:

> The GOC decided to concentrate everything on TRACY-BOCAGE feature 174. That is now being successfully carried out. This Pt 174 dominates the village. The Div attacking has been identified by means of PW as the 2nd SS [*sic*] Pz Div. The axis of supply is precarious as there are small gps of enemy operating on the left flank, some of which have had to be silenced by artillery fire. 5 RHA have actually been under small-arms fire while manning their guns. [A full transcript appears in Appendix IV.][1]

The 8th Hussars' war diary records: 'The enemy [was] attacking from the North, South, East & West. The centre line to Division was cut and the Group was temporarily surrounded. The Regt Leaguered in the area 783579.' Other than some mortaring and German movement, the night was surprisingly quiet.

Brigadier Hinde wrote in his report that

> On 14 Jun, 5 R Tks moved out at first light to their dispositions of the previous day; I made a tour of the defences to make sure they were strong,

my orders being to hold the posn. The inf bns had been ordered to patrol actively outwards from their posns; these patrols disclosed that the enemy were in BRUYERE-TRACY BOCAGE and LE HAUT DE ST LOUET; AMAYÉ-SUR-SEULLES was reported clear after a night patrol and we occupied it with a standing patrol in the morning.

That morning as remembered by Lieutenant Wilson:

> ... every crew in the Fifth was waiting and watching for the expected counter-attack. I recall one junior officer sending a message on the regimental net to the effect that two enemy tanks had got round his position and were heading for RHQ. Whereupon Colonel Gus swiftly replied: 'They may have got past you, but they won't get past me. Out.' He slipped quickly into his Cromwell and traversed his gun to the expected spot.

Gunner Coombs of G Battery commented that 'At first light we became aware of the Island Position and how exposed it was when two gunners delivering ammunition to the SP [Sexton] guns were sniped and there were several casualties from shell fire close by.' As the morning wore on, shelling of the Island Position increased and 'several vehicles were brewed up' and as Hinde reported: 'The congestion of vehicles in the 'Box' was a disadvantage and the ground to be held was not favourable to all-round def – hull down positions for tks were extremely difficult to obtain and the ground sloped away in thick woods and orchards.'

Vehicles of all types were crowded into every clump of trees and orchard. Sergeant Markham was G Battery's quarter master sergeant:

> We had heavy casualties because we were packed tightly in a defensive box. There was a vehicle to every 10 yards. The first shell to arrive was an American one which was a bit off-putting and that was followed at once by German shelling. One landed on my own Q2 truck, ruining the engine and wounding the driver and forcing us into a half-completed slit trench for eight hours except for a dash to get our Bren which was buried under

22 Armoured Brigade carried its own brigade symbol, the stag, as well as the 7th Armoured Division's Desert Rat because of their own strong fighting pedigree from North Africa.

The RHA cap badge. It was unofficially adopted by the senior regiments then in existence.

scrimmage in the back of the truck. We had never expected to use it. Now we were told we were cut off.

At about 1000 hrs on 14 June 1/7 Queen's at the eastern end of the position noted that 'it became clear that enemy infantry were feeling their way forward' through the thick hedges that provided them with a covered approach to the two forward companies:

> Both mortars and Arty were used with good effect. By 1100 hrs a definite attack had materialised on the left forward Coy ('C' Coy) and a small-arms battle of great intensity raged for the next two hours with the MGs of the tks lending valuable assistance. The mortars and 5 RHA were continually in support switching from one area to another and meeting every call for fire with speed and intensity and accuracy.[2]

In the close country the 5 RHA fired at ranges of just 800 yards range and as the Germans closed in they engaged over open sights at ranges of less than 100 yards from the forward trenches. Gunner Coombs recalled that the services of an American 155mm battery were called on:

> ... attached to our CP was a Captain of artillery from the US Army called Chuck ('Just call me Chuck' was how he introduced himself), and from time to time he called down fire from his regiment way back in the main battle area. So it was that at about midday when a G Battery OP reported a large force of tanks and infantry assembling to attack, he said he would call on the whole of his corps artillery. He set off running towards his jeep about 100 yards away just as a load of shells landed on our position. Looking over the rim of my trench I watched him run and drop in between shell bursts like John Wayne in a WW2 movie. When he got there, his signaller was in the trench and refused to get out, so we heard Chuck shouting fire-orders himself down the mike. Before he got back to us, the shells came over like 400 express trains and seemed to land in the next field, so we were surprised when shouts of 'Apples' (code for shells on own troops) came over the radio, followed immediately to everyone's relief by 'Apples OK'. The whole 'stonk' came down on target.

Oberfeldwebel Braun was on several occasions 'on the receiving end of the bombardment fired by all of V US Corps' and British artillery in range:

> For fifteen minutes there was a continuous howling and shrieking all around the orchards. Shells thunder-clapped, throwing up clouds of smoke and dust; red-hot splinters, lumps of earth, shattered branches and splintered tiles from the farmhouse roof behind us flew round our ears at each detonation. But this was only the beginning. Minutes later, after we had just carried two of our wounded to safety, it seemed that the very earth around us was going to burst.

A US self-propelled 155mm gun in action.

Hundreds of shells of all calibres literally ploughed up the gardens. Dozens of hits shook the walls of the farm and set its roof on fire. Thick smoke clouds as bitter as gall from the high explosive made breathing difficult and irritated our throats so that we developed a dry cough. A hurricane of fire raged through the countryside, wrapping everything in grey smoke and dirt.

The German attack when it finally came fell on C Company 1/7 Queen's, whose historian wrote:

One platoon which was sited in front of the others was overrun, but C Company counter-attacked with Stens and grenades and restored the situation, though at some cost ... The men were very tired from their two days of hard fighting and put up a fine performance. Battalion Headquarters, within 20 yards of the front line, as being the only position not in full view of the enemy, had been in considerable danger. The padre, Rev. J. Macintosh, had at one time to be physically restrained from going forward into the enemy positions, where some of our wounded could be seen lying.

The attack had been beaten off, but a decision was being made to withdraw 7th Armoured Division from the Island Position where they were all but surrounded. At 1600 hours Major General Erskine made his second trip forward to give his orders at 131 Brigade's headquarters. Brigadier Hinde wrote:

> The gist of the orders was that owing to the slow progress of 50 Div and consequent vulnerability of the Div CL [line of communication] 22 Armd Bde would be withdrawn during the night 14/15 Jun through 1/6 QUEEN'S at Briquessard 1/5 and 1/7 QUEENS reverting to comd 131 Bde on reaching Briquessard. Brig EKINS to hold open CL to Briquessard with 1 R TKs and 1/6 QUEEN'S until 22 Armd Bde were through.

The withdrawal was to be covered by the sound of RAF bombing raids on Évrecy and Aunay.

At 1830 hours reports were circulating that Panzer IVs were again moving between Bruyères and Tracy-Bocage. Brigadier Hinde reported that

> By 1900 hrs it was evident that the enemy was putting in an inf attack from the SOUTH supported by tks, having apparently given up the idea of getting into our posn from the EAST and NE, where he had been most active during the day. I made it clear to the Bde that all tps would hold their present posns and that there would be no movement of any kind other than rft or counter-attack by 4 SHARPSHOOTERS in res.

An account in the *Rifle Brigade Chronicle* reads:

> I Company were on the Southern flank and had a very busy time, and the whole area was fairly heavily shelled and mortared. At about 7 in the evening the enemy put in an attack on I Company's area and got quite near to I Company's positions.

Sergeant Markham recalled that 'The shelling became very heavy and we were told that German infantry were coming into attack; they were now about half a mile away. The guns of our battery took them on over open sights with air-burst fuses and halted them.'

Brigadier Hinde continued:

> The enemy pressed his attack home with some vigour but little skill – his inf were able to get within some 300 yds of our posn without great difficulty but as soon as they were located they came under a withering fire from the inf and supporting tks and our arty fire was devastating and all calls for it were promptly and accurately answered.

The commanding officer of 1 RB wrote in his report:

> The enemy had quite appreciable artillery and mortar support and his infantry were supported by some of his heaviest tanks ... but this time it was we who were sitting still and the German tanks who were moving and ... quite a number of them were brewed up ... and after that the infantry rather lost heart ... the Horse Gunners firing air bursts at 400 or 500 yards ... really rather enjoyed their party.

British infantry with their close-range anti-tank weapon, the PIAT.

Gunner Coombs was up near his battery's gun position:

> The eight guns of G Battery were blasting away non-stop making speech impossible, but we all knew, without being told, that only those guns separated us from the enemy. It was not a situation we were used to. Our little trench was about 10 yards behind the left-hand gun, which completely obscured my view but I was dead calm and determined to fight it out with anything in grey or black that came around the corner of the Sexton in front ... I had picked up a Sten gun from somewhere and I carefully cocked it and made sure the safety catch was off, but I was denied my moment of glory. There was a muffled cheer from up front and the guns fell silent while the empty shell cases came clanging over the side of the SP, and the adjutant careered off in a tank to claim some prisoners ...

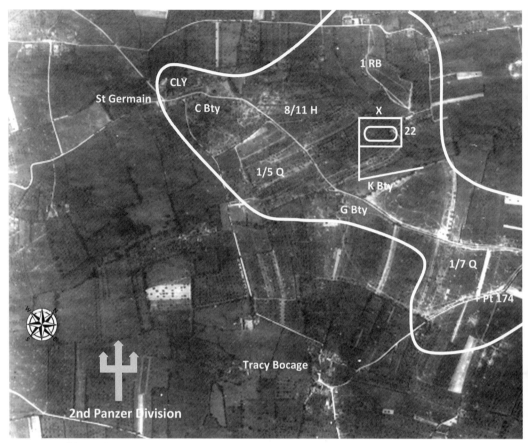

Air photo with the main and battery gun positions shown.

As they had done at Waterloo 129 years (almost to the day) before, Mercer's Troop (G Battery RHA) had broken up an enemy attack, not French Cuirassiers this time but SS Panzer Grenadiers [*sic*], and I, for one, was very relieved. We had no more excitement that day; the Typhoons came over to add their bit of punishment.

In addition to the medium and heavy guns of 5th Army Group Royal Artillery (5 AGRA)[3] the US forward observation officer was still with 5 RHA. I Company, 1 RB beat off the attackers in their area 'admirably assisted by 5 RHA firing air bursts over open sights' and

> Then the Americans took a hand ... their SP 155s had been supporting us throughout ... We had an OP officer ... who certainly knew all the answers. As the firing died down ... there were quite a number of German infantry in a certain wood to our right front. The American OP then called for a special concentration on it. I think its code name was Pandemonium: at all events ... it meant that every gun within range had to engage and it could only be ordered by an American general. However, it came down within about a minute and a half and it certainly was a real 'pandemonium'. Afterwards, two Germans who surrendered said ... in the wood they must have had some

800 or so casualties. Although this is no doubt a gross exaggeration it will give you some idea of the sort of shoot it was. It may have caused telegrams from Washington due to the colossal amount of ammunition expended but it certainly put 'finis' to any further German attack.

As the artillery fire lifted, in swept a squadron of seven Typhoons to attack *Oberfeldwebel* Braun's position:

Instantly, several of our vehicles, parked out of sight in a sunken road, went up in flames, marking our positions for the enemy with columns of jet-black ascending smoke.

Hell broke loose. Machine-gun bursts mingled with the screeching of rockets. We lay huddled here, pulses beating, while the ricochets went zinging through the bushes, or hit with a crack against the stone walls. Then the bombs came whistling down, nearly bursting our eardrums, and men, weapons and fragments of shattered vehicles were thrown into the air. Explosive rockets came howling away from under the wings of some of them. They burst on the ground, brightly glaring as a lightning flash, leaving behind a

A 5.5in gun of one of the medium regiments of 5 AGRA.

A Typhoon of 2 TAF. A week after D-Day the first air strips in Normandy were opening at this point for rearming and refuelling, but at last light aircraft returned to UK bases for maintenance and pilot rest.

spray of a thousand splinters. For an eternity of minutes, the screaming of my wounded comrades and the terrified roaring of mortally-wounded cattle which had been grazing in the fields was mingled with the chaotic sound of the low-level air attack.

Brigadier Hinde recorded that by 2200 hours 'the attack had fizzled out and quiet reigned once more': 'It is questionable whether the expenditure of arty and SA amn was justified by the scale of the enemy's effort but there is no doubt that he must have suffered severe cas and a very disagreeable experience.'

Oberfeldwebel Braun would almost certainly have agreed with Brigadier Hinde.

The Withdrawal

The start time for the withdrawal from St Germain was to have been 2330 hours, but due to the enemy attack it was put back to 0030 hours. It was covered by flights of Lancasters flying in and dropping 1,700 tons of bombs on Évrecy and Aunay-sur-Odon. The operation started promptly with three companies of 1/5 Queen's riding on the tanks of the CLY on the road to Briquessard and 'the move proceeded with no confusion and comparatively minor delays.'

The enemy, no doubt reeling from the earlier bombardment and the noise of RAF Bomber Command, were slow to realize what was happening. Last to move was the rearguard, which was a well-balanced infantry/armour grouping based on

5 RTR, their motor company (I Company, 1 RB), a company each from the two Queen's battalions and a squadron of the 8th Hussars' tanks. Hinde wrote:

> The enemy did not interfere at all with the move – the rear gd was subject to some sniping before it moved off but by 'brassing-up' the area generally it soon discouraged the enemy from closing in. Some delay was caused by two carriers of the motor battalion being brewed up on the rd by shell-fire during the move.

The CLY at the head of the column reported being leaguered up just before dawn at 0400 hours, while the final vehicles of the rearguard only cleared Briquessard at 0550 hours.

The withdrawal of 7th Armoured Division on the night of 14/15 June 1944 and 131 (Queen's) Brigade redeployment.

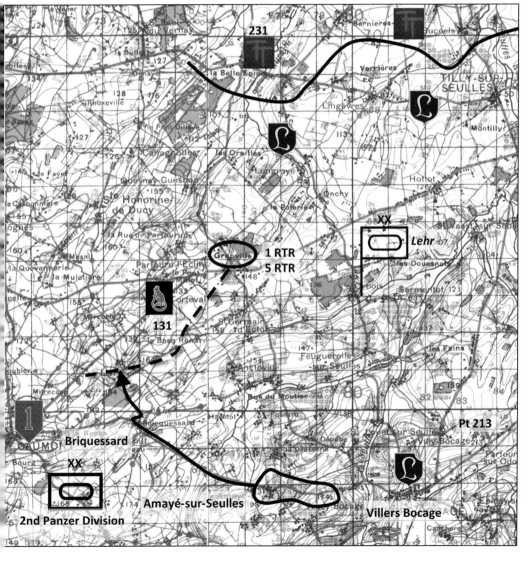

Final Thoughts

Lieutenant Colonel Gordon of 1/7 Queen's wrote in his report:

> The myth that the Tiger was invincible has now been exploded.
>
> The Bn experienced its first enemy counter-attack, which was driven back at a heavy cost to the enemy. The result of that has shown that if every soldier stands firm and fights hard with all his weapons, he has nothing to fear in the Hun.

On 15 June General Bucknall sent a message to General Erskine: 'Hearty congratulations on successful actions yesterday. You have dealt 2 Pz the hell of a smack. A major contribution to the general plan. Well done all ranks.'[4]

The German view was that the forced withdrawal of 7th Armoured Division was a success, as this XXX Corps note indicates: 'An officer PW from 2 Panzer Division remarked rather caustically to one of our interrogators "It's about time the *Wüsten-mauser* (Desert mice) realised that they're no longer operating in the desert with those tanks of theirs."'[5]

General Dempsey, in a post-war interview, said:

> This attack by 7th Armoured Division should have succeeded. My feeling that Bucknall and Erskine would have to go started with that failure. Early on the morning of the 12th I went down to see Erskine – gave him his orders and told him to get moving and that I would tell the corps commander what he was doing. If he had carried out my orders he would never have been kicked out of Villers-Bocage but by this time 7th Armoured was living on its reputation and the whole handling of that battle was a disgrace. Their decision to withdraw [was] made without consulting me; it was done by the corps commander and Erskine.

In the aftermath of Operation PERCH, Bucknall, Erskine and Hinde were on borrowed time. After another performance that Montgomery and Dempsey considered to be below par during Operation BLUECOAT, in early August all three were replaced.

Out of the Line

While the tanks were pulled back out of the line, for 7th Armoured Division's four infantry battalions there was to be no long rest. 131 Brigade took up defensive positions filling the gap between the Americans and 50th Division and, as recorded by the Rifle Brigade:

> We were only given a few days' respite (with the exception of the remnants of A Company which was sent back to refit) and the Battalion was concentrated and sent up to fill a gap in the line near Le Pont Mulot some 4 miles south of Caumont. The frontage was about 2,500 yards and with only two motor companies and the support company there was no depth to the position whatever. We remained in position for eleven days and found

Tank Regiment

In contrast with the cruiser tanks (Cromwells and Shermans) of the armoured regiment, whose role was one of exploitation, the tank regiments, with their slower-moving and more heavily armoured Churchill tanks, were organized for the support of infantry attacks. Tank brigades consisted of two or three regiments, but did not have either an organic infantry motor battalion or a self-propelled artillery regiment and their slim brigade headquarters, certainly at the beginning of the North-East European campaign, was more for administration than command in battle.

Based in the Aldershot area, 34 Tank Brigade had been issued with 75mm guns in February 1944 to replace the 6-pounders (57mm). The new gun had a breech to take the US 75mm ammunition and the 6-pounder barrel was bored to 75mm. Some 6-pounders were retained in the squadrons to exploit the emerging Armour-Piercing Discarding Sabot (APDS) round that was beginning to enter service in early 1944. The decision to recalibrate the Churchill's gun to 75mm had been made when progress in developing new armour-piercing ammunition was only moving slowly and the significant improvement that APDS subsequently delivered was far from certain.

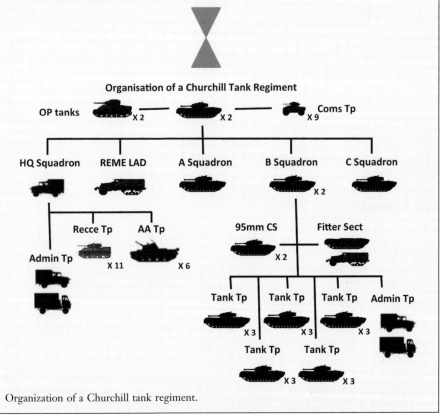

Organization of a Churchill tank regiment.

22 Armoured Brigade's workshop carrying out repairs to Cromwells in the field during the aftermath of Operation PERCH.

the long hours of daylight desperately trying. Stand-to in the morning was at 4.15 and in the evening at 10.30 each for an hour, so that there was no opportunity for a good night's rest. Still there were certain compensations in the form of delicious Camembert and Port Salut cheeses from Bayeux, eggs and fresh butter from the farmhouses and plenty of Calvados, a highly potent and lethal form of applejack which tasted like fire water.

In their leaguers the armoured commanders had much to dwell on, realizing that in the thick bocage country tanks could not operate on their own but only with the closest of co-operation with the infantry to their mutual benefit.

Chapter Thirteen

50th Division's Operations: 13 and 14 June

The 50th Division's part in Operation PERCH was to maintain the pressure on *Panzer Lehr* in order to minimize redeployment against 7th Armoured Division and 'once the presence of our tanks in the German rear area had unhinged their defence at Tilly, advance south towards Villers-Bocage.' This would form a salient with Villers at its head adjacent to that of the Americans at Caumont.

The GSO1 Ops' diary reads: 'Plans made rather late tonight for an attack by Div starting early 13 June.' Inevitably that meant that the 50th Division's attack would not be coordinated with 7th Armoured Division's advance to Villers-Bocage and would lack coordination within the division. As a consequence, General Bayerlein was not under pressure at Tilly and further west and was able to redeploy troops to contain 7th Armoured Division at Villers-Bocage and Point 213.

The 50th Division attacked with 151 Brigade left and 231 Brigade right. As a result of the the enemy stoutly resisting attempts by 1 Hampshires to advance south from Bernières-Bocage towards La Senaudière the previous afternoon, Brigadier Stanier's plan for 231 Brigade on 13 June was to attack from the forward position held by 1 Devons at la Belle Épine. This had the benefit of being on the inner flank of 7th Armoured's right hook and the advance would take the brigade via L'Oraille to their objective at Les Landes on the Juvigny-Caumont road.

151 (Durham) Brigade would, meanwhile, resume the attack on the high ground overlooking Tilly-sur-Seulles, with the village of Hottot their ultimate objective, also on the Juvigny-Caumont road. 56 Brigade held the line in front of Tilly and 69 Brigade, having been relieved of responsibility for Point 103 by 49th West Riding Division, were in reserve near Condé-sur-Seulles.

The Mobile Bath and Laundry Unit

Before considering the attacks, it is worth contrasting the experience of British and German infantrymen of the *Hitlerjugend* and 69 Brigade and the issue of lice and other vermin after nine days in battle. Living on and under the ground is inevitably dirty, but the German system of getting clean clothes or bathing had broken down. *Sturmmann* Decker of 25 SS *Panzergrenadiers* provides an insight

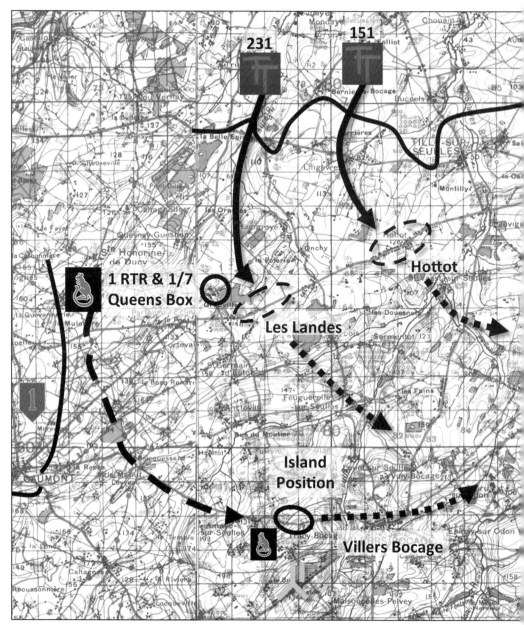

The 50th Division's concept of operations for 13 and 14 June 1944.

into some of the practicalities of life for German infantrymen at the front during this phase of the Battle of Normandy:

Disruption on the railways caused by Allied bombing and increased partisan activity meant supplies were no longer reaching the fighting troops at the front. As a result, we were given permission to enter French houses and to take whatever was necessary for personal use, such as clean underwear and so on, but nothing more. We were not allowed to take any more than was absolutely essential ... I can remember cutting up a bedsheet and wrapping the strips around my feet because I didn't have any socks. Fortunately, I had one chap in my mortar team who could always find food, so we never went hungry, as he always returned with a chicken, a duck, a rabbit, whatever he could find.

Conditions in the field meant we were unable to wash or clean our uniforms regularly and this led to many of us catching lice. The lice used to gather in the crotch of our trousers and drive us mad. When we had time, we would remove our trousers, turn them inside out and hold the crotch over a lighted candle. This was a horrendous job, but it killed most of the little blighters. When we were finally taken prisoner, one of the first things they did was to delouse us with DDT. They sprayed every nook and cranny; they had to.

Private Tateson of 7 Green Howards recalls being relieved by 49th Division:

> ... and we marched off to a rest area near Condé-sur-Seulles. Here were bivouacked in the orchards adjoining Manoir de Ghene. The following day were taken to Bayeux and visited the bath unit for the luxury of a shower. We also had an hour or so to ourselves and a few of us indulged in the exotic pleasure of visiting a wine bar.

A division's Mobile Bath and Laundry Unit (MBLU) would normally be set up in a central location, most often in a barn with an ample supply of clean water and a visit was something all ranks looked forward to. Units would take turns to bathe when not in action, which was about fortnightly. Dirty shirts and underwear, which of course had been worn continually since the last visit, were handed in and a good, hot shower was followed by clean towels and the issue of shirts, vests and 'drawers, woollen, long'. Clean battledress, blankets and greatcoats were issued less frequently. At full capacity, Royal Army Ordnance Corps MBLUs required 36,000 gallons of water a day and could wash 12,000 sets of personal clothing a week, plus 16,000 blankets, etc. from a division's units and medical facilities. MBLUs were considered to be a vital part of maintaining not only health and hygiene but morale as well.

Out of the line there were other opportunities for something approaching normal army life, as Lieutenant Taylor of 6 Green Howards' signals platoon recorded in his personal diary:

> Tuesday 13 June: There seems to be plenty of buckshee Compo[1] at present and with enormous numbers of eggs produced by Robertson we feed very well indeed. 49 Div arrived to relieve us in the afternoon, fresh from England and first time in action. All wearing steel helmets, with faces blackened, they amuse us rather, and were treated with superior grins.
>
> Moved out in the evening to a Manoir near Condé-sur-Seulles. Told at least 24 hrs rest, Bn HQ in the Manoir. Slept in a room, ate at a table, sat on

British soldiers, having been cleaned up, enjoyed a short period of normality in Bayeux.

A fourteen-man composite (Compo) ration box of tinned and packeted food including cigarettes and toilet paper.

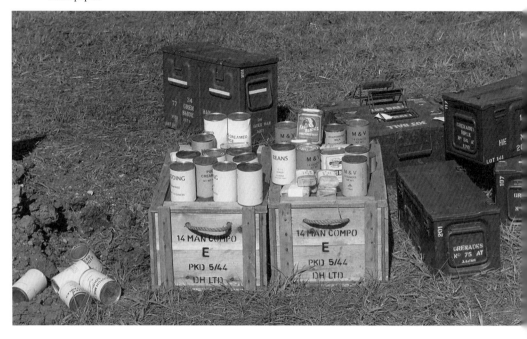

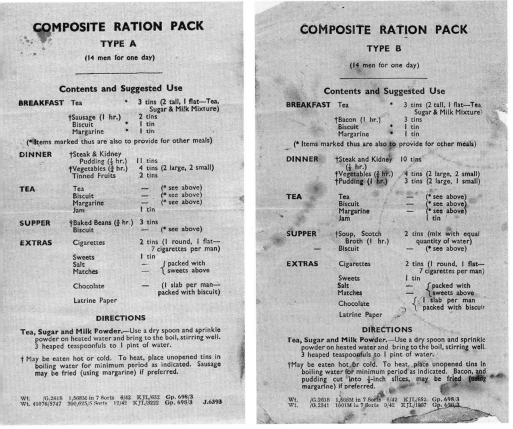

COMPOSITE RATION PACK

TYPE A

(14 men for one day)

Contents and Suggested Use

BREAKFAST	Tea *	3 tins (2 tall, 1 flat—Tea, Sugar & Milk Mixture)
	†Sausage (1 hr.)	2 tins
	Biscuit *	1 tin
	Margarine *	1 tin

(* Items marked thus are also to provide for other meals)

DINNER	†Steak & Kidney Pudding (¾ hr.)	11 tins
	†Vegetables (¾ hr.)	4 tins (2 large, 2 small)
	Tinned Fruits	2 tins
TEA	Tea	— (* see above)
	Biscuit	— (* see above)
	Margarine	— (* see above)
	Jam	1 tin
SUPPER	†Baked Beans (¾ hr.)	3 tins
	Biscuit	— (* see above)
EXTRAS	Cigarettes	2 tins (1 round, 1 flat—7 cigarettes per man)
	Sweets	1 tin
	Salt	— { packed with
	Matches	— { sweets above
	Chocolate	— (1 slab per man—packed with biscuit)
	Latrine Paper	

DIRECTIONS

Tea, Sugar and Milk Powder.—Use a dry spoon and sprinkle powder on heated water and bring to the boil, stirring well. 3 heaped teaspoonfuls to 1 pint of water.

† May be eaten hot or cold. To heat, place unopened tins in boiling water for minimum period as indicated. Sausage may be fried (using margarine) if preferred.

Wt. /G.2618 1,568M in 7 Sorts 8/42 KJL/652 Gp. 698/3
Wt. 41076/5747 200,625/5 Sorts 12/42 KJL/3222 Gp. 698/3 J.6393

COMPOSITE RATION PACK

TYPE B

(14 men for one day)

Contents and Suggested Use

BREAKFAST	Tea *	3 tins (2 tall, 1 flat—Tea, Sugar & Milk Mixture)
	†Bacon (1 hr.)	3 tins
	Biscuit *	1 tin
	Margarine *	1 tin

(* Items marked thus are also to provide for other meals)

DINNER	†Steak and Kidney (¾ hr.)	10 tins
	†Vegetables (¾ hr.)	4 tins (2 large, 2 small)
	†Pudding (1 hr.)	3 tins (2 large, 1 small)
TEA	Tea	— (* see above)
	Biscuit	— (* see above)
	Margarine	— (* see above)
	Jam	1 tin
SUPPER	†Soup, Scotch Broth (1 hr.)	2 tins (mix with equal quantity of water)
	Biscuit	— (* see above)
EXTRAS	Cigarettes	2 tins (1 round, 1 flat—7 cigarettes per man)
	Sweets	1 tin
	Salt	— { packed with
	Matches	— { sweets above
	Chocolate	{ 1 slab per man packed with biscuit
	Latrine Paper	

DIRECTIONS

Tea, Sugar and Milk Powder.—Use a dry spoon and sprinkle powder on heated water and bring to the boil, stirring well. 3 heaped teaspoonfuls to 1 pint of water.

†May be eaten hot or cold. To heat, place unopened tins in boiling water for minimum period as indicated. Bacon, and pudding cut into ½-inch slices, may be fried (using margarine) if preferred.

Wt. /G.2618 1,568M in 7 Sorts 6/42 KJL/652 Gp. 698/3
Wt. /G.2341 1001M in 7 Sorts 9/42 KJL/1907 Gp. 698/3

The day's menu for one of the types of compo.

a chair, talked to a pretty French girl who, however, chewed gum and much preferred to sleep with the SS.

Everyone feeling happy to be out of the line – not having to stand-to and lay lines. Unfortunately, a Medium Regt has set up shop in a neighbouring field and fired regularly during the night. Slept well though. Monsieur le Marquis also had a bath in his establishment – cost 10 cigarettes. These people very polite and hospitable but obviously not glad to see us.

151 (Durham) Brigade: 13 June 1944

With direct assaults down the axis of the Bayeux road over the previous two days having failed, 6 and 9 DLI were called forward to take a more westerly route via the hamlet of Marcel and the high ground south-west of Pont de la Guillette. They were supported by two squadrons of 4th/7th DG, which having been in action since D-Day were at the rear when 'Unexpectedly the Regt was called on in the afternoon to go to support 6 and 9 DLI (151 Bde) in an attack on the high ground dominating TILLY-SUR-SEULLES.'

6 DLI had been in reserve in the area of Condé-sur-Seulles since 8 June and was to lead in the first phase of the attack with 9 DLI following. That battalion would take over the lead to complete the advance on Hottot. 6 DLI's A Company

led down the Bayeux-Tilly road, but as they passed through 56 Brigade west of Pont de la Guillette they were heavily engaged by mortars and machine guns and under this fire all the company's radios were damaged by mortar and shell splinters. Consequently, the only communication with the Battalion Tactical (Tac) HQ was via liaison officers and runners, who often worked under very heavy fire and often failed to get through with their messages. Leading the attack onto the high ground, 1 Platoon almost reached some farm buildings before the platoon commander was wounded and the rest of the platoon was driven to ground. The rest of A Company was soon similarly pinned down and casualties from mortar fire mounted.

The report on the battalion's operation written by the adjutant describes their attempts to take the high ground:

> It was obvious that the farm was strongly held, so the CO decided to put in a company attack on the right flank to try and take the enemy in the rear. B Company, under Major Atkinson moved off to carry out this flanking movement and followed the line of a small stream. As the forward Platoon was moving up a salvo of *Nebelwerfer* bombs fell amongst them, killing two men and wounding six. The line of this stream was continually engaged by the enemy and Major Atkinson decided to push over the high ground towards the farm with his two reserve platoons. During this period the enemy positions had been heavily engaged by our mortars and artillery, and a troop of tanks was brought up to support the attack.[2]

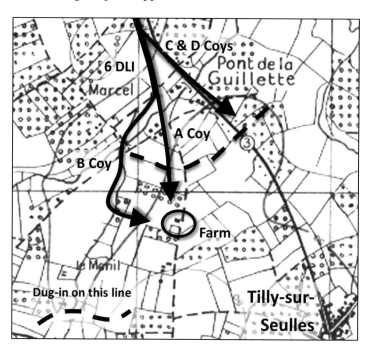

6 DLI's attack on the high ground west of Tilly.

The battalion's war diary highlights the difficulty that the Shermans of C Squadron had in identifying well-concealed machine guns and riflemen in the bocage: 'Tanks were brought up to try and deal with snipers and machine guns at 833690 [the hedges around the farm] but not effective.'

However, with the covering fire of the 4th/7th DGs' Shermans, 12 Platoon of B Company attacked the farmhouse, which it reached with the help of the

The German army was not fully prepared for war in 1939 thanks to Hitler's adventurism. As the army expanded, it was easier to invest in the 80mm mortar and ammunition than artillery.

platoon's 2in mortar firing smoke but 'was shot up badly by enemy infantry in hedges to the right and from immediately in front from the road.' They were forced back, and the company commander reorganized his platoons again before launching another attack supported by a tank. This final attempt was again broken up by heavy machine-gun and mortar fire and B Company withdrew from the open ground and reorganized along a hedgerow some 200 yards from the farm.

Here A and B companies dug in with their remaining men to establish a line astride a track. A Company were left and B Company right, while C and D companies were sent forward to dig in astride the main road to Tilly and to link up with A Company's left: 'Casualties had been heavy and at 2030 hours the Brigade Commander ordered the Battalion to withdraw.'

The commanding officer praised his stretcher-bearers and the attached Royal Army Medical Corps personnel who, covered by fire from the two leading companies and the tank, evacuated all casualties to an advanced RAP at Pont de la Guillette. Five officers were wounded, seven other ranks killed and forty-two wounded. Only when all casualties had been brought in did the companies withdraw to the Battalion RV at Bucéels. At the end of the day the adjutant concluded:

> There is no doubt that the line from Tilly to Lingèvres was the enemy's first defensive line, strongly held by determined troops. Both units attacking on our flanks reported very stiff opposition and had been unable to break through. The enemy had built a formidable defensive line and it was evident that a big attack would be necessary to break through.

A 2in mortar – the platoon commander's own 'artillery' – firing smoke, HE and illuminating rounds.

Nebelwerfers

There had only been a single battalion of *Nebelwerfers* in Normandy on D-Day, which was in action against the Americans on the Cotentin peninsula, but on 11 June 7 *Werfer* Brigade had arrived to bolster the defence and were in action around Tilly by the 13th. The brigade consisted of two regiments each of three battalions, established for twenty-two of the multi-barrel launchers. Two battalions had 150mm launchers and the third 300mm, with seven launchers per battalion mounted on vehicles. Three battalions of the 84th *Werfer* Regiment were under command of I SS Panzer Corps, with a battalion in direct support of *Panzer Lehr*.

For newly-arrived divisions such as the 49th the scream of the incoming rockets and the series of six crashing explosions were quite a shock, but for troops such as the veterans of 151 Brigade the appearance of the *Nebelwerfer* in Normandy was the meeting of an old foe from Sicily. Their nickname for the weapon was the 'Moaning Minnie', while the Germans referred to it as the *Heulende Kuh* ('Howling Cow') and the Americans as the 'Screaming Meemie'.

Having a range of more than 6,000 yards, it had double the reach of the 80mm mortar of the day and it alone contributed to 21 per cent of British casualties that were attributed to mortars. In manpower terms, in common with mortars, it was an attractive weapon for the Germans, requiring a smaller crew than a conventional artillery piece.

As the British intelligence sketch (see page 249), which was circulating in formation 'intreps' within days of the *Werfer* brigade's arrival indicate, the initial

A 150mm *Nebelwerfer*.

The *Nebelwerfer*'s signature.

A 210mm version of the *Nebelwerfer* being manhandled into action by its crew.

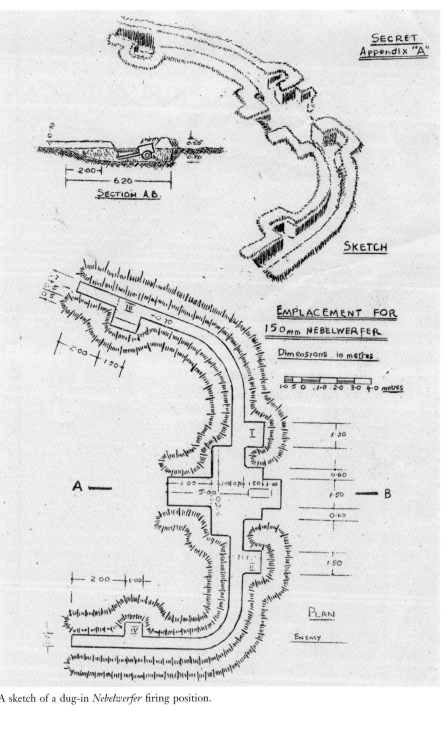

A sketch of a dug-in *Nebelwerfer* firing position.

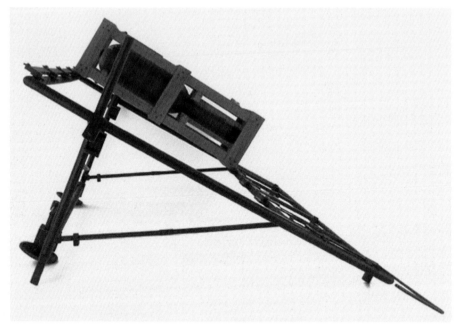

The *Wurfkörper* was fired directly from crates mounted on stands.

practice was to dig the launchers in but the signature of the rockets' fiery trails and, as the campaign went on, success in plotting firing positions with anti-aircraft radar, the Germans resorted to 'shoot and scoot'.

The *Wurfkörper*, however, continued to employ dug-in positions to fire their 280mm and 320mm crated cousin of the *Nebelwerfer*.

231 Brigade's Advance: 13 June 1944

Further west 231 Brigade were to exploit south from the only toe-hold 50th Division had on the Tilly-Balleroy road at la Belle Épine towards Les Landes. Brigadier Stanier's plan was for the Devons to advance from there, while the Hampshires attacked on La Senaudière from their positions just forward of Bernières-Bocage, before continuing on towards the Jurques-Caumont road. 1 Dorsets, having rejoined the brigade, was in reserve at Vichy and the brigade still had a handful of the tanks of 79th Armoured Division under command reluctantly operating as ordinary armour, 'patrolling the area and its rather open flank'.

2 Devons led off south from la Belle Épine with C Company. They initially succeeded in pushing back the men of 130 *Panzer Lehr* Recce Battalion but halfway to Les Landes they were stopped at L'Oraille. Meanwhile, on their left the Hampshires still could not get south from Bernières-Bocage to La Senaudière less than a mile distant. The enemy were well dug in and concealed in the numerous hedgerows.

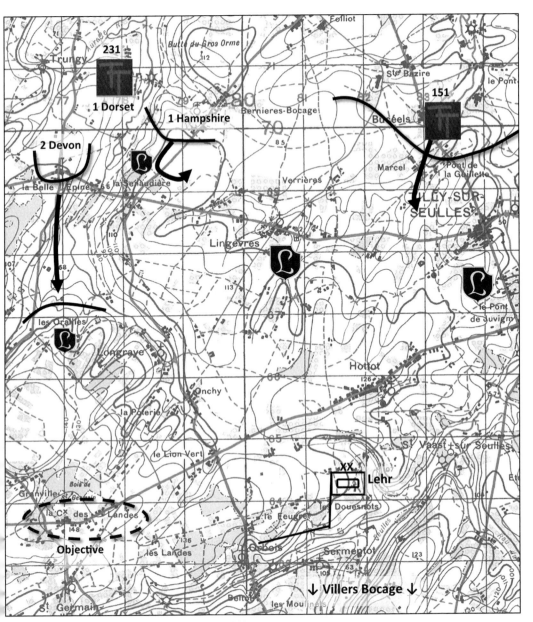

The 50th Division's operations, 13 June 1944.

The result of the fighting at La Senaudière was that 2 Devons, which had started the day on a bit of a limb at la Belle Épine, were now a further 2 miles ahead of the rest of the division. Consequently, both the Devons and the Dorsets were withdrawn to their starting-points and the Dorsets' commanding officer recalled that 'It was now decided that the Brigade must clear the area around La Senaudière before any other operations on our front could take place.' Given the situation that 7th Armoured Division was in the attack, the following day would be well resourced.

A Changed Situation: 14 June 1944

With 50th Division's failure to make progress south along with PERCH's abrupt halt at Villers-Bocage the previous day, along with its aim to roll up I SS Panzer Corps and envelop Caen, General Dempsey was faced with a new situation and a new phase of the campaign in Normandy. He wrote that there was

> ... no chance of a snap operation with airborne troops to either seize Caen or deepen the bridgehead on XXX Corps' front. It is now clear that Caen can only be taken by a set-piece assault and we do not have the men or ammunition at this time.

1st Airborne Division, which had been on call in the UK for a drop south of Caen or around Évrecy, despite the airmen's reservations, recorded in their war diary with a note of frustration that 'Operation WILD OATS is dead.'[3]

With 7th Armoured Division's right hook having been halted at Villers-Bocage and the division virtually surrounded in their Island Position, it was expected that a renewed attack by two of the 50th Division's brigades on 14 June would not only gain ground but salvage something from Operation PERCH. Having been relieved of Point 103 during the 13th, General Graham shifted his main effort further to the west. Attacking on a 3,500 yard frontage the objectives of 151 and 231 brigades were again on the Juvigny-Caumont road including the villages of Hottot and Les Landes, but first they would have to break through *Panzer Lehr* on the Tilly-Balleroy road at Verrières, Lingèvres and La Senaudière, all of which were still strongly held. Prisoners reported that the

General Bucknall's XXX Corps' planning conference. He is sitting on the ground wearing the light-coloured jumper. Seated to the rear, Major General Graham (50th Division) is on the left and Major General Erskine (7th Armoured) on the right wearing the cap.

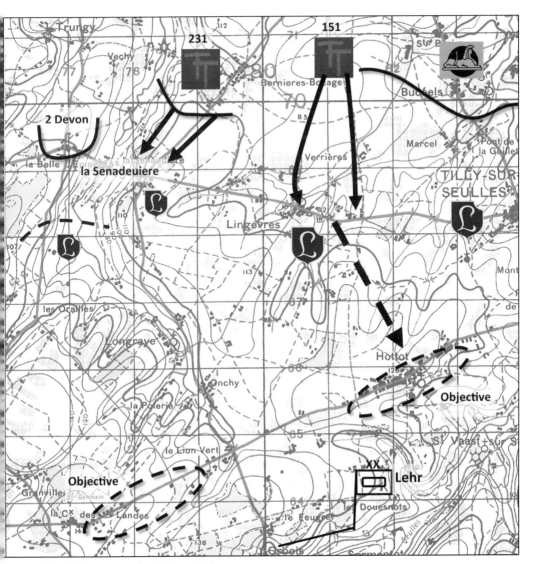

50th Division's plans for 14 June 1944.

front from Tilly westward was held by 901 *Panzergrenadiers*, 130th Pioneer Battalion and 130th Recce Battalion. All had, however, suffered significant attrition but were backed up by panzers and *Panzerjäger*, and it was all too apparent that their ability to resist in the bocage was not diminished in proportion to their losses.

231 Brigade: La Senaudière, 14 June 1944

The plan was this time for the brigade to attack with two battalions: the Hampshires on the left and the Dorsets on the right. 2 Devons would remain 'as a firm base' at la Belle Épine. The three Crocodiles from 141 (Buffs) Regiment RAC, one of which had been 'salvaged', and flail tanks of the 22nd Westminster Dragoons were still with the brigade.

To help blast the Germans out of their entrenched hedgerows, an impressive fire plan was developed, including the guns of six British field regiments, three mediums and the US 155mm battalion, plus naval gunfire and close air support; all timed just before the 1130 H-hour. No. 83 and 84 groups were to carry out strafing attacks and bombing of the enemy defensive line in the villages and along the Balleroy road with 120 tons of ordnance. This, however, required the Hampshires to withdraw for safety reasons to the northern end of Bernières-Bocage.

The Dorsets moved forward to their FUP through what the commanding officer described as 'difficult country' with A and B companies leading. The monthly summary appended to the war diary records that

> Misfortune overtook us from the outset when our own barrage came down on our start line and inflicted severe casualties on B Coy and to a lesser extent on A Coy – the former Coy being considerably shaken and disorganised and Major Chilton wounded. The unfortunate mistake had occurred owing to our 'start line' being taken by the Gunners as the 'opening line' of their barrage.

The Hampshires' war diary describes the mechanics of the attack, the support available and the effect of the safety withdrawal:

> Arty barrage covering 100yds in three minutes was laid on. Spting [supporting] arms consisted of a troop of Crocodiles and a troop of M10s of the NH [Northumberland Hussars]. The Bn moved off already deployed and opposition was met N of LA SENAUDIÈRE, showing the enemy had occupied same ground which we had given up when the air attack began.[4]

The Crocodiles went ahead of the infantry into the village and although doing considerable damage, 'all except one were knocked out and again provided no immediate assistance to the Bn.' The Hampshires, however, do not do justice to the bravery of the Crocodiles of 15 Troop, C Squadron, in leading the attack!

With the Hampshires looking on, the three Crocodiles advanced towards the buildings grouped around the crossroads, firing a smokescreen as they went. As the Crocodiles passed the first house they came face to face with a Panzer III.[5] The moving Crocodiles and stationary panzer all fired at the same time. The panzer missed, while the Crocodiles' 75mm rounds hit but ricocheted off the sloping turret armour. The panzer promptly withdrew, reversing at speed.

A close-range game of cat and mouse continued as the three Crocodiles advanced into the village, this time with a Panther which stalked its prey. Manoeuvring into a firing position around a corner of a building, it fired two rounds into one of the Crocodiles flame fuel trailers but remarkably it did not burn. The Panther, however, was itself confronted by the other two Crocodiles as they emerged from their smoke. One engaged with its 75mm main armament, but even at close range the AP round failed to penetrate the Panther's frontal armour, while the second flamed the Panther, setting the whole thing on fire.

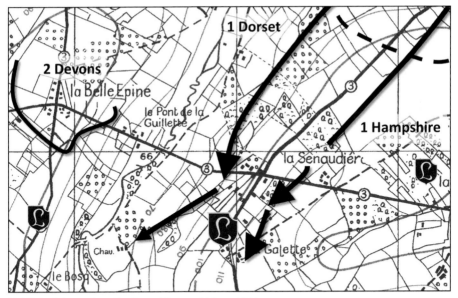

231 Brigade's attack on La Senaudière on 14 June 1944.

While concentrating on the considerable threat of the Panther, the Panzer III had reappeared and disabled one of the Crocodiles with a shot to its tracks. The panzer, however, was quickly knocked out and the remaining Crocodiles continued to advance into the village where another Panther was waiting, which knocked out another Crocodile. The remaining Crocodile withdrew.

To add to the destruction of days of bombardment, some of the houses were burning largely from the result of shelling and mortaring, but while the Crocodiles had used their flame to deal with the *panzergrenadiers'* supporting armour, some would have set fires alight. The Buffs' war diary reads

> The action was successful and advanced down the main road to the X rds using a small quantity of flame. They were fired on by German armour. One CROCODILE completely wrecked having its turret blown off and caught fire. This was due to a penetration of the thickest armour on the front to the right of the driver.

Meanwhile, the Dorsets had resumed their advance at 1215, having reorganized. They also reported increased opposition as they approached the area west of La Senaudière crossroads, with the war diary recording at 1300 hours that B Company was 'advancing slowly through heavily wooded country mopping up MG posts and snipers in conjunction with 1 Hamps on left'. Progress was indeed slow: it wasn't until 1600 hours that B Company reached the Balleroy road, which A Company on the right had gained with little opposition. This company continued to advance to some château building some 600 yards south of the road, which they reached at 1700 hours.

Flail tanks of the 22nd Westminster Dragoons moving forward to join the fighting.

The Dorsets' C and D companies were called forward and swung to the left to assist the Hampshires in clearing La Senaudière in detail but as the Dorsets' war diary reports, the inevitable German counter-attack was launched:

> 1930. Enemy opposition made it advisable to conc the Bn north of the main road, but one PANTHER is captured, and its crew killed, one PANTHER KO'd by one of our A/Tk guns which was manhandled forward under the direction of Capt HEBDEN. D Coy lose CSM O'CONNELL, who was killed whilst rallying a part of the coy. A Coy is withdrawn north of the road. The area of the important X Rds at La SENAUDIÈRE was in our [1 Hampshires'] possession.

The enemy remained in close contact throughout the night, but withdrew towards Longraye at dawn.

151 Brigade: 14 June 1944

While 6 and 9 DLI were pulling back from the attack on the high ground southwest of Tilly on the evening of 13 June, the commanding officers[6] reported back to Brigadier Walton's headquarters to attend orders for the following day's attack on the villages of Verrières and Lingèvres. However, they did not like what they heard, and Colonel Woods said: 'Brigadier, you know if we do this we shall have a tremendous number of casualties. We ought to do this attack at night and we ought to have some time for reconnaissance.'

Brigadier Walton replied:

> I know that, but I have been told this is a desperately important battle. We've got to get this village. We've got to go on so that the break-out can continue from the beachhead and if we don't do it now, we may well find that the opposition is stiffening up all the time, so we've got to do it.

The battalion's history makes it plain that when he gave his own orders Colonel Woods showed true leadership by not revealing his doubts.

Following the same heavy bombardment and creeping barrage as 231 Brigade, 151 Brigade planned to attack Lingèvres on the right, with 9 DLI in their first action since D-Day, while 6 DLI attacked Verrières on the left. Both battalions were supported by a squadron of 4th/7th DG. The barrage, which according to German sources included white phosphorus smoke, was designed to help the tanks and infantry across the open cornfields and 3 ft-high standing crops that had given 2 Essex such trouble days earlier.

9 DLI had an advantage over 6th Battalion, which was of course still committed to battle on the high ground west of Tilly, as they were able to mount a reconnaissance with B Company:

> In order to estimate or indeed confirm the enemy strength here, it was decided to carry out a reconnaissance in force at almost company strength that evening in daylight. B Company was selected to do this, supported by the Carrier Platoon and a FOO. I watched this attack from my company position and it gave me a fair indication of what we might expect the next day ... They were allowed to get right out into the standing corn with only some mortaring and sporadic automatic fire until they were within 60 or 70 yards of the edge of the woods. They were then subjected to withering fire and forced to withdraw very hurriedly suffering considerable casualties. Two German tanks were seen during this attack and one of them was, in fact, brewed up by ... the Northumberland Hussars, from my company position. This reconnaissance in force had shown that without doubt the enemy were in strength and probably seasoned and well-trained troops, capable of withholding their fire until it would be most effective.

According to his Military Medal citation, Lance Corporal Smith in the B Company headquarters carrier

> ... then volunteered to collect the wounded. In face of enemy MG fire, he drove in front of the enemy's positions four times. He drove the carrier himself and collected the wounded without help other than smoke and supporting fire from a troop of tanks behind him. It was not until he satisfied

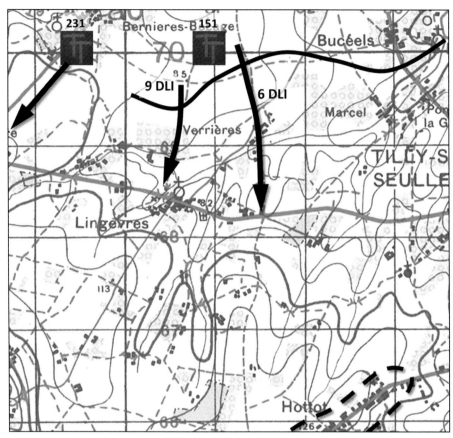

151 Brigade's plan, 14 June 1944.

himself that all that could be done had been done that L/Cpl. Smith returned to his own lines.

As the last heavy shells ploughed into the villages at 1015 hours on 14 June, 151 Brigade followed the creeping barrage of 90 Field Regiment's 25-pounders and advanced south across open fields towards the orchards, woods and villages.

6 DLI: Verrières

At 1015 the battalion crossed the start line supported by a squadron of tanks in an open formation in order to minimize casualties from mortars and artillery and the advance went well for the first mile. The platoons all had yellow marker panels tied to rifles to ward off friendly aircraft and when waved and pointed in the direction of a concealed enemy position used to indicate targets to tank commanders: 'It proved to be a simple but effective system.'[7] However, progressing south, 'On reaching the open ground 8169 [see map on page 262] leading companies came under heavy machine-gun fire from the line of trees running north-east and south-west along a track north of Verrières. Companies [were] unable to move forward.'

Private Harvey recalled:

We were all going into the attack and we were going across this cornfield . . . when Jerry opened up with Spandaus. Well, [there was] a small groove in the ground where, fortunately, I got into it. I got down. The men were getting mown down left, right and centre. In fact, the Company was being slaughtered; it's as simple as that. As those were going down more men were coming up and these were getting knocked down. The cry then was, 'Mother! Mother!'

Eventually two tanks came up behind us. This was after a long while and all the corn had been completely mown down, as though it had been with shears, by the Spandaus . . . We couldn't move. If you moved, you got shot. You had to stay down and, I remember, two tanks came up eventually and they blasted this hedge.

The 'wood' that the Germans occupied was a belt of trees along the road immediately north of the village and was bounded by a ditch in which the German infantry, who it was later found to have been there for six days, had prepared positions. The battalion's post-action report described the problem facing them:

The enemy positions were found to be in a ditch and a large amount of enemy equipment was taken in the ditch. Some machine guns had been set up on tripods and they had been fired by men who were well dug in to the side of the ditch and protected against anything but a direct hit by a shell or mortar bomb.

An MG 42 mounted on a Lafette tripod in the sustained fire role.

Captain Perry was the FOO attached to Major Spike Galloway's A Company and was in cover with his radio-operator at the company headquarters:

> This really is a rough battle; everything on earth seems to be landing in our fields, and if we poke our noses above this corn the Spandaus in those farm buildings will knock us down like ninepins. We cannot get the guns onto them because Ted and his company [C Company] are coming round the right of the farm [on the outskirts of Verrières]. We lie in the open for about half an hour while the Battalion Commander sums up the situation. Then we get orders to advance. It seems suicide to stand up in the corn with a dozen Spandaus just in front, ready to knock us down, but Spike Galloway is a grand chap, and with a cheerful 'Come on chaps', we all get onto our feet and start walking forward; the Spandaus open up and a dozen of our chaps go down. After 100 yards down again into the corn and get ready for the assault; as we go down there is a shout from Spike; he is shot through the shoulder; we help him back to the stretcher-bearers and, oh Hell, the wireless has packed up. We will have to dash back and get another. I walk back to the carrier, thinking that every moment will be my last, but for some reason nothing opens up.
>
> Meanwhile, we are going into assault; the Durhams go like mad with fixed bayonets, and we are in the farm building at last. No wonder we have had a tough time getting here. In this farmyard alone there are two 75s, three SP guns, a half-track and seven Spandau positions dug into the bank of a sunken lane. As we are going in, a bullet whistles through my battledress but does no more damage than a graze on my shoulder blade.[8]

It had taken five hours of battering away at this position with tanks and artillery to wear down the Germans and an attack by the reserve companies to secure the defended ditch: 'The quantity of ammunition left behind indicated that the enemy had every intention of holding this line in strength.' Getting short of ammunition, the Durhams turned the German machine guns on their erstwhile owners, while the companies reorganized in the ditch and prepared to resume the advance.

While B and D companies went forward to clear Verrières, A and C companies remained in the ditch. B Company went through to Verrières without opposition, crossed the stream into the thick bocage and halted to the left of a track to allow D Company on the right to move up alongside them. With B Squadron having lost five Shermans 'after strenuous fighting', there was a single tank advancing in close support during this move to the road at Les le Gallois. A Panther was sited where the track crossed the Balleroy road, covering the track north and the approaches to it. D Company was heavily engaged from the front and right and was unable to get on.

B Company pressed forward and reached a position 200 yards from the main road where they were shot up by machine guns and a panzer. The left platoon of B Company had made their way forward using the cover of the hedgerows

Major Spike Galloway MC and Bar in the process of being evacuated.

and a section reached the road where it was cut off by fire from the left flank, losing half its strength. The company commander, with his platoons exposed to counter-attack, decided to withdraw and with no prospect of a further advance, the battalion reorganized in the area of Verrières: C and A companies were combined on the left; a battered B Company occupied the ditch, which had been captured earlier; and D Company remained forward just to the north of the stream.

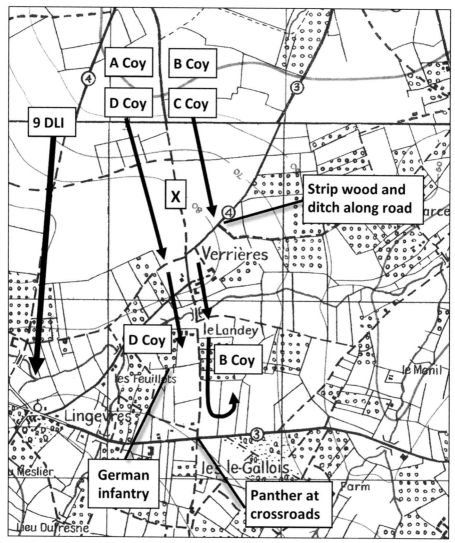

6 DLI's action at Verrières on 14 June 1944.

During this time, after fighting hard the Germans started to surrender. Dispatch rider Gunner Mawson of the 86 Field Regiment took a surrender in unusual circumstances:

> ... the chain came off my motorcycle and I was busy with it when someone tapped me on the shoulder. I nearly jumped 6 feet. It was a German giving himself up! He even helped me with the chain. I told him to get on the back and took him several miles to a prisoner of war cage – I made sure he didn't get shot.

6 DLI lost in the region of 100 men in the fight for Verrières and B Squadron
7 crewmen. A Durham officer, however, wrote after the attack:

> This was by far the most successful attack the battalion carried out during
> six days of heavy and continuous fighting, and the perfect co-operation of
> artillery, tanks and infantry really showed what could be done. There was
> no doubt that the enemy had to be blasted out of his positions in that very
> close country – and after several not-too-successful attempts we seemed to
> have come upon the best method of doing it. The weary look in the eyes of
> the men was once again replaced by keenness and eagerness, and even after
> six days of fighting the defences in our new positions were dug more quickly
> and better than ever.

Lingèvres

9 DLI had a much shorter expanse of open ground to cross but instead had the
extensive battle-scarred orchards, which 2 Essex had captured and withdrawn
from several days previously, to fight through before reaching the village of
Lingèvres. Supported by a troop of Shermans from A Squadron 4th/7th DG,
the forward companies waited in the FUP for H-hour. Lieutenant Williams was
with them:

> We were treated to a front seat at a very accurate and sustained 25pdr.
> barrage and the woods literally jumped and danced in front of our eyes and
> not 300 yards away ... The Typhoons, each one, did a dive and each one
> released two bombs and ten rockets, straddled and plastered that wood.
> Surely nothing could live in that now.[9]

As the aircraft departed, 9 DLI moved forward and as with 6 DLI to the battalion's left there was initially little enemy fire. Gunner Bullen was driving Major
Swann in an artillery command Sherman belonging to 342 Battery:

> We were now advancing across a large field of corn in company with eight
> other Shermans in a rough line abreast with each tank well separated from
> the next one. As a driver I was getting many changes of direction unneces-
> sarily I thought until I realised that we were driving through our own
> infantry who were invisible to me through my periscope. The corn was
> almost at eye level.
>   About 500 yards from the village I saw a Dragoon's tank hit way over to
> our right. Suddenly one to our left stopped and the crew bailed out. That too
> was hit. Then suddenly all hell was let loose.

Sergeant Eagles, leading one of 9 DLI's mobile tank-hunting teams mounted in a
carrier, recounted:

> We entered a large cornfield. The men were well spread out, with rifles
> at port position, as they waded waist-high through the corn. We would
> be about 500 yards up the field, which was triangular in shape, and were

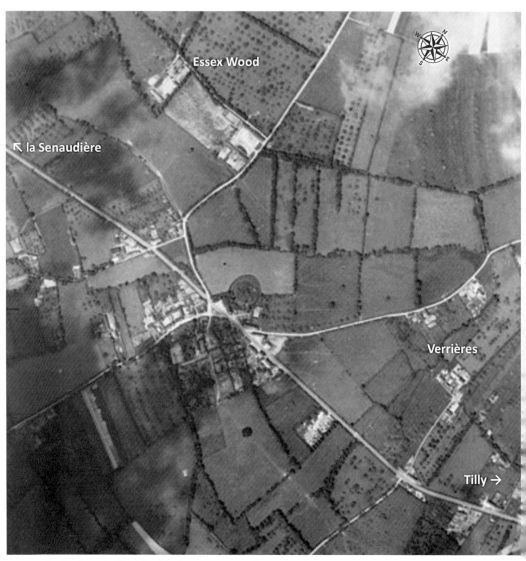

Essex Wood

↖ la Senaudière

Verrières

Tilly →

An air photograph of the Lingèvres area.

advancing towards the apex when all hell was let loose: withering Spandau, snipers and mortars caught us in the crossfire. Men were falling left, right and centre and I jumped from the carrier ... We ran over to the other carrier, which had been hit and pulled the Corporal clear. He was screaming in agony as his leg and arm had been blown off. The driver, a young ginger-headed lad, was in a terrible state but he was dead – killed immediately. There were dead and dying all around us and gruesome screams filled the air, mingled with the sound of gunfire, which was so intense it was cutting the corn like a scythe.[10]

'All hell' was indeed 'let loose', with A Company suffering particularly badly. Infantrymen fell and tanks were soon burning, but the Germans were not having things entirely their own way, with a panzer being knocked out. Battery OP tank driver Gunner Bullen recalled:

> The main armament of the tanks fired at targets I couldn't see and the wireless sets which I could hear in the background were constantly receiving and sending messages. I can remember one in particular: 'Mike target – Mike target – Mike target' followed by a grid reference. This was from my own commander and seconds later a barrage of shellfire burst on the village. It seemed to go on for an hour or more. In reality it was only a few minutes.

Colonel Woods ordered up the reserve companies with B Company passing through A Company to reach the woods. The company commander Major D'Arcy Irvine recalled that

> My left forward platoon reached the woods and quite a considerable number of Germans climbed out of their weapon pits with their hands above their heads. I cannot to this day understand why some of them were not shot but the Geordies paid no attention to them, despite the havoc they had wrought among us and the fact that their compatriots were still keeping up a continuous hail of fire. It was at this stage, just short of the edge of the woods, that I was hit.

Major Mogg, the battalion's second-in-command who was controlling the companies to the west of the road, recalled a radio message from Colonel Woods:

> We are running into terrible trouble here on the left. Most of A Company's officers, in fact all A Company's officers, are casualties. I'm trying to get on with B Company. I will try and see how it happens and if not, if we don't make any ground, you go on with whatever you do with your side of the village. I will try and collect as many of them and try and come round behind you. It's obviously going to be easier at your side [see map on page 226].

While A and B companies were stalled in their wood, Major Mogg ordered D Company up alongside C and together they cut through the orchards (Essex Wood) towards the village, which the battalion reached at further cost:

> I was the right-hand man of A Company, with C Company on my right. As we went across the cornfield, a shell of our own creeping barrage fell not far in front of me and the left-hand man of C Company fell. I knelt quickly beside him and thought he had been killed by the blast, but I had to carry on. As we came out of the high corn, Spandau machine guns opened up all along our front and many men fell. I was so close to the one nearest me, I saw the dust thrown up in little spurts as the bullets left his gun. He was firing straight ahead as I ran forward with Sten gun firing towards him. As I got close, the firing stopped, and I pulled the Spandau away. He lay dead in the trench and I hauled his very terrified comrade out. He had to stand on his dead mate. 'Hands on head! Walk!' and I think he was glad to do so, back

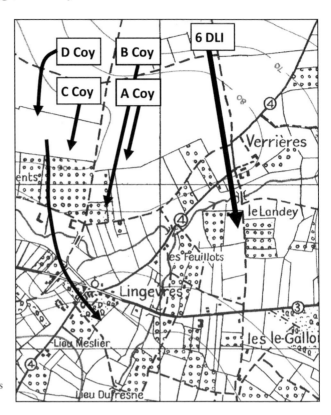

9 DLI's attack on Lingèvres
on 14 June 1944.

across the cornfield, whilst I went to the next trench … I stood back to see
what was happening but saw no one else standing. Just then a burst of
Spandau from deeper in the woods hit me and I fell.

Among those killed during this phase were two of the artillery forward observation officers and the commanding officer, Colonel Woods, was mortally
wounded by a mortar bomb. Consequently, Major Mogg took command of the
battalion.

Lingèvres was reached by C and D companies around midday, but for 9 DLI
and 4 Troop of A Squadron the battle in the village was far from over. First there
was the clearing of the houses and then the inevitable German counter-attack.
Major Mogg recounted:

By 12 noon, I found myself in command of what was left of 9 DLI in the
village of Lingèvres – with D Company fairly strong, C Company at about
one platoon strength and the remnants of A and B on their way to reinforce us.[11]

The fighting in the village went on into the afternoon as determined resistance by
6th Company of 902 *Panzergrenadiers* in the buildings had to be subdued house

by house, room by room. Major Mogg then needed to put Lingèvres into a state of defence:

> Having been well trained at my Battle School, I had a quick O Group. I ordered D Company to occupy the East and SE edge of the village, facing towards Tilly and one platoon of C Company to look after the approaches from the South. I made a defence fire plan with my gunner, [Major] Ken Swann of 86 Field Regiment. I ordered the support weapons to move forward, putting the carriers to guard the Western approach and set up my Bn HQ in the area of the bridge over the stream just North of the village and on the Bn axis.

The inevitable counter-attack consisted of Panthers of I Battalion, 130 *Lehr* Regiment, luckily with little infantry support. Major Ritgen recalled that it was less powerful than it could have been. His panzers were assembling in some woods in a valley near Longraye some 2 miles south-west of Lingèvres:

> As II Battalion, 130 *Pz Lehr* Regt prepared to counter-attack against Lingèvres, the British thought these were preparations to attack the 7th Armoured Division and ordered 'Pandemonium' against the forest ... The Panzer attack was brought to a halt in the marshy forest by an enormous expenditure of ammunition.

Private Casson of 9 DLI.

Major Ritgen, commander of II/130 Panzer Regiment.

Few of the Panzer IVs were knocked out but nonetheless, as Ritgen wrote: 'The author remembers well that his battalion was not destroyed yet, but it could not be controlled, as antennas and vision slots were destroyed.' Even without Ritgen's Panzer IVs it was going to be a tough fight in which Lieutenant Morrison's 4 Troop were going to bear the brunt. He was sent forward to find Major Mogg who was in the doorway in the western end of the church, where the RMO had already set up a forward RAP behind the substantial building and was busy with casualties that were being brought in every few minutes. Mogg gave his straightforward orders: 'We've got to capture the village ... and when we've got it, we must hold it. I want you to give me all the support you can.'

Morrison deployed the two Sherman 75s on the roads south and west out of Lingèvres and Sergeant Harris's Firefly covering what he had been briefed by Major Mogg was the greatest threat: the road east to Verrières and Tilly. He kept his own tank in the centre of the village near the church. Other tanks entered the village and joined in fighting the protracted and confused action that saw Panthers manoeuvring in and around the village. Gunner Bullen driving Major Swann's Op tank was entering the village when the counter-attack began. He wrote:

> As we got closer [to the village] I could see more infantry setting up machine-gun positions. I then turned into the village square and found far more destruction. The church, houses and shops had obviously been caught in the Typhoon raid. A few dead Germans and British soldiers were scattered about. A Sherman [Morrison's] was positioned by the entrance to the church and on the other side of what I call a square but was in fact just a road junction, a Firefly stood with its gun pointing north-west.

A Firefly commanded by Sergeant Roberts reported a panzer advancing towards him down the Balleroy road from the west. He pulled back with his turret to the rear and engaged at probably 1,000 yards with his 17-pounder. Not only did the flash obscure the fall of shot, but it set the camouflage nets on the back of the Sherman on fire. Consequently, Roberts had to withdraw to extinguish the fire.

Meanwhile, approaching up the road from the south, which was covered by 9 DLI's 6-pounders, were a pair of Panthers. Major Mogg wrote that he had

> ... sited the five remaining anti-tank guns singly, facing down the road approaches. This was a fatal mistake as in the first counter-attack four of the five were knocked out by advancing tanks coming down the road. It taught me never to site A/Tk guns to fire frontally but always to engage tanks from a flank.

Sergeant Harris was positioned on the Tilly-sur-Seulles road making use of a slight rise which provided him with a 'hull-down position'. He recalled: 'I was there about ten minutes before it was reported over the radio that two Panthers were coming towards us. I couldn't see them at first, but I didn't have long to wait.'

The Lingèvres war memorial looking east down the road where Sergeant Harris engaged the German Panthers.

What came into sight was a surprise: it was a Sherman, but shortly afterwards two Panthers drove past it:[12]

> Keeping my eyes open I picked up the two Panthers about 1,200 yards away creeping down a hedge. I was confident they couldn't see me, so I held my fire and let them get closer. By this time my gunner Tpr McKillop had the leading tank well in his sights and when it was about 400 yards away he opened up and to my amazement the first shot sent it into a mass of flames and with the second shot we did the same to the second Panther.

With Panthers closing in seemingly from every direction, the battle became reminiscent of that in Villers-Bocage the previous day, with tanks hunting tanks at short range in the village. Captain Garton Ash explained that the artillery could not play its usual highly destructive role:

> A German tank was spotted on the far side of the stream close against the side of farm buildings, and thus protected from shellfire. The crew was just scrambling into it. The whole village was full of dust and debris and I searched round the back of houses to try and find anywhere to provide a decent OP looking south, but this was impossible because of the bocage.

Gunner Bullen was waiting while Major Swann talked to one of the DLI's officers:

> I was told to stop by a Sherman and wait, engine running. The Commander called a greeting and waved. In answer to a request from our skipper he

Photographed then and now ... the road into Lingèvres from Tilley, up which the Panthers advanced before being knocked out.

A 4th/7th DG Sherman knocked out in the centre of the village.

pointed to the Firefly. Our Commander ran across the road, climbed on the Firefly and pointed to something out of my vision. I didn't have a chance to wonder what he was pointing at. Our own wireless operator shouted into the intercom: 'Driver reverses, right-hand down and go like ****!' I didn't hear the last word – I was already going!

The tank lurched, a building to our right collapsed, followed by a loud explosion and pieces of flaked enamel came flying around inside the driving compartment of the tank. For a minute I couldn't gather my thoughts. I remember saying to the co-driver: 'Christ!' His reply was something to the effect that his wireless had gone 'diss'.

We learned from the skipper [Major Swan] that he had seen an SP gun that required the attention of the Firefly's 17-pounder. While he was directing the fire, he spotted a Panther up the Tilly road bringing its gun to bear in our direction. He shouted to our operator to move. The shell – an HE – took us on the right-hand side while we were in reverse. It ricocheted off and exploded in the shop we were going behind for cover. When we examined the damage sustained, outwardly there was not too much to see. The shell had left some score marks about a foot long and about an inch deep.

The side of the tank was slightly concave for about 2 feet. Inwardly, the front set was out of commission, as was the forward Browning. Flakes of white enamel covered the driving compartment.[13]

With shells and mortar bombs ploughing into Lingèvres, a German attack developed from the west where A Squadron's second-in-command was observing from a hull-down position. He spotted a Panther's turret moving and waited for it to approach along the Balleroy road and engaged with his 75mm gun at a range of less than 100 yards, hitting with all three rounds, at which the panzer burst into flames. For the Germans this was the signal to 'Go'. Three Panthers charged down the road into the village, past Stirling's tank and knocked out Corporal Johnson's Sherman by the church. Sergeant Harris had, meanwhile, been back to A1 Echelon to replenish his ammunition and on returning towards the village was fortuitously in an ambush position from where he knocked out the leading Panther with a 17-pounder round into its rear flank. This set the engine compartment on fire, while the other two Panthers pressed on into the centre of the village at speed but in doing so they presented their flanks and rear to Trooper McKillop, whose next round destroyed the drive sprocket, broke the track and with its momentum sent the panzer spinning off the road near the memorial. The third Panther pressed on and presented its rear to Harris's Firefly and thus McKillop earned a Mention in Dispatches for knocking out five Panthers. Sergeant Harris was awarded the Distinguished Conduct Medal for his actions in Lingèvres on 14 June 1944.

As the battle progressed the artillery came into its own and along with the RAF's Typhoon fighter-bombers broke up German attacks all afternoon, while

Sergeant Harris of A Squadron, 4th/7th DG, and the Distinguished Conduct Medal.

the Durhams did their best to dig in and prepare positions in the buildings while under fire. Gunner Bullen commented of one FOO: 'He must have found it a little sticky as he was bringing fire down on or very close to his map reference.' With panzers often at close quarters around them, tank-hunting patrols set out to stalk them with platoons' PIATs and sticky bombs. One of these was led by Major Mogg who led several men, including a private who had carried the PIAT since D-Day! The target was a Panther that had got into the village and needed finishing off taking. Having stalked into a firing position, Mogg ordered the PIAT gunner to fire, but he confessed that he didn't know how it worked! Major Mogg took the shot, which disabled the panzer.

Another Panther, this time one that had looped around to the north-west, was reported as coming into the village from the direction of Juaye-Mondaye, probably to take the defending tanks in the rear. Gunner Bullen was alarmed when it stopped on the road on the other side of a hedge to his unarmed OP tank!

We were relieved when it moved off again, but our relief was short-lived. It stopped at the crossroads and started traversing its gun in our direction. Whether it was going to fire at us with co-ax or finish off our Sherman, we didn't know. Fortunately, a Firefly of the 4th/7th Dragoons, which looked as if it had been following the Panther, stopped where the German tank had originally halted. It fired two quick shots of AP at 300 yards; the Panther had no chance with two 17-pounders up its stern!

The road into Lingèvres is the one down which the Panther advanced from the north. The field on the left with its much-reduced hedge was where Gunner Bullen was parked.

The overflowing aid post of one of the Durham battalions. Visible are medics, a padre and both British and German wounded.

The Panther had driven past A Squadron's reserve in the hedgerows north of the village, where tanks were being rotated for replenishment and a short rest. Duly spotted, the Panther was, as Bullen described, stalked by a Firefly.

Panzer Lehr had lost about nine Panthers and self-propelled guns during the day-long battle and 6th Company of 902 *Panzergrenadiers* was virtually destroyed. 9 DLI had, however, suffered almost 50 per cent casualties and was in no state to continue the advance towards Hottot. That evening they were relieved by 2 Gloucesters of 56 Brigade.

The four battalions of 50th Division had fought to gain the Balleroy road as their initial objective on the way south to the Caumont road. The Dorsets and Hampshires had captured the crossroads at La Senaudière and 9 DLI Lingèvres, and both dominated a stretch of the lateral road which had been so important for the enemy at the cost of approximately 500 casualties across the division. While two of the initial objectives had been fully secured, XXX Corps' attempt on 14 June to salvage appreciable results from Operation PERCH had failed. Consequently, with 7th Armoured Division out on a limb and under increasing pressure from 2nd Panzer Division, there was no alternative but for them to be withdrawn.

The DLI memorial in Lingèvres.

130 *Lehr* Panzer Regiment

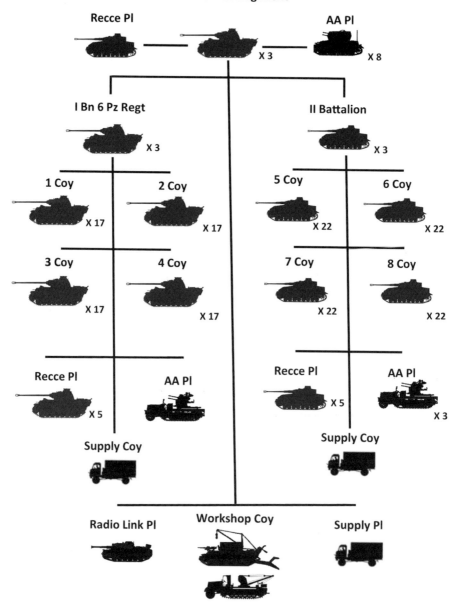

Chapter Fourteen

Hiatus

After over a week in action 50th Division was exhausted and their intention to advance south to Hottot and Villers-Bocage had been recognized as unachievable, and 7th Armoured Division had been withdrawn from their front to form a line on the flank of the British Second Army linking up with the Americans. On the other side of the hill *Panzer Lehr* had been very badly battered, with prisoners reporting substantial losses of both men and equipment. 50th Division's GSO1 recorded in his diary: 'On our front there is still 901 Pz Gr bn; from all accounts these are not in too good shape.'

Of course, with almost First World War-scale casualties to the likes of 9 DLI and whole companies of *panzergrenadiers* being virtually destroyed, both sides were suffering. The big difference was that the British had replacement equipment and, at this early stage in the campaign, plenty of reinforcements. With few replacements and a falling strength in his division, Major Ritgen wrote:

> In order to preserve the force, it was necessary to shorten the *Panzer Lehr* front. The 902nd Rgt had become too weak to be able to hold the entire sector. Its remnants were reorganised near Sermentot. The reduction of the front was made possible by the arrival of the 2nd Panzer Division on the left of *Panzer Lehr*.

Most British units as well as the division had an immediate supply of reinforcements to replace casualties known in the case of armoured regiments as 'spare crews'. A veteran of 4 CLY writing under the *nom de plume* of 'Desert Rat' describes life in A2 Echelon waiting to be called forward as a casualty replacement:

> The spare crews moved around the invasion area in 3-ton trucks following the progress of the regiment. There would be about ten men to a truck. We lived, slept and ate as a group and were issued with compo rations which came in wooden boxes containing tinned food enough for fourteen men for one day. The compo rations boxes contained everything necessary to maintain normal subsistence. All the food was tinned and was very good, but there was no bread, only hard tack, which we put in stews to make it palatable.
>
> We made every effort to get fresh vegetables, and of course eggs were a great prize. On one occasion I went with a colleague searching for eggs, going across fields, through hedges and along lanes until we arrived at a farmhouse. It was intact, but all the shutters were closed, and it seemed

deserted ... but suddenly the shutters of one of the upstairs windows were flung open and someone shouted, 'English, English!' (in French, of course).

Then we asked about the Germans and were told that they had been in the farmyard only a short while before us. The farmer thought we were the advance guard and that was the reason the Germans had gone. Needless to say, it did not take us long to leave in the direction we had come. It appeared that we had wandered into or through the front line, which of course was very fluid at that time. What we had done was very foolish, to say the least ... Our guardian angel was certainly watching over us that day, because, apart from the risk of running into the enemy, it was common practice to mine and booby-trap tracks and lanes, in particular gaps in hedges.

By 15 June most of the spare crews and officers in 8 Armoured Brigade had been called forward to the squadrons, some taking with them the newly-arrived diesel-engine Sherman IIIs to replace knocked-out petrol-driven DD Sherman Vs.

Shermans of 4th/7th DG. M4A2s (Sherman IIIs) replaced the DD Sherman Vs.

Second Lieutenant Bill Bellamy had commanded A Squadron 8th Hussars' echelon since the arrival of 7th Armoured Division in Normandy:

> I heard that Mike Browne, another of my friends and a very capable troop leader in A Squadron, had just been killed. I was devastated; that was three out of the five troop leaders in A Squadron killed or wounded in two days of action. I had hardly assimilated this news when Jack came over and told me that Philip de May, with whom I had shared all the excitements of the journey out to join the regiment in Egypt, had just been killed by shelling in the leaguer ... I was told to leave at once, adding that I was to inform Titch Kirkham that I would be leaving the echelon forthwith to become a replacement troop leader as soon as A Squadron had had a chance to reorganise.

As ever, the infantry's casualties were proportionately higher and the 50th Division's immediate supply of reinforcements that landed with them was quickly used up. From D+2 to D+8 further reinforcements were sent forward to units from XXX Corps' Reinforcement Camp in an ad hoc manner with little recognition of training or employment. 1 Dorsets' second-in-command, Major Bredin, commented on the poor quality of the replacements, many of whom, as Private Powis of 2 Devons mentions, were suddenly thrust into a regiment that was not their own:

> The number of reinforcements which arrived to rebuild our strength meant that very few Devon shoulder flashes could be seen for a while, there being so many men from other regiments attached to our unit to renew our effectiveness. The name Green Howards stands out in my mind, but I cannot remember any of the other regiments involved.
>
> There were insufficient reserves of men immediately available to bring our Brigade back to full strength so we had to rely on a number of our own wounded who were considered to be fit for further action after having been patched up for return to the fighting lines by the Field Hospital and CCPs (Casualty Clearing Posts). Some of the men were well below fighting standard, but because they could walk and were able to use the 'trigger-finger', they were passed as fit enough to carry on. Many of them who were definitely not fit enough to continue were passed and somehow kept going.

By D+8, 101 Reinforcement Group was established in Bayeux with some 6,000 replacement officers and soldiers in pre-planned allocations.[1] This greatly

Regimental shoulder flashes or 'titles'.

improved matters of quantity, if not necessarily quality. Major Bredin commented: 'The most welcome event of the day was the arrival of reinforcements, mostly from the 9th Battalion [Dorset Regiment].'[2] Where possible cap badge integrity was maintained, but in the case of heavy casualties, building a unit back up to full strength was of overriding importance.[3]

In what was now the rear area, where 50th and 7th Armoured divisions and 8 Armoured Brigade had fought through during the days immediately following 6 June, the scene was greatly changed. The 50th's divisional historian described what he saw:[4]

> On the whole, the British bridgehead did not expand at the same rate as troops poured into it, and by the 15th of June the small area of Normandy we held presented an amazing scene.
>
> Along the beaches and on their fringes was strewn the wreckage of the German defences and our landing craft and tanks, rusting memorials to the first encounters of the Normandy campaign. Where they needed space the beach groups had bulldozed the debris out of the way and set up their own installations for the handling of supplies and equipment coming in from the sea. And on the roads between the beaches and the British first line there crawled, and stopped, and started again endless streams of lorries, tanks, armoured cars and jeeps.
>
> Although the sea was rough, the sun shone, and the little roads of Normandy, subjected to a strain for which they were never built, began to disintegrate into dust. Every journey became a nightmare compounded of traffic jams, dust, heat and engine fumes. The smallest and most primitive tracks were pressed into service as one-way roads. Suitable leaguer areas for units coming ashore became harder and harder to find as airstrip after airstrip came into commission. Life in the villages became a torment to the French, for throughout the twenty-four hours heavy traffic pounded past their doorsteps in a never-ceasing stream, shaking the little cottages to their foundations and coating them with white dust.
>
> But amid all this seeming confusion and crowded bustle a great British army was being concentrated for the day when it would burst its bonds and flood through France and Belgium to the very frontiers of the Reich.

Squadron Leader Duff, an RAF Logistician (402 Air Stores Park) who supported a Typhoon Wing in 84 Group, recalled repeated journeys to the Mulberry harbour that was taking shape at Arromanches:

> Many of the roads in the bridgehead were in a one-way circuit, so as you drove up to the Mulberry you came in at one end. This meant there would be trucks carrying POWs and ambulances offloading whilst your vehicles were loading up; it was all well organised to get you out of the target area as quickly as possible. You then headed off along the one-way system back to base. If you made a navigation error you quite often had to go all the way

Summer 1944: a typical road sign in the forward area.

Squadron Leader Duff OBE.

around the circuit which took you close to the front line where your dust – it was very dry – could be spotted by the Germans and shelling followed. It was amazing how quickly the drivers improved their navigation skills. Luckily, we had no one killed.

Physical casualties were not the only ones admitted to the casevac chain. After days of intense fighting, 50th Division was suffering psychological casualties as well. Sergeant Gray of 7 Green Howards noted in his diary: 'D Coy lads all out Ok, but they've had it. We've been at it all this time without a break.'

By 15 June XXX Corps' Exhaustion Centre was open and admitting more than twenty cases a day. The majority of casualties were found among those who had returned with 50th and 7th Armoured divisions from the Mediterranean and those who had previously been treated. At this early stage in

A convoy of trucks bearing the sign of XXX Corps moving to the front on 'Club Route' in Normandy. The ace of clubs was painted on tac signs to indicate their main supply route.

the campaign most of those who went back to the Corps Centre did not return to their units. Once unit management of what were colloquially described as the 'bomb happy' improved and divisional rest centres, within the sound of the guns, were established, rates of return improved greatly from 15 per cent to 50 per cent.[5] For the Normandy campaign as a whole psychological casualties stabilized at a figure of 14 men per 1,000 who were admitted for treatment, which represented 11 per cent of all casualties.[6]

At the Front

The 15th was a relatively quiet day while both sides took stock and reorganized and adjusted their defensive positions. The war diary of 1 Dorsets recorded that after a tense night at La Senaudière, with the enemy at close quarters, the Germans withdrew towards Longraye:

> Resultant on a slight German withdrawal during the night, the Bn occupies more favourable positions S of the main Rd with Bn HQ at 777689 [see map]. A Coy in buildings 775686, B. 777688, C. 780679, D. Pt 110 and a protective OP, consisting of the I Section with a Sec of Carriers is established at 784674. Enemy are known to be still in occupation of LONGRAYE.

The battalion mounted patrols to pinpoint the enemy positions around Longraye and Onchy in order to assist 69 Brigade who were to advance through the Dorsets to Les Landes on the following day.

Private Powis of 2 Devons recalled an incident of a type that crops up surprisingly frequently in war diaries and accounts while readjusting positions around la Belle Épine:

> Our Intelligence Section left the road and entered a field with our tanks following us into the same field when the sniper shot and killed the officer who was giving instructions from the turret of the leading tank. Our 2nd Devons' men on foot pointed out to the man in the turret of the following tank that the shot had come from the hedgerow, so he immediately fired a salvo of shells at the area of hedgerow where the shot had come from. Immediate investigation of the place revealed the body of a French civilian and his damaged sniper's rifle. Anger against the French people was now outstandingly evident.[7]

In his diary for the 15th Lieutenant Taylor of 6 Green Howards (69 Brigade), who were out of the line at the time, gives a different but qualified perspective:

> Morning's rest. Stacked up to move in the afternoon. Went as far as Folliot without incident. This village bombed and shelled to hell. Spent evening talking to two men and a woman of the Resistance. Grand people, who have no resentment of their village being destroyed. Watched Thunderbolts diving. People said all France is behind us – slight exaggeration. Went to bed early.

Following 7th Armoured Division's withdrawal, out to the west 131 Brigade's right flank rested on the boundary with the Americans 2 miles east of Caumont, on a line running through Briquessard and Torteval. To 131 Brigade's left there was a 3-mile gap east to 50th Division's positions at la Belle Épine. While all the rest of the armour was leaguered to the rear, a squadron of 8th Hussars was deployed to cover this gap: 'C Sqn [the most recently-arrived squadron] came under comd 131 Bde and moved to the BRIQUESSARD area 7459 and put out a screen of observation around the position held by 1/6 Queens.'

5 Company of 304 *Panzergrenadier* Regiment of 2nd Panzer Division were opposite to them in this area and launched in several attacks: 'C Sqn were involved in close and confused fighting, but all attacks were beaten off. Lt Pegler was killed during the night.' On the Hussars' left were 130 Panzer Pioneers and elements of the recce battalion. *Unteroffizier* Henning commanding an Sd.Kfz.250 half-track reconnaissance vehicle recalled:

> To reinforce our defensive line in No. 2 Company's area we positioned our vehicles behind the earth banks. The nightmare of every panzer reconnaissance man was to lose manoeuvrability and be forced to function as protection for the infantry with its light weapons. Now we found ourselves behind

Panzer Lehr recce troops mounted in a half-track.

the earth banks in range of enemy artillery and mortar fire which went on day and night.

Each crew had to dig a large hole behind the bank and park the vehicle over it. When the enemy opened fire we crawled into this protected trench. To give ourselves a field of fire we had to cut away some of the prickly hedgerows. Daily we could see how the green meadows grew ever greyer from the dust of enemy shelling. During the day we often set off on patrol and if it was decided to adopt a new location then we had to dig a new hole.

One early morning there began a fearsome howling and screeching. Half asleep, we were rolled up near our panzer and wondered what this new racket could be. It was a battery of six-tube 15cm rocket-launchers [*Nebelwerfers*] firing at the enemy positions. This must certainly have woken the Tommies up, for shortly afterwards their answer came back ten times as powerful. The German battery had already moved on, but the reply fell around our ears and we were forced to drop swiftly into the trench below our vehicles.

Unteroffizier Henning of 130 *Panzer Lehr* Reconnaissance Battalion.

The basic form of the Sd.Kfz.250 vehicle which came in twelve special-purpose variants.

Losses among the division's *panzergrenadiers'* towed 75mm anti-tank guns, which required a large and vulnerable open gun pit, meant that 'The panzer battalions had to act as *Panzerjäger*, each having to detach a panzer company to the infantry battle groups for their anti-tank defence.'

Lieutenant Bill Bellamy, now a troop commander, recalls deploying his three Cromwells from the squadron leaguer before dawn to cover the road south and to observe the village of Granville and the valley beyond in the gap between 50th and 7th Armoured divisions:

> The sun was well up by this time and we had a splendid view over the valley. We watched and waited. This was the moment when an enemy would be likely to appear if they had detected our presence or if they were mounting an attack in our area. As the visibility improved, so we began to see enemy movement on the opposite hillsides. The noise of tracked vehicles was clear in the early morning air and there was a frenzy of activity in some woodland below the ridge which was slightly hidden from us by trees. There was no movement near us, although I had a long discussion about a possible infantry position 400 yards to our left front astride the road.

During the day a pair of 61 Recce Regiment's armoured cars patrolled down the road Bellamy was observing in the direction of Granville. They were immediately engaged:

> There was a very loud bang and the front car stopped dead in the middle of the road while the second vehicle, a lightly-armoured Humber reconnaissance car, slewed over to the right and stopped on the grass verge by the

hedge. It was all over in a fraction of a second and I looked in stunned silence as smoke billowed from the foremost vehicle. The enemy gun, probably a 75mm anti-tank gun, had been well sited to cover the crest of the hill and although we heard the crack as it fired, we could only hazard as to its exact location.

Bellamy very bravely rescued the two surviving crew members.

For the infantry in the close country with the Germans regularly changing the location of their outposts, patrolling was a dangerous business. A point in no man's land that was safe one day may not be the next: riflemen lying in wait,

Lieutenant Bill Bellamy receiving his MC from Montgomery.

a machine gun covering a low point in a bank, *Schu minen* (anti-personnel mines) planted in gaps in the hedgerows and booby-traps abounded. A 9 DLI patrol lost half a section of men to *Schu minen* laid in a gateway and some soldiers claimed to have developed a sixth sense warning them of trouble.

The 15th was also a time to reflect on operations so far. Having visited front-line units, 50th Division's GSO1 commented: '... we haven't the technique for this country yet. Our tactics fall short and we don't take advantage of this country. Worth much thought.' Major Mogg, who now commanded 9 DLI, commented:

> There is no doubt the Durhams were too slow to appreciate it as first-class infantry country to be made use of and not feared. At first, we were slow to dig slit trenches; we were inclined to use houses, which were apt to become artillery targets and were more frequently booby-trapped. We were slow to use the ground as infantry country and expected to move behind heavy artillery barrages and air strikes in the nature of the battles in the Western Desert. Carrier platoons were of little value except to help in quick consolidation or dismounted as an extra infantry platoon. The anti-tank platoon had to be content with short fields of fire and the mortars came into their own with a vengeance, learning to fire off maps instead of by direct observation and doing so with deadly effect.

DLI wounded receiving treatment at an aid station.

While officers pondered their tactics, the pause in operations on the British right flank could not be allowed to last long as Montgomery needed to 'keep the battlefield alive'. In his *Memoirs*, he explained:

> On the eastern [Second Army] flank ... the acquisition of ground was not so pressing; the need there was by hard fighting to make the enemy commit his reserves, so that the American forces would meet less opposition in their advances to gain territory which was vital in the west.

With the 49th Division now fully committed to its left, the 50th Division was to renew its attacks on Tilly and south towards Hottot and Les Landes on D+10, 16 June 1944.

The Infantry Carrier Platoon

In addition to Universal Carriers found across a battalion and the anti-tank platoon's Loyd Carriers, the infantry fighting in Normandy in 1944 had a dedicated carrier platoon. The role of this platoon and its thirteen Universal Carriers, developed from earlier Bren and Scout carriers, had morphed into one of providing mobile logistic support and a number of tactical roles, again based on mobility.

Being both armoured and tracked, a carrier platoon could be more successful in reaching infantry positions across country and/or under fire that could not be reached by the battalion's soft-skinned wheeled transport. During attacks some carriers typically accompanied the advance, but most were used for ammunition resupply and the evacuation of casualties. Tactically, a carrier platoon using its mobility could conduct more wide-ranging reconnaissance than the traditional dismounted patrol. Using its protection and the fire-power of their Bren guns they could manoeuvre into position to give fire support or act as cut-offs. The Dorsets' carrier platoon did just this at Bazenville on D+1 (see page 44).

Training manuals stressed that the Universal Carrier was not a light tank and should not be used as such. The carrier's armour was only proof against small arms and smaller shell splinters.

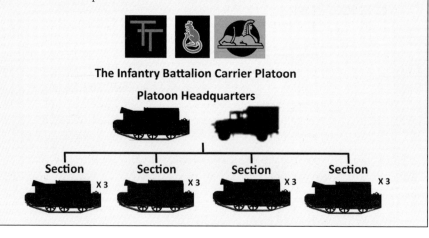

The Infantry Battalion Carrier Platoon

Platoon Headquarters

Section   Section   Section   Section

X 3   X 3   X 3   X 3

Chapter Fifteen

Tilly-sur-Seulles: 16–18 June

Lieutenant General Bucknall's plan for XXX Corps' renewal of operations on 16 June was for the 49th Division to repeat 6 Green Howards' attack on Cristot but this time a little further north from Audrieu, while 69 Brigade, after something over thirty-six hours out of the line, were to attack through 231 Brigade in the direction of L'Oraille (see Chapter 16).

Meanwhile, 2 Essex were to return to the front and recce the German positions around Tilly, prior to a renewed attempt there. To the west 7th Armoured Division was to mount tank and infantry patrols to coincide with 69 Brigade's attack. They were to probe 'from BRIQUESSARD towards AMAYÉ-SUR-SEULLES. Some confusion rose as to the exact locations of enemy and own troops. Tanks of the 1 RTR and the 1/6 Queen's were able to penetrate as far as ST-GERMAINE and were able to secure useful information.'[1]

For almost a week *Panzer Lehr* had stoutly held Tilly as a bulwark against a direct advance south to Villers-Bocage by 50th Division and Bayerlein's command had also thwarted all attempts to bypass it to both the east and the west. For the next attack, 2 Essex were brought forward and came under command of 151 Brigade, having had a period out of the line to reorganize after their blooding at Essex Wood. Brigadier Walton's plan was for 2 Essex to attack Tilly using the Bayeux road as their axis, with 6 DLI echeloned to their right rear. The Durhams would start from the village of Marcel an hour after the Essex, on an axis 500 yards to the west of the Tilly road. This line of advance would take the Durhams through the area where they had fought on 13 June.

On the evening of the 16th the Essex occupied trenches around Bucéels where orders were issued for recce patrols to provide Colonel Elliot and his battery commander with vital information on topography but above all the enemy positions that they would face the following day. After dark patrols pressed carefully towards Pont de la Guillette, where they located German outposts covering the road and flanks. Slipping between them they crept on, looking and listening, towards Tilly, which they found to be still heavily defended. A renewed attack on Tilly was, however, expected by *Panzer Lehr*. Major Ritgen wrote:

> The anticipated attack against Tilly started with the commitment of strong artillery and with the support of simultaneous attacks conducted along the entire front … Tilly was held by *Kampfgruppe* Schone (II/Battalion, 901 *Panzergrenadier* Regiment) with support from assault guns of the *Funklenkkompanie*.[2]

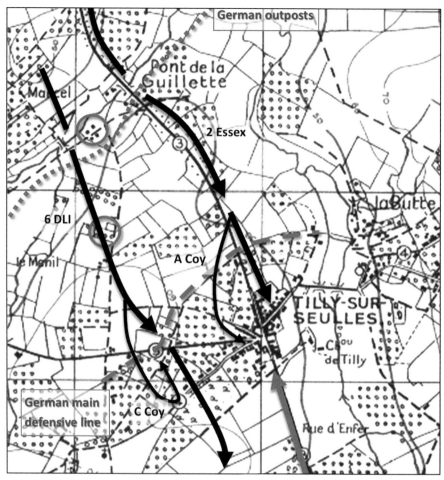

151 Brigade plans, 16–18 June 1944.

2 Essex

With 69 Brigade attacking further to the west on the afternoon of 17 June, 2 Essex's advance got under way at 1600 hours, with A and D companies leading, supported by a troop of Shermans of A Squadron, 4th/7th DG. According to the battalion's history: 'It was a stiff fight forward, with the main Bayeux-Tilly road as a directional guide to the two forward companies advancing astride it through the thick bocage country.' Nonetheless, the companies pushed south through the German outpost line and within the hour were at their positions for the assault on Tilly. A war diary entry timed 1700 hours reads: 'Arty support called for to help Coys onto objective.' The regimental history adds details:

> Again, the enemy observation points had been well selected, and soon artillery support was necessary to help A and D Companies forward. Snipers,

Spandaus, artillery and booby-traps in ditches and hedges all hindered but did not stop the 'Pompadours'[3] advance, until right in front of the main defences the advance slowed and finally lost momentum.

The following war diary entries paint a picture of slowing progress and greater resistance despite considerable artillery support:

1913 hours: A & D Coys temporarily delayed by snipers.
1948 hours: A Coy meeting opposition – difficult to deal with.
Still well short of the village, one of the supporting Shermans was disabled by a Teller mine.

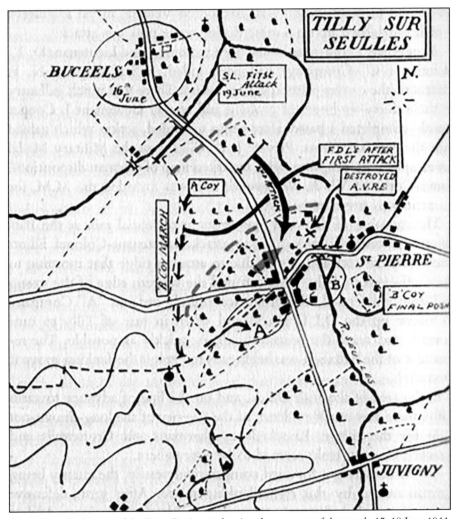

A map from the history of the Essex Regiment showing the progress of the attack, 17–18 June 1944.

2018 hours: D Coy temporarily held up by SPANDAU fire.
2045 hours: D Coy report two left-hand objectives taken.
2200 hours: D Coy report objective reached.

At 2227 hours Colonel Elliot called a halt, as the remainder of the companies were pinned down still about half a mile short of the centre of the village and darkness was falling. Consequently, they were ordered to hold their ground and dig in. Battalion Headquarters was brought forward to an orchard about 500 yards south-east of Pont de la Guillette.

The Essex's attack had started well; but it was met with determined resistance to their front by II Battalion, 901 *Panzergrenadiers* and by nine *Sturmgeschütz* of 316th *Funklink* Company in their conventional role.[4] Both were supported by Flak 36/37 88mm guns firing HE and armour-piercing rounds in the ground role.

Not only did the Essex have a strong force to their front, but were also hampered by fire from the left flank, where enemy infantry had infiltrated up the Seulles valley onto the western slopes of Point 103. The Essex were halted short of the hedgerows and orchards through which the Gloucesters had fought the main German defences during their attack on 11 June.

6th Durham Light Infantry

The battalion began its part of the attack at 1700 hours, but the leading companies, C and D, were soon in difficulty under machine-gun, rifle and mortar fire from the farm buildings by the stream between them and the Essex at Pont de la Guillette. Meanwhile, B Company on the battalion's right rear was being engaged by small-arms fire from that flank.

The enemy outposts by the stream were cleared by the Durhams who, on familiar ground, made good tactical use of the cover provided by undulations and the hedgerows, with the vulnerable Shermans of A Squadron, 4th/7th DG providing fire when they could from the rear. The veterans of the Western Desert and Sicily were learning to cope with the bocage, in the same way that the Fourteenth Army found that the 'jungle was neutral'. The hedgerow country provided the attacker with covered approaches for movement, infiltration and fire positions. As Major Mogg reflected after Lingèvres, 'it was good infantry country'. Corporal Root recalled:

> It helped that we knew a bit about the ground from the last time we were there. Rather than going across the fields deployed as a platoon, we [sections] worked our way up the hedges and ditches with another section or platoon ready to give covering fire. As we did the time before, we used smoke but when Jerry got wise, we fired it to his rear to worry him and draw his fire. It wasn't quick but it worked, and I remember when we got around him, we used a lot of grenades.

Making steady progress, D Company on the left reached and cleared a second farm complex and continued on south, driving back the German outposts until

A Company, 6 DLI moving tactically to the FUP for the attack.

darkness settled, upon which they dug in to the left of the axis track. C Company, on the right, however, had forged on and reached the line of the Tilly-Balleroy road, but they were out on their own without radio communications. The company commander could not contact either battalion headquarters or his platoons, which made the task of command very difficult, particularly coordination with the Shermans.

If the lack of radio contact was not bad enough, C Company now found themselves halted in the uncomfortable position of being behind a hedge on one side of the road, with the road as no man's land between them and the enemy in the opposite hedge. Any sound or movement by either side prompted the exchange of grenades; fortunately, the supply of these was limited. Having almost reached their objective, isolated and at far too close a proximity to the enemy, C Company withdrew some 200 yards into line with D Company. B Company dug in behind, providing depth to the battalion's defences.

The Attack Renewed: 18 June

The weather had been unseasonably cold for some days with regular rain showers, but on this day the rain set in with a vengeance along with increasing wind. The deteriorating weather grounded most close air support and air ops; the latter in turn reduced the amount of naval gunfire available as well as its accuracy.

With Brigadier Walton, who had only been in command of 151 Brigade for two days, being wounded on 16 June, Colonel Lidwill of 8 DLI was again back in charge of the brigade. He held orders at 1000 hours, confirming details of the attack, which was to be a continuation of the previous day's advance to the Hottot road. It was already apparent that 151 Brigade would be aided by the progress made by 49th Division, which following the capture of Cristot had recaptured Saint-Pierre and was maintaining pressure on the boundary between *Panzer Lehr* and the *Hitlerjugend*. In particular, 10 DLI had already mounted an attack on an orchard south of Saint-Pierre at 0400 hours.

The commanding officers and the commander of B Squadron, 4th/7th DG were briefed that the advance of two battalions would be preceded by a creeping barrage fired by three field regiments, which would advance at a rate of 100 yards every five minutes. The armour was instructed to move forward with the infantry companies, engaging hedgerows and identified enemy positions as required. Machine guns mounted in carriers were to harry the enemy from the flanks. The artillery fire plan duly began at 1430 hours and fifteen minutes later the creeping barrage set off into the enemy position.

6 DLI, as they had the previous day, advanced with C Company on the right and D Company on the left. Communications within the battle group on this occasion worked well and the coordination of both artillery and 4th/7th DGs'

A knocked-out Panther on the way up the Bayeux road from Pont de la Guillette.

Shermans was very effective. All three arms worked together to overcome the enemy hedgerow by hedgerow. By 1540 hours, B Squadron's tanks were reporting being on a line half a mile north-east of Tilly. In the words of one of the Durhams' officers who took part:

> Tanks crashed through hedges, shooting into hedge junctions and giving magnificent support. The fire brought down on the enemy was simply terrific, and he was well and truly blasted out of his positions. Once the attack started to move there was no stopping it, and the forward companies had a magnificent day; they kept pace with the barrage and D Company had the good fortune to see the Boche get up and run for it.

The combination of effective British tactics and days of being pounded by naval gunfire, artillery and air attack had done their work on the German fighting spirit and for the first time the *panzergrenadiers*, rather than standing and fighting, were seen pulling back as the Durham infantry platoons' assaults went in.

At 1700 hours, 6 DLI were reporting digging in on their objective, the high ground to the south-west of Tilly. While the infantry dug as quickly as possible,

A knocked out Panzer IV and its dead crew.

the gunner FOOs prepared fire plans to help defeat the inevitable enemy counter-attack. In another sign that the German grip on their defences was slackening, no significant counter-attack was launched, although the Durhams reported that the supporting M10 tank destroyers and Shermans knocked out two Panzer IVs, while the artillery put down defensive fire. Casualties had been light and the men's spirits were high. The lessons so painfully learned by both the infantry and tanks over the previous twelve days were now in regular use across the 50th Division when fighting in the hedgerows.

For 2 Essex, however, it was another day of hard pounding and slow but steady progress towards well-defended Tilly. During the morning it was reported that the church tower was being used by the Germans as an OP, probably by artillery and/or mortar observers. Consequently it was included as a target in the early stages of the afternoon's pre-attack fire plan. This would help to blind the German artillery just as it would be needed most, as the Essex advanced.

The regimental history describes Lieutenant Colonel Elliot's plan:

> He knew that the 6th DLI was due to attack a ridge that morning to the south-west of Tilly, passing round the western edge of the strong and stoutly-defended village. He accordingly ordered A Company to follow up the DLI attack, and when in rear of Tilly to turn inwards and reach the central square as quickly as possible. The remainder of the Battalion was held ready to exploit the flanking move if successful.

At the same time as 6 DLI began their advance through the bocage at 1445 hours, the Essex attacked the main German positions dug in in the battered remains of the orchards north of Tilly with D Company right and C Company left. As the barrage lifted onto the edge of the village the battalion's leading companies, which were well within 'danger-close',[5] were up and on top of the forward German positions and fighting through. Three troops of 4th/7th DGs' Shermans and a troop of AVREs from 81 Assault Squadron RE accompanied the infantry. The battalion's war diary records that at 1555 hours C Company was in the out-skirts of Tilly and was clearing the houses. Other companies closed up, finding difficulties moving forward through the rubble but it wasn't just rubble blocking the way: 'There was much evidence of the severity of the long-drawn-out fight for the village. Knocked-out Shermans and Cromwells and wrecked German tanks seemed to be everywhere.'

The wreck of an AVRE that had previously fallen victim to a mine was found almost totally blocking one avenue of approach and another AVRE supporting the Essex in making its way over a pile of rubble ended up on its side in a ditch. The Essex's B and D companies, tanks and AVREs continued to batter their way through the *panzergrenadiers'* well-established positions. Colonel Elliot knew that he was going to have to fight to hold his gains and had arranged for the bat-talion's 6-pounder anti-tank guns to be brought into the village by D7 armoured bulldozers, which would also prepare positions for them in the rubble.

The 79th Armoured Division's D7 and D5 armoured bulldozers had been used to clear beach obstacles but now found another role amid the rubble of Normandy.

Meanwhile, A Company, despite successfully getting around the western flank of Tilly as far as the Balleroy road, did not precipitate a collapse of the German defence. The ring was, however, steadily closing on the defenders and A Company dug in on the western outskirts of the village. *Panzer Lehr* was not ready to give up the fight and at 1642 hours 10 DLI in Saint-Pierre reported 'ten Panthers or Tigers' assembling; this was the expected counter-attack. Major Ritgen wrote:

> After heavy fighting, the enemy was able to suppress a portion of the combat positions, formed out of the ruins of houses, in Tilly. The counter-attack conducted that evening by the Panther Battalion made only slow progress. Its commander, Major Markowski [I/130 *Panzer Lehr* Regiment], was wounded by artillery fire. *Hauptmann* Jahnke took over the battalion.

The infantry element was provided by 2nd Company, 130 *Panzer Lehr* Pioneer Battalion. Private Cordon of C Company recalled that

> We were working our way through the wreckage of people's houses. After days of shelling most had lost their roofs and bits of stone were constantly falling around us, dislodged by bullets and shell splinters. Our tanks would shoot up a building with HE and MG and in we would go. We quickly discovered to avoid doorways which could be booby-trapped with a jumping mine [*Schu Mine*] and went through the windows which were all smashed or holes blasted by the tanks.
>
> We were getting on when their artillery and mortars started up seriously and we heard the sound of German tanks coming our way – by now we knew what Shermans sounded like.

With both British tanks and German panzers in the village the armoured battle around the crossroads was conducted at very close range. One AVRE took on a Panther that crossed the main road with its petard mortar,[6] but the round hit a telegraph pole a yard from the panzer; nonetheless, the detonation of the demolition round was enough to immobilize the Panther, probably as a result of the blast. Other than this, the surviving AVRE's demolition gun was able to reduce a number of troublesome buildings for the Essex.

As the panzers came into the village it transpired than not all platoons had brought their PIATs into Tilly and now they regretted it! Private Cordon continued:

> The sound of the tanks firing their main guns at each other, machine guns going and shells exploding was terrible and the building I was in was collapsing around me. All we could do was to keep our heads down until our

The AVRE's petard or spigot mortar and its 290mm 'flying dustbin' demolition round.

Corporal shouted 'Enemy infantry' and kicked those who were too slow
getting to their feet. Across this open area we could see between the burning
smoke, figures moving through the houses heading towards our boys there
[D Company]. We shot at them, taking care to fire from well inside the
rooms – if a tank saw the flash of a rifle or Bren, the next thing would be
boom – and you would be gone!

The counter-attack failed, with the German armoured advantages of fire-power
and protection being largely negated in the close-range engagements, but the
Essex could not complete the capture of the village and were left holding the
northern part. They had, however, with A Company to the west and D Company
to the east almost enveloped Tilly. Further out, with 6 DLI on the high ground
south-west of the village and 10 DLI firmly holding Saint-Pierre to the south-
east, Tilly was now a very narrow salient and an inevitable trap for continued
defence. Consequently, General Bayerlein gave the order to withdraw overnight
but not before instructing the pioneers to redouble mine-laying and the placing
of booby-traps. Major Ritgen commented: 'Due to the shortage of forces, the

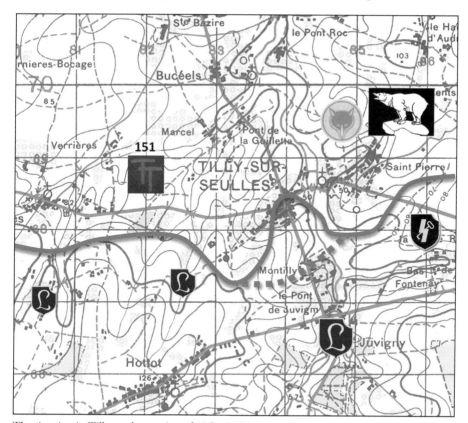

The situation in Tilly on the evening of 18 June 1944.

hotly-contested Tilly was given up, after it was mined, and the main line of resistance was withdrawn to the Montilly-Sagy line.'

The Fall of Tilly: 19 June 1944

With the rain still falling, it was a damp and muddy 2 Essex, unaware that the enemy had gone, that prepared to renew their attack and complete the capture of Tilly:

> 0800 hours: The Bn were ordered to attack again by the right flank. Enemy shelling was then reported as falling on Tilly. Accordingly, the CO decided to push on for the village as it appears that enemy might have pulled out. This was done. Bn was able to secure the village.

The companies had to advance into the village through heavy artillery fire, including 88mm HE and mortars, to their objectives. A Company worked from their flanking overnight position through the buildings to the centre of the village

Destruction in Tilly.

Even after the German withdrawal from Tilly, it remained a dangerous place.

A wrecked carrier in the centre of Tilly being checked with a mine-detector after the battle.

Tilly, a puppy found in the ruins of the village, became a somewhat disrespectful mascot of Headquarters Second Army.

to secure the south-west quadrant, while B Company moved up from reserve and went forward to clear the château that dominated the approaches from the south and south-east. The regimental historian concluded that

> After some defensive mortar fire and shelling, the enemy pulled back to Juvigny. And so Tilly-sur-Seulles was finally taken, the last advance into the village being at the cost of eight ranks wounded. The village and all roads leading to it had been most thoroughly mined and booby-trapped, and its entry and occupation were extremely hazardous. Further casualties were caused in the village by the numerous Teller mines.

> All through the 19th the Battalion was subjected to very heavy artillery fire, German 88mm guns firing air-bursts in some of the most brilliantly accurate shooting experienced during the whole campaign.

Chapter Sixteen

The Western Flank:
16–19 June

While 151 Brigade were preparing to renew the attack on Tilly, with 2 Essex under command, 69 Brigade was back in action on 50th Division's right flank. The brigade had originally been moved west where it was to have exploited success by 231 Brigade in their attack south from la Belle Épine and La Senaudière on 14 June. However, without a breakthrough, General Graham's plans for 69 Brigade had been revised; now they were to take over the attack and secure L'Oraille and clear the woods that the Germans were known to be using for assembling armoured counter-attacks west of Longraye.

69 Brigade: L'Oraille, 16 June

The operation saw all three battalions in action. 6 Green Howards were to lead off from Bernières-Bocage, through 2 Devons' positions south of la Belle Épine and secure L'Oraille as a firm base by 0900 hours. From here the brigade's axis of advance was the road leading south-east from L'Oraille, with the task of 'mopping up woods west of LONGRAYE'. 5 East Yorks were to advance on the northern side of the road, led by C and D companies, supported by a troop of AVREs, while 7 Green Howards were to the south, supported by a squadron of 24th Lancers. H-hour for the attack towards the woods was 0930 hours.

Batteries of 90 and 147 Field regiments were to fire in support of 69 Brigade's advance, but due to a lack of detailed tactical intelligence regarding German deployment, plus limited planning time, a proper fire plan was not possible. For example, artillery support to Yorkshiremen of 6 Green Howards south of la Belle Épine was limited to 'known enemy positions and one hedge ahead of the advance'. The 4.2in mortars of 2 Cheshires from the divisional machine-gun battalion were also in support.

6 Green Howards' signals officer, Lieutenant Taylor, recorded in his diary: 'Set off early. No trouble to la Belle Épine. Resistance on way to L'Oraille held us up. Went thro' L'Oraille and had to stop.' Nonetheless, the battalion had secured the start lines for the remainder of the brigade by 0900 hours.

A section commander in 7 Green Howards' carrier platoon, Sergeant Gray, recorded in his diary: 'Reveille 0300 hrs and Battalion started to move forward,

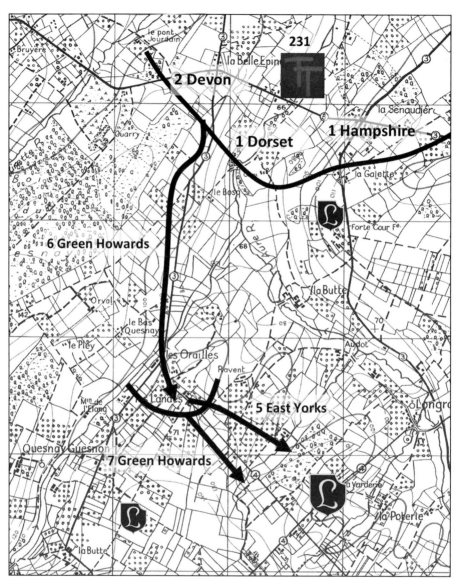

69 Brigade's advance on L'Oraille and attacks south on 16 June 1944.

carriers leading, at 0530 hrs to form up on start line at L'Oraille by 0900 hrs, a squadron of tanks with us.' The war diary covers their phase in the operation:

> After mortar (4.2in) barrage bn crossed SL. D Coy on the Rd followed by B Coy. C Coy on the right followed by A Coy. Carriers and 1 Sqn 24 LANCERS were making sweep patrols to the sides of the road. The going for tanks off the road was bad and progress was slow.

Sergeant Gray's entry for the day described the battalion's short-lived advance on the Longraye Woods:

> Started to advance but didn't get far before boys ran into hellish Spandau fire and tanks. Casualties rising and we are kept busy getting them out [Casevac], Christ but it's hell and old Jerry certainly knows his ground. Tanks unable to move on account of the closeness of the country.

Private Tateson, also of 7 Green Howards, recalled:

> On coming under fire, the men would go to ground in the standing crops and I was constantly hearing the message that one or other platoon was pinned down. The tanks which were endeavouring to give support lost contact since they had no clear field of vision. On one occasion our section was crawling along the side of a hedge when the chap in front of me disturbed a wasps' nest. The wasps came up in a swarm round our heads, but round his in particular; he immediately came up on his knees and started beating around with his hands in spite of our urgent demands of 'For Christ's sake get down.' Whether he was seen or not I don't know but soon afterwards a burst of machine-gun fire rattled through the hedge and twigs dropped on me as we lay motionless. Perhaps it was simply desultory fire at any hedge where we might be lurking, since after a time we were able to press on.

A casualty being evacuated by 7 Green Howards' carrier platoon.

In close country enemy positions were missed and the *panzergrenadiers* infiltrated in from the flanks. Sergeant Gray MM in a frank entry in his diary reveals the ferocity of the fighting south of L'Oraille:

> Boys reached first objective but had to pull back because of fire from the rear. You can't see the bastards, which makes things so nerve-wracking. Wish that we were back in the old desert. Moved into TAC HQ and consolidated. Strengthened A Company front with our Brens. Nearly copped us that time. In a cottage with Captain Murray and brigadier when Jerry whipped a tank up and let bang at close range. Brigadier wounded and two killed, but my luck held out again. Wish I could stop a cushy one. About time they brought a fresh division in, as our lads have had it, but they still stick in. Brassed hell out of us all night. Very few old lads left now.

Captain Isaac, the intelligence officer of 69, was with Brigadier Knox watching the attack by 7 Green Howards. During the battalion's advance Major Boyle, D Company's commander, had been mortally wounded and some fifteen men became separated from the rest of the company and, leaderless, were pinned down in a ditch by very heavy fire. Captain Isaac dashed forward and led the soldiers back to the company. Here, due to officer casualties, Isaac, who had previously served in the sister battalion, 6 Green Howards, took over command, reorganized the company and through sheer force of personality that earned him an immediate Military Cross[1] led the whole company forward. Regardless of heavy machine-gun and rifle fire, D Company took the enemy position. By the time the enemy were dealt with both of the commanders of the leading companies had been killed. Private Tateson wrote: 'The sudden loss of these two officers had a depressing effect on us all, particularly those who had served with the battalion all throughout the Western Desert. We were in a very sombre mood.'

7 Green Howards and their supporting tanks had advanced just 800 yards.

Meanwhile, 5 East Yorks advanced south-east on the Longraye woods, which proved to be strongly held and the fight was far from the 'mopping-up' quoted in their orders:

> 0930: Bn with one Tp AVREs under command advances south from track 765667 [L'Oraille]. C and D fwd. Heavy opposition from MGs in wood 7765–7766 [Longraye].
>
> 1130: On rt of axis on rd running south from L'ORAILLE met heavy opposition including SP 88mm guns.[2] Bn ordered to reorganise where it was. Mortaring and shelling of Bn area throughout remainder of the day.

5 East Yorks had made similarly little progress south before being halted in the southern portion of the woods, adjacent to 7 Green Howards' leading companies.

Carefully sited in the hedges and woods ahead of 69 Brigade were panzers. *Hauptmann* Ritgen commented on the tactics, which been forced on the panzer regiment, of deploying Panthers and Panzer IVs in lieu of anti-tank guns:

> The commitment of panzers in small groups was contrary to the principles of armoured warfare, but it was unavoidable, because there were not enough *panzergrenadiers*, and the air situation, terrain and artillery fire limited the mobility of our panzers. These tactics, however, proved effective in holding the front but they depleted our panzer strength and prevented the withdrawal of the division for its proper mission, the conduct of mobile combat.

69 Brigade's arrival in L'Oraille and the prompt advance by two battalions had meant that a dangerous situation had emerged for *Panzer Lehr* and General Bayerlein hastily assembled a counter-attack, including II Battalion of Panzer Regiment 130 and the *Hitlerjugend*'s Escort Company. When it was launched, the British gunners were waiting. Even though the quantity of artillery support was less than would normally be expected, *Hauptmann* Ritgen wrote of its impact:

> Particularly dreadful was the heavy artillery barrage that broke over us when we were jammed in a sunken road between other panzers. The fragments rained down like hail, damaging periscopes and antennae and covering everything in smoke. My driver lost his nerve, cried for his mother and got us stuck.
>
> From the outside our panzers looked a mess. Antenna, vision blocks, etc., as well as *zimmerit*[3] were no feast for sore eyes. We could not fight without communication and we withdrew unsuccessful.

Even though the initial counter-attack had not forced 69 Brigade back, it had ensured that they remained halted digging in. Tactical headquarters of the

A *Jagdpanzer* IV.

6th Battalion was established in a farm complex in L'Oraille. Lieutenant Taylor described an unpleasant and dangerous situation:

> Tanks and 88s shelling our positions. 88 thro' window five feet above my head. Dug in rather quickly near farm buildings. Shelled steadily all afternoon and evening. A few casualties. Pte Bready became very drunk on local brew[4] and had to be evacuated under close arrest. Shelling struck me as most unpleasant so far as we had to sit and do nothing. Could not attempt our objective – Le Lion Vert.

69 Brigade's advance on a broad front across the Tilly-Balleroy road had greatly alarmed the Germans, with *Obergruppenführer* Sepp Dietrich from HQ I SS Panzer Corps signalling Rommel that British tanks had broken through at Longraye. To contain 69 Brigade General Bayerlein had been forced to form *ersatz* units of clerks, drivers and cooks. Unaware of the brigade's near success, as far as 50th Division were concerned, the attack against *Panzer Lehr*'s determined resistance had been halted, having gained very little ground beyond L'Oraille. In contrast to the despairing notes to be found in British war diaries, words of praise

A 4.5in gun of 211 Battery in action in support of the 50th Division. The battery was a part of 5 AGRA, which was getting stronger by the day, with arrivals across the beaches daily.

Every Normandy farmer produced cider and Calvados from his apple trees.

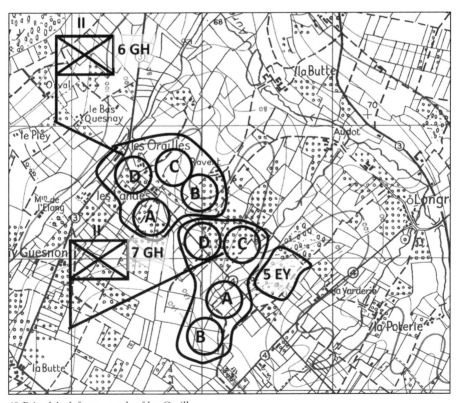

69 Brigade's defences south of les Orailles.

for *Panzer Lehr* are everywhere in German reports: '*Panzer Lehr* has especially distinguished itself.'

As the axis road was covered by enemy fire, 7 Green Howards built a track to the west of the road for resupply and communication with the forward companies, and overnight both the forward battalions dispatched patrols to locate the enemy.

At the eastern end of XXX Corps' area 49th Division's attack on Cristot during 16 June had been successful. The *Hitlerjugend* had, unlike *Panzer Lehr* at Longraye, retired, leaving only a handful of outposts to be swept aside by the well-supported attack.

The Attack Resumed: 17 June 1944

69 Brigade's patrols brought in information on enemy positions well to the south and orders were duly issued for a resumption of operations. This time, however, they were designed to expand the salient they had created to the east of the River Aure, closing up towards 151 Brigade at Lingèvres and Verrières. Brigadier Knox's plan was for 7 Green Howards to relieve the 5 East Yorks in the Longraye Woods and for that battalion to extend the area held into the northern part of those woods. The 5 East Yorks in turn were to relieve 6 Green Howards in L'Oraille, freeing up that battalion for the offensive operation. Once 6 Green Howards' attack developed east of the Aure, 7 Green Howards were to advance from the woods towards Longraye in a pincer movement.

6 Green Howards were to march back 2 miles north cross the Aure and form up in orchards near La Senaudière, which had been secured by the Hampshires. From here they were to strike south-east to Point 113 and from there to the hamlet of La Taille where 69 Brigade's pincers would close.

At 1030 hours 6 Green Howards were in the orchards near La Senaudière and preparing to advance at 1330 hours. Their war diary describes the action:

> … the Bn moved forward to occupy the area of the crossroads at LA TAILLE, intention being to advance along both sides of the LINGÈVRES-CUNCHY road. Owing to the close country progress was slow and the battalion was continually engaging the enemy who offered stiff resistance with mortars and Spandaus.

By 1600 hours they had reached Point 113. Here they were halted until reorganized and helped forward again by artillery down the axis of the Lingèvres-Cunchy road, but by 1800 hours they had been halted about halfway to La Taille and were digging in.

During the morning 7 Green Howards extended their control of the woods and sent a platoon-sized patrol from A Company down into the river valley, but they were beaten back. At 1345 hours A Company, which had been relieved in their position by the Carrier Platoon, began their part in the day's fighting. The war diary records that 'A Coy commence to pass through D Coy and B Coy with one pl on the west of the road which pass through C Coy.'

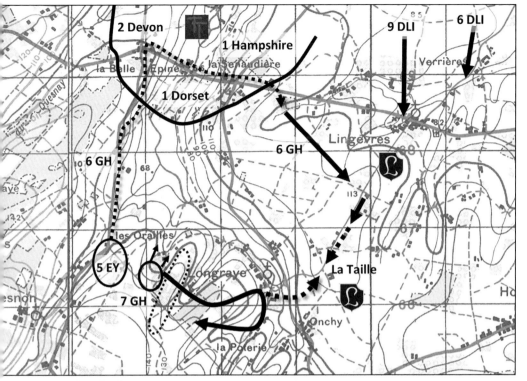

69 Brigade's plan for 17 June 1944.

Carrier section commander Sergeant Gray provides a flavour of the day's fighting:

> Took over from [5] East Yorks and once more we tried to push forward but it's sheer suicide. The country's absolutely rotten with snipers and Spandaus. The lads have had it and they'll have to pull them out.
>
> My section [of carriers] takes over A Company's position while they try to advance; did we get hammered, but we had to stop there. Poor old [Sergeant] Topper runs into a Spandau and gets five bullets in him. Marvellous piece of work by an officer getting him out. Doc thinks he might pull through. Hope so, as he's the best sergeant in the Battalion and hates Jerries more than anyone, on account of him seeing his brother killed next to him at Akarit.[5]

A Company supported by a second company changed tactics and 'infiltrated to within 200 yards of the GRANVILLE–LONGRAYE rd and were then held up with enemy MG and Mortar fire'. With 6 Green Howards halted short of their objective, the companies withdrew back to the woods. Sergeant Gray continued his account of the day:

> A Company starts to pull back about 1600 hrs and Jerry spots 'em – sent over everything he had and I just missed it again – saw three chaps killed by the same shell that knocked me daft, not 3 yards off me and Ike. Dick Staveley and Allen wounded and that left three of us to go and get them out. God

knows why we weren't hit. Much more and I'll have had it; shaking like a leaf so we'll get the brew on before it gets dark.

Kampfgruppe Gerhardt (130 *Lehr* Recce Battalion) reported that they counter-attacked 'enemy forces that had penetrated south-west of Longraye and captured fourteen prisoners'.[6] Longraye remained in German hands and overnight, when one of 7 Green Howards' patrols approached the village, it was rebuffed by heavy fire.

Panzer Lehr recce troops mounted in a well-camouflaged half-track vehicle.

Attack and Counter-Attack: 18 June 1944

The morning of 18 June was relatively quiet across the divisional front but, as Sergeant Gray recorded in his diary: '. . . then, more "fun and games" as the brass hats call it, in the afternoon. God, but they're sending us in again.'

At 1430 hours, the task of attacking, as Sergeant Gray feared, fell on 7 Green Howards. This attack, designed to precede and draw enemy reserves away from that by 2 Essex on Tilly-sur-Seulles, had as its objective some high ground east of La Croix des Landes, which dominates the Hottot road. B Company remained north of the road, while D Company relieved by A Company moved across the advance south of the road. A Company would subsequently 'mop up' La Varderie Farm, which would be bypassed in the initial advance (see following page).

The attack went well against slight opposition, but by 1600 hours panzers were reported to the front. Anti-tank guns were rushed forward, but could not get into a position to knock them out and C Company was moved up to provide depth.

The adjutant recorded at 2000 hours that an 'Enemy tk passed A Coy travelling from LONGRAYE stopped at X rds 777654 [X on the map] and was quickly brewed up by an M10 of 99 A/tk Bty.' This was a part of increased enemy activity and fire which by 2100 hours was preventing all movement and the commanding officer, Lieutenant Colonel Williams, was pinned down, stopping him from coordinating the battalion's defensive position, but just before last light at 2200 hours, as recorded by Sergeant Gray: 'I knew it would happen, Jerry let us get right through and then counter-attacked with tanks. What hell.' The war diary reads: 'Strong enemy counter-attack of infantry supported by tanks. B Coy was overrun and the OC and others believed taken prisoner.'

Major Ritgen wrote of events on the 18th:

The 69th (British) Brigade tenaciously continued to try and break through the thinly-occupied positions of the 130th ALA [Recce Battalion].[7] However, the old line was always restored by counter-attack. On 18 June 3rd Company of 130 ALA were attacked after a strong mortar preparation. The company withdrew but was able to create the prerequisite for a counter-attack to restore the original line with the support of eight-wheel armoured cars, light infantry guns and the engineer platoon. The 3rd and 4th companies of 130 ALA conducted this counter-attack with such surprise and motivation, together with the 12th SS Panzer Division Begleit [Escort] Company that the enemy was overrun.

Sergeant Gray was altogether less dispassionate:

The OC, Major Hudson and all B Company lost. Absolutely overrun before we could dig in. What confusion, but would the lads be blamed for it?

At it every day since D-Day with only one break and still no sign of any relief. I thought that we were the assault Division and after that finish, but it

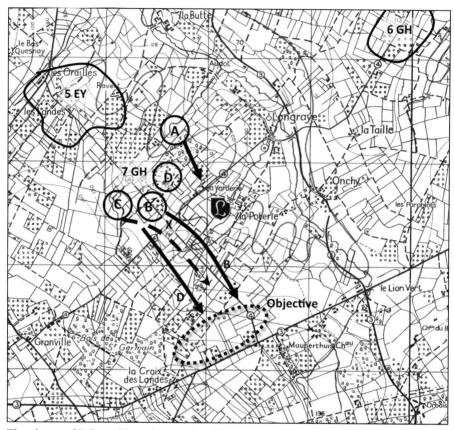

The advance of 7 Green Howards on 18 June 1944.

looks as if we're going to get all the shit again, just as it was in the desert, but we've got to keep going and something will turn up, but God knows what.

The battalion, with D and C companies forward barely dug in, now faced a withdrawal in contact with the enemy; one of the most difficult phases of war and in increasing darkness too. D Company fell back through C Company as the light failed. Sergeant Gray and the other carriers covered the withdrawal back towards 5 East Yorks:

> Had to fall back to where we started from and carriers fought a rearguard while what was left of the Battalion regrouped. Casualties for the day about 250 including the CO and stacks of arms and equipment. Ike's section and mine took up positions with the East Yorks for the night and then went to strengthen C Company in the morning.

The battalion's losses were grievous with some 125 casualties, plus 120 taken prisoner. Lieutenant Colonel Williams escaped and returned to the battalion.

Major von Fallois (left), commander of 130 Reconnaissance Battalion, and General Bayerlein.

The following day 4 officer and 144 other rank reinforcements arrived with the battalion.

A note in the 50th Division's operations diary for 19 June reveals that Sergeant Gray was not alone in thinking that 'The lads have had it.' 'Brig Knox represented that his bde was not fit for further offensive action.' To make matters worse, 'heavy rain and therefore no air support or observation.'

Despite the increasingly bad weather, the following day Sergeant Gray was more positive:

> If it wasn't for this diary I wouldn't know what day or date it was. Battalion more or less regrouped as much as possible. Pouring with rain and a cold north wind blowing, everybody soaked to the skin and very miserable. Must be great to be in England right now. I'd give a hell of a lot for a few more nights out like we used to have at the Spa in Weymouth. Two more letters from Bids today, bless her, and feel 100 per cent better after receiving them. Still no sign of any relief.

The Attack on Hottot: 19 June 1944

After several quiet days it was 231 Brigade's turn to 'keep the front active', with an attack on Hottot and the next important lateral route the Juvigny-Caumont road. Brigadier Stanier's plan was to attack the long straggling village, which was reported to be held by two companies of *panzergrenadiers*, with 2 Devons on the left and 1 Hampshires right. 1 Dorsets were to take over the defences around Point 103 from 6 Green Howards during the morning and subsequently advance, protecting the brigade's right flank, with Château de Cordillon as their objective.

One of 2 Cheshires' 4.2in mortars in action against Hottot.

288 Battery of 102 Anti-Tank Regiment provided a troop of M10s to each battalion and the Vickers machine guns and 4.2in mortars of the Cheshires were in support in addition to the divisional artillery and the guns of 5 AGRA.

Due to the heavy artillery barrage, the FUP was on the Tilly-Balleroy road with the actual start line, which was marked by the battalions' intelligence sections, with white tape, some 600 to 700 yards south. Due to the heavy rain that persisted all day, there was no close air support to the attack. Lieutenant David Holdsworth, a platoon commander in B Company on the battalion's left, wrote:

> Someone, we were told, had laid out white tapes to mark the place from which our attack was to start. In bright sunshine these white tapes might have been easy to find. In teeming rain, they were very nearly invisible. However, we found them, took up our positions, and prepared to advance on Hottot behind a 'creeping barrage'.[8]

The preliminary barrage opened at 1300 hours and the Germans, knowing that the attackers would be forming up, replied. The Hampshires recorded that 'Enemy mortars & 88mm guns shelled the area of the

Brigadier Stanier, commander of 231 Brigade.

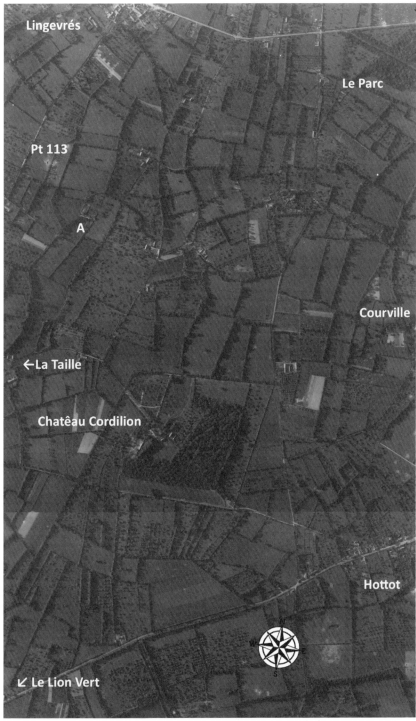

Lingevrés

Le Parc

Pt 113

A

Courville

←La Taille

Château Cordilion

Hottot

↙ Le Lion Vert

A montage of air photographs of the area covered by 231 Brigade's advance taken two days earlier and used by 1 Dorsets during the attack.

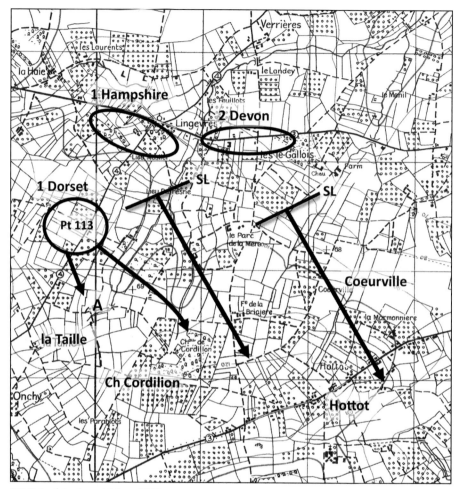

231 Brigade's plans, 19 June 1944.

start line mercilessly' and the Dorsets lost their commanding officer, Lieutenant Colonel Norrie, who was badly wounded along with both the mortar and anti-tank platoon commanders.[9] The Devons recorded that 'The right-hand coy, C Coy, came under MG fire about 200 yards short of the start line', which is never a good start.

2 Devons

Under continuing heavy fire and pouring rain, the first phase of the operation began: the clearance of more than a mile of bocage. The Devons' left-hand company, B Company, with Lieutenant Holdsworth to the fore, crossed the start line, dubious about the creeping barrage: 'With my platoon I scrambled over a hedge and into the field on the far side. Shells burst only about 100 yards ahead of us. But the artillery were as good as their word. As we advanced, so they increased their range.' Holdsworth continued:

> We were halfway across the field when enemy bullets began to zip round our legs and bodies. We didn't need much training to help us to decide what to do next. We threw ourselves down onto the soggy, dripping grass. And then we remembered that we too had firearms. I doubt whether we hit the enemy, but it did us the world of good to fire back.

The war diary states: 'So now both forward coys were under rather heavy but inaccurate [partly suppressed?] MG fire from about 300 yards range. The country was extremely close with high standing corn and grass, and very thick hedges.'

Meanwhile, to the Devons' right, as noted by the Hampshires' adjutant: 'The Bn advanced in spite of the shelling and stiff resistance of the opposing Pz Grs supported by tanks dug in north of HOTTOT.' B Squadron of the 4th/7th DG were available to support 231 Brigade's infantry, but

> For the first time the tanks were not called for by the infantry brigadier in impossible or unnecessary tasks, the country again being close and most unsuitable for tanks. The infantry, using their own anti-tank weapons, claimed four enemy tanks, believed to be Tigers. B Sqn did not have much of a shoot and were largely occupied in getting themselves into proper positions to meet any tank threats, which was very difficult. Up to 1600 hrs there was tremendous artillery support (the whole of the Corps artillery being available) ... B Sqn remained in mobile reserve.[10,11]

Major Ritgen wrote:

> ... the enemy attacked at the junction between the 901st and 902nd Regiments. While *Kampfgruppe* Welsch (902nd) was able to eliminate all penetrations, the enemy pushed back the German line in the *Kampfgruppe* Scholze's sector of operations to the edge of Hottot.

Colonel Neville's plan for 2 Devons saw C Company advancing on the right and B on the left, with D Company following 'mopping up'. A Company remained in the FUP. In the bocage the Devons record that the creeping barrage was 'on an optimistic schedule, moving further and further ahead until its value was almost gone' and the Devons were halted:

> The Commanding Officer called for D Coy, only to find that it did not exist as a company. In the close country the coy had become split up and platoons and sections had lost contact. Thus the Commanding Officer called for A Coy, who were at this time in the FUP providing the firm base.

With A Company coming up on the left and C Company going around to the right, the German position was outflanked and with the barrage marching onwards, the Devon companies were left to battle 'against successive lines of close-set, well-sited machine-gun posts'. The battalion made slow but steady

Panzer Lehr grenadiers and a Panther. The half-track mounts a 75mm gun as found in the Heavy Company.

progress and reached Coeurville, with A Company covering the brigade's open left flank and advancing to cut the Hottot road east of the village. A pair of *Sturmgeschütz* IIIs approached from the left, but were knocked out by an M10 Tank Destroyer.

With D Company reorganized and brought up to Coeurville, at 1820 hours B and C companies reported being in Hottot having driven *Kampfgruppe* Scholze from the village. Lieutenant Holdsworth wrote:

> We got up and continued our advance. Through the trees on the hill in front of us we could make out the vague outlines of some buildings. This was Hottot.

The rain stopped and the sun came out. The gunners behind us stopped shelling. We reached the main road which ran through the village and looked up and down. To our right, about 400 yards away, was a monster of a tank with a gun on its front that was so long as to make it look ridiculous. Men could be seen alongside it and on its turret.

Three members of my platoon, which had been necessarily split up during the attack, made their way towards the tank. It wasn't clear to me whether they had recognised their first German Tiger tank or not. They ought to have done because the men beside it certainly weren't wearing British uniforms. Nor was it clear whether the German tank crew had recognised us as British soldiers. The three members of my platoon weren't taking any particular care as they made their way down the road. Equally casually, the Germans clambered onto their tank and slowly disappeared, one by one through the turret. As the last German heaved himself into the turret a rifle shot rang out. The man in the turret dropped out of sight. The lid of the turret clanged down and the road was sprayed with German machine-gun bullets for about ten seconds.

Holdsworth, looking back towards the half of his platoon on the 'dangerous side of the road', found them ignoring the battle, picking strawberries from the French gardens!

The war was temporarily forgotten. The German Tiger tank need not have existed. The German crew firing the machine gun down the road was of no account. The strawberries in Hottot were delicious and my troops were

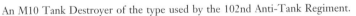
An M10 Tank Destroyer of the type used by the 102nd Anti-Tank Regiment.

determined to make the most of them. They were kind enough to offer me some.

Strawberries eaten, rejoining the rest of the platoon on the other 'safe' side of the road was the next issue:

The road through Hottot ran perfectly straight, but there was a bit of a kink in it a few yards away from us, and it was a little narrower. I decided that we'd have to dash, one by one, across the road at this narrow kink and so rejoin the rest of my command.

The first man hurled himself across the road. There was a burst of machine-gun fire, but he was safe. The second, third and fourth man each made it safely, with the machine-gun fire just a fraction too late. The fifth man stumbled as he reached safety and jettisoned a large part of his equipment into the road. Numbers 6, 7, 8, 9, 10, 11 and 12 all made it, to the accompaniment of cheers from their comrades and machine-gun bullets over the last few feet. Then it was my turn. Number 13. Whether the rest of the platoon realised this I don't know. I did.

A Panther hull-down below the level of the bank in a Normandy lane.

He made it, but with the tank rumbling towards them the platoon stared into the road to where number 5 had dropped their PIAT. The platoon disappeared into cover and the panzer ground on past:

> A few minutes later shells crashed into the streets of Hottot, ripping up trees and gardens all around us. We dug ourselves deeper into whatever cover was available. We had great confidence in the Royal Artillery but wondered why it was considered necessary to be firing on us!

1 Hampshires

The Devons had a tenuous hold on Hottot, but to their left the Hampshires had been halted by *Kampfgruppe* Welsch short of the village, where they dug in. Lieutenant Blackmore of A Company described the action:

> We pushed forward under a heavy barrage with our Brens fighting a staccato duel against the faster b-r-r-r-p of Jerry's Spandaus. In the din it was difficult at first to know which was his artillery and which was ours, but one soon

An oblique air photograph looking south, showing the dense network of hedges that brought the Hampshires to a halt short of Hottot. The Dorsets' objective, Château de Cordillon, is bottom right.

realised where the 'receiving end' was when we reached a sunken lane, evidently well pinpointed by the enemy. Several men in D Company (the leading formation) were also held up in this lane. But the place was decidedly too hot for comfort, so we climbed up the bank and dashed across the next field through a hail of mortar bombs and bullets, luckily without any casualties. We shoved over a lot more artillery than the enemy; he seemed to rely more on his mortars.

We got to close quarters with him at a farm. One of his Panther tanks came rumbling forward right up to our position, firing everything it had. With great presence of mind, one of our anti-tank gunners caught the Panther amidships, but not before it had managed to get one of our Shermans [probably an M10]. Both caught fire but the Sherman crew managed to get out all right. The 'brewed up' tanks, now well ablaze, began to attract heavy mortar fire, and although A Company were still supposed to be in reserve, we moved forward towards the farm where Major J. Littlejohns (commanding 'D' Company) had set up his headquarters.

No sign of the rain stopping after ten hours. Everyone is tired and wet; we have moved forward nearly a mile from La Senaudière, with Hottot just another 1,000 yards ahead.

1 Dorsets

Meanwhile, the Dorsets covering the right flank had been advancing from Point 113 on Château de Cordillon, having recovered from the loss of their commanding officer. A and C companies led the battalion south. Almost immediately, they too came under mortar and machine-gun fire, this time from La Taille out to their right, with A Company suffering particularly heavy casualties. The advance stalled, having made less than 500 yards. The war diary records that 'Communications broke down, several sets being damaged, and line parties are sent out to try and lay [telephone] lines to coys.' Major Bredin, who had assumed command, ordered A and C companies to reorganize, while D Company on the battalion's left pushed on and reached an orchard north of Château de Cordillon at 1530 hours: 'There they encountered two or three PANTHER tanks. One is hit by a PIAT and the crew were shot whilst climbing out. D Coy are ordered to remain in position, whilst B Coy continue to advance towards the château.'

To the relief of the company the three Panthers, including the one damaged by the PIAT, drove away south but not for long. While A and C companies were still stationary just south of Point 113, B and D companies were ordered to resume the attack on the château. D Company would provide the fire support and B Company were to carry out the assault.

With B and D companies reorganizing around the château, Major Bredin, reduced to moving on foot, returned to Point 113:

It became obvious that so long as the strong enemy positions at La Taille on our right flank remained, any further advance by A and C companies towards

A section of 1 Dorsets' mortars in action near Château de Cordillon.

the château was for the time being out of the question. This also meant that no anti-tank guns could be moved up to B and D companies, who were now being heavily counter-attacked. (Determined efforts were made to get some of the anti-tank guns up to B and D companies, risking the mines, but the carriers became stuck or bogged.)[12] Some very bitter fighting ensued and many brave deeds were performed, but parts of both companies were overrun.

With the companies' appeals for anti-tank guns impossible to answer, they only had PIATs with which to contain the six or seven Panthers that spearheaded the counter-attack at 1630 hours. Officers, NCOs and soldiers of the two companies had to fight hard to extricate themselves and rally the surviving platoons. Thirty-one men were listed as missing from these two companies.

Meanwhile, the much-reduced A Company out to the right had 'a severe fight' for a small gain in ground towards La Taille and reached some buildings (A on the map), where they were halted.

Panthers and *panzergrenadiers* assemble for a counter-attack.

At the End of the Day

At 1820 hours 2 Devons were reporting that three of their companies were in Hottot, with D Company in Coeurville covering the open left flank. At this point the remains of the two Dorset companies were being withdrawn from Château de Cordillon, which allowed the Germans to switch their attention to the Devons in Hottot. With low cloud, wind and rain, *Panzer Lehr* could deploy and redeploy without fear of Allied fighter-bombers, which in good weather paralysed movement during daylight. Major Ritgen wrote: 'The counter-attack by the reinforced Panther Battalion first swayed to and fro and then enjoyed some success.'

Lieutenant Holdsworth recalled that

> At last a message arrived by runner from the company commander telling us to hold our position overnight and to withdraw at first light. It was the longest night I can remember. Even a tin of cold mixed vegetables was welcome.
>
> As we withdrew at dawn in single file, we had to negotiate a barbed-wire fence. One of my soldiers bent down to get under the wire. He slipped and his finger touched the trigger of his rifle. The soldier in front of him was shot dead.
>
> A wet, tired and depressed platoon dug itself into a defensive position not very far from the point at which it had been launched into the attack.

The positions held by XXX Corps on 20 June 1944.

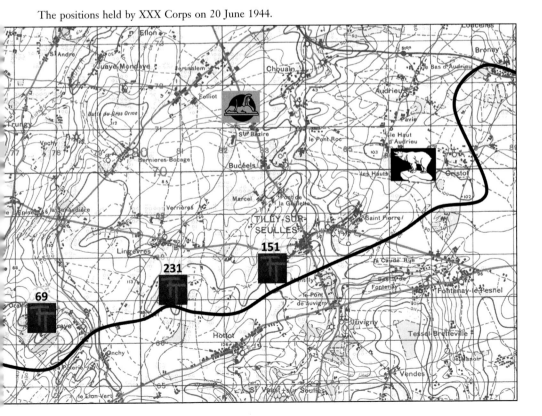

That morning the Germans reoccupied the village of Hottot and the 50th Division's operations diary noted:

> Very expensive fighting in this close country. Arty barrage seems to be good. Prisoners (one a Pole) say that *Lehr* Div may have only 3,000 effectives, 4.2in mortar fire devastating and many infantry killed. Counter-attacks appear to be almost unsupported by infantry now. Enemy will probably try to reinforce this div soon.

After two weeks in action 50th Division was 'fought out' and even though tactics were improving, the cost of fighting in the bocage was all too apparent. Further east the ground was more open and 49th Division, though suffering heavy casualties in fighting the *Hitlerjugend*, was still fresh and with the 15th Scottish and 11th Armoured divisions arriving, the plains towards Caen would be where

Montgomery and Major General Graham during a visit to Headquarters 50th Division.

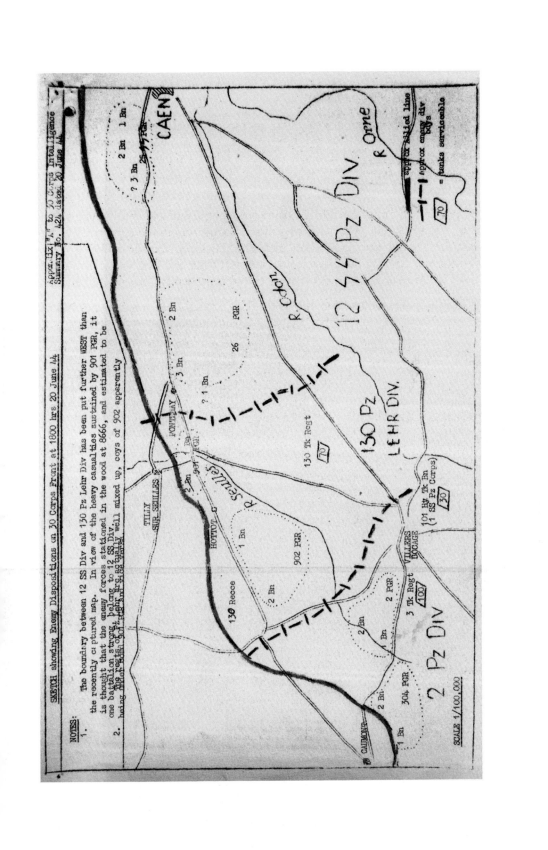

SKETCH showing Enemy Dispositions on 30 Corps Front at 1800 hrs 20 June 44

NOTES:

1.   The boundary between 12 SS Div and 130 Pz Lehr Div has been put further WEST than the recently captured map.   In view of the heavy casualties sustained by 901 PGR, it is thought that the enemy forces stationed in the wood at 8666, and estimated to be one battalion strong, belong to 12 SS Div.

2.   being the Regts of Pz Lehr are actually well mixed up, coys of 902 apparently

CAEN

2 Bn 1 Bn

25 PGR

? 3 Bn

2 Bn

26 PGR

R Odon

3 Bn

? 1 Bn

PONTIGNY

2 Bn

901 PGR

TILLY
SUR SEULLES

R Seulles

HOTTOT

1 Bn

902 PGR

2 Bn

130 Recce

2 Bn

2 Bn

Bn.

2 Bn

304 PGR

1 Bn

CAUMONT

2 Pz DIV

3 Tk Regt 100

2 PGR

VILLERS
BOCAGE

101 Hy Tk Bn
(1 SS Pz Corps) 30

130 Tk Regt
TU

**130 Pz
LEHR DIV.**

12 SS Pz DIV.

R Orne

= approx Allied line
------- = approx enemy div boys
70 = tanks serviceable

SCALE 1/100,000

Montgomery's next blow would fall. The rainstorms that had soaked 231 Brigade had, however, been accompanied by strong winds that slowed the in-load of men, equipment and combat supplies across the beaches to a trickle for vital days. Consequently, it wasn't for a further six days that the next of Montgomery's 'colossal cracks', Operation EPSOM, was launched.

For the 50th Division, however, having been fighting for 'nearly a fortnight while the main force was coming ashore, there was a further long and arduous spell in the line without relief'. War diaries, memoirs and histories are united in saying that for the division this was one of the most unpleasant periods of the entire war. It was not just sitting quietly in defence, but as the Hampshires' war diary records, there was 'A policy of continuously punching the enemy at various points in his defences was put in place. And maintained relentlessly. Aggressive fighting patrols penetrated the enemy lines by day and by night and engaged the enemy with all arms at their disposal.'

The division would keep the front active as Montgomery required and attacks such as that on Hottot on 15 July continued until the break-out began at the end of that month.

For *Panzer Lehr*, the division was being progressively destroyed before General Bayerlein's eyes, with Major Ritgen estimating the division's losses by the end of the first fight for Hottot as '160 officers and 5,400 men killed, wounded or missing with only 66 of the 190 panzers operational'. For them there was little rest, inadequate food and few replacements of men or equipment.

Orders of Battle
8–19 June 1944

50th (Northumbrian) Infantry Division – Major General Graham

Headquarters 50th Division

69 Infantry Brigade – Brigadier Knox
5th Battalion, East Yorkshire Regiment
6th Battalion, Green Howards
7th Battalion, Green Howards

151 Infantry Brigade – Brigadier Senior,
  Lieutenant Colonel Lidwill and
  Brigadier Walton
6th Battalion, Durham Light Infantry
8th Battalion, Durham Light Infantry
9th Battalion, Durham Light Infantry

50th (Northumbrian)
Infantry Division

231 Infantry Brigade – Brigadier Stanier
1st Battalion, Hampshire Regiment
1st Battalion, Dorsetshire Regiment
2nd Battalion, Devonshire Regiment

Divisional Troops
61st Reconnaissance Regiment
2nd Battalion, Cheshire Regiment (Machine-Gun and Mortar Battalion)
90th Field Regiment, RA (SP)
86th Field Regiment, RA (SP)
74th Field Regiment (towed), landed D+2
102nd Anti-Tank Regiment (Northumberland Hussars), RA
25th Light Anti-Aircraft Regiment, RA
50th Division, Royal Engineers
233rd, 295th and 505th Field Companies, RE
235 Field Park Company, RE
50th Division, Signals
50th Division, Provost Company
149th Field Ambulance, RAMC
186th Field Ambulance, RAMC
200th Field Ambulance, RAMC

50th Division, Ordnance Field Park RAOC
50th Division, Royal Electrical and Mechanical Engineers

Attached to 50th Infantry Division

56 Infantry Brigade – Brigadier Pepper
2nd Battalion, Essex Regiment
2nd Battalion, Gloucestershire Regiment
2nd Battalion, South Wales Borderers

56 Infantry Brigade

8 Armoured Brigade – Brigadier Cracroft
4th/7th Royal Dragoon Guards
Nottinghamshire (Sherwood Rangers) Yeomanry
24th Lancers
147 (Essex Yeomanry) Field Regiment, RA (SP)
8 Armoured Brigade Workshops
265th Forward Delivery Squadron
552nd Company, RASC
168th (City of London) Light Field Ambulance,
   RAMC
987th Field Artillery Battalion, US Army (SP 155mm)
B and C Squadrons, Westminster Dragoons (Flails)
C Squadron, 141st (Buffs) Regiment, RAC (Crocodiles)
73rd Anti-Tank Regiment, RA
81st Assault Squadron, RE (AVRE)
82nd Assault Squadron, RE (AVRE)

8 Armoured Brigade

7th Armoured Division – Major General Erskine

Headquarters 7th Armoured Division

22 Armoured Brigade – Brigadier Hinde
1st Royal Tank Regiment
5th Royal Tank Regiment
4th County of London Yeomanry (The Sharpshooters)
1st Battalion, Rifle Brigade (Motor)

131 (Queen's) Infantry Brigade – Brigadier Ekins
1st/5th Battalion, Queen's Royal Regiment (West Surrey)
1st/6th Battalion, Queen's Royal Regiment (West Surrey)
1st/7th Battalion, Queen's Royal Regiment (West Surrey)

Divisional Troops
3rd Support Company, Royal Northumberland Fusiliers
8th King's Royal Irish Hussars (Reconnaissance)
263rd Forward Delivery Squadron
3rd Royal Horse Artillery
5th Royal Horse Artillery
15th Light Anti-Aircraft Regiment

7th Armoured Division

65th Anti-Tank Regiment (Norfolk Yeomanry)
4th and 621st Field Squadron and 143rd Field Park Squadron
7th Armoured Division, Signals
58th, 67th, 507th Companies, Royal Army Service Corps
2nd Light Field Ambulance, 131st Field Ambulance, 29th Field Dressing Station,
 70th Field Hygiene Section, 134th Mobile Dental Unit
7th Division, Ordnance Field Park, RAOC
7th Division, Royal Electrical and Mechanical Engineers

*   *   *

130th *Panzer Lehr* **Division** – *Generalleutnant* Bayerlein

Divisional Headquarters

Panzer Lehr **Regiment 130** – *Oberst* Gerhardt
I Battalion (Panthers)
II Battalion (Panzer IV)
316 Funklenk Kompanie

*Panzergrenadier-Lehr-***Regiment 901** – *Oberst* Scholze
I Battalion, 6th Panzer Regiment
II Battalion
Infantry Gun Company (SP)
Pioneer Company
Light Flak Company

Panzer Lehr

*Panzergrenadier-Lehr-***Regiment 902** – Oberst Welsch
I Battalion (Detached)
II Battalion
Infantry Gun Company (SP)
Pioneer Company
Light Flak Company

Divisional Troops
Panzer-*Artillerie-***Regiment 130** – Major Zeister
I Battalion (Detached)
II Battalion
III Battalion
992 Medium Artillery Battalion (attached)
Feldersatz-Bataillon 130 (Medical)
Panzer-*Aufklärungs-Lehr-Abteilung* 130 (Recce) – Major von Fallois
Heeres-Flak-Artillerie-Abteilung 311 (88mm Flak)
Panzerjäger-Abteilung 130 (*Jagdpanzer* IV)
Panzer-*Lehr-Pionier-Bataillon* 130 (Engineers)
Panzernachrichten-Abteilung 130 (Signals)
Panzer-*Versorgungstruppen* 130

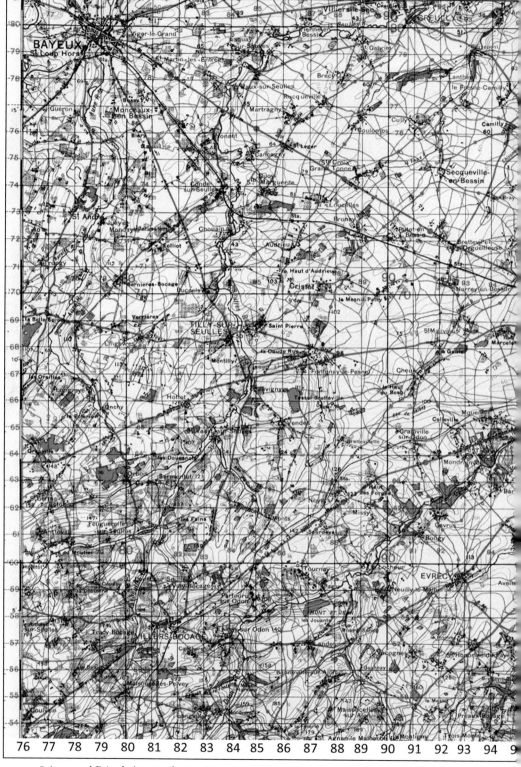

8 Armoured Brigades's area of operation.

8 Armoured Brigade's Operation Order

This is a detailed extract from Brigadier Cracroft's Operation Order No. 25 regarding the advance to Villers-Bocage via Point 103. It was issued to his units on 25 May 1944.[1]

INTENTION

5. 8 Armoured Brigade Group will advance to and dominate the area VILLERS BOCAGE 8157, with the object of holding up German forces moving towards our Bridgehead.

METHOD

6. On receipt of codeword YAR from 50 (Northumbrian) Division HQ, [8 Armd Bde] units will assemble in area MARTRAGNY 8676 – BRECY 8878. Trace in Appendix 'B' shows unit assembly areas. The codeword will be followed by a time by which units which have already landed will reach the assembly area. Unit commanders including Battery Commander and 2 OPs from 86 Field Regiment will report for orders to Brigade Tactical HQ at the time by which assembly is to be complete.

   If it is necessary to alter the assembly area the codeword YAR will be followed by a map reference in the new assembly area to which unit commanders will report for allocation of unit areas.

7. Axis
   RIGHT: ST LEGER 8675 – Road junction 876747 – ST. PIERRE 8568 – JUVIGNY 8466 – VILLERS BOCAGE.
   LEFT: Road junction 905731 – Road junction 872680 – Road junction 880678 – Road junction 868674 – MONTS 8561 – VILLERS BOCAGE.

8. Bounds
   1st Bound: Point 103 – Point 102 8769. Codeword THAMES.
   2nd Bound: High ground East and West of wood 8666. Codeword OUSE.
   3rd Bound: High ground just NORTH-EAST of VILLERS BOCAGE. Codeword SHANNON.

9. It is intended to move forward in three parties –
   (a) Forward Reconnaissance
   (b) Main party
   (c) Rear party

10. Forward Reconnaissance
    (a) Commander: Lieutenant Colonel Sir W.M. MOUNT, Bt TD
    (b) Composition: 61 Reconnaissance Regiment (less one Squadron)
        One Squadron 24th Lancers
        Two detachments 505 Field Coy RE
        OPs of 86 Field Regiment
        Possibly one Battery 147 Field Regiment
    (c) Task
        1. On D-Day to recce routes on axis and to advance and make good
           second bound, and if light permits to send reconnaissance further
           forward.
        2. On D plus 1 to advance and make good third bound.
    It is vital to move some vehicles on axis so that this can be reported clear for
    subsequent use.

11. Main Party
    (a) Advance Guard
        Commander   Lieutenant Colonel W.A.C. ANDERSON
        Composition 24th Lancers (-)
                     One Company 1 DORSET
                     OP 147 Field Regiment
        The Advance Guard will probably move on both routes dependant [*sic*]
        on reports of Forward Recces.
    (b) LEFT Axis   Brigade Tactical HQ
                     One Advanced Dressing Station from 168 Light Field
                     Ambulance
                     Detachment 505 Field Coy RE
                     Section Valentine Bridgelayers
                     147 Field Regiment less one battery
        RIGHT Axis   1 DORSET (less one company) with under command:
                     'A' Company (Machine Guns) 2 CHESHIRE
                     288 Anti-Tank Battery (less one Troop)

12. Rear Party
    (a) Commander   Lieutenant Colonel R.G. BYRON
    (b) Composition 4th/7th Dragoon Guards
                     Sherwood Rangers Yeomanry
                     Main Brigade
                     Brigade 'B' Echelon
                     Brigade HQ OP Tanks
    (c) Task To be prepared to move out not before 1200 hrs on D Plus 1 on
        either axis to join Brigade on final objective.

13. Artillery
    Tasks
    (a) 86 Field Regiment and one Battery 147 Field Regiment will support
        from the bridgehead area movement out of forward reconnaissance on

D-Day and to continue support of forward reconnaissance on second bound.

(b) One Battery 147 Field Regiment moving with forward reconnaissance on D-Day will support forward reconnaissance on to third bound at first light D plus 1.

(c) 147 Field Regiment, on reaching third bound, to register all likely approaches with a view to denying enemy use of roads into the VILLERS BOCAGE area.

14. Anti-Tank

Tasks

(a) To be prepared to co-ordinate an anti-tank layout on first and second bounds.

(b) With support of armour to co-ordinate an anti-tank defence of firm base on third bound.

15. Machine Guns

Task to assist in defence of firm base on third bound or before if required.

16. Royal Engineers

Each of two detachments with Advance Guard will consist of one M14 and [?] men equipped with mine detectors and explosives. Detachment with Main Body will consist of one 3-ton truck and two bulldozers.

Task

To develop left axis as a two-way route. If left axis proves unsuitable then on orders from Brigade to develop right axis in lieu.

17. Marking of Routes

Rear Party will mark axis from Tactical Divisional HQ to Tactical Brigade HQ, with Brigade axis signs. See Appendix 'C'.

ADMINISTRATION

18. Issued separately.

INTERCOMMUNICATION

19. Brigade Tactical HQ

Location of assembly RUCQUEVILLE 8777.

Route on left axis.

20. Signal Instructions

Issued separately.

21. Liaison

LO (Lt Northern) on frequency of 'C' Squadron Inns of Court Regiment on D-Day.

LO (2/Lt Burgess) on frequency of 2 Canadian Armoured Brigade on D plus 1.

German infantry advance supported by a StuG III and an engineer company halftrack.

A lightly camouflaged Panzer V panther.

101st *Schwere* Panzer Battalion and Tiger Reliability

by Richard Hone

The Route to Normandy

The Battalion's start point was in the vicinity of Gournay-en-Bray where the battalion had been located since 3 April 1944.

7 June. March on the D316 to the junction of St Jean de Fromelles via Gournay-en-Bray and Mornay. 1st Company strafed by *Jabos* at Mornay. The march continued on the N14 to Paris, passing the Arc de Triomphe to Versailles. The 2nd Company and Maintenance Company are hit by an air strike near Versailles.

8 June. 1st and 2nd companies continue via Verneuil L'Aigle. From there 1st Company proceeds via Vimoutiers to the area south of Caen. The 2nd Company marches via Argentan to Falaise. The 3rd Company returns to Paris and starts single tank movement to the west the next day. Numerous attacks by *Jabos*.

9 June. Road marches carried out only at night due to the Allied air threat.

10 June. 2nd Company were strafed by fighters in Argentan and again hit by fighters at Occagnes. One enemy plane shot down by *Unterscharführer* Warmbrunn. 2nd Company arrives in Falaise during the night.

12 June. 1st and 2nd companies arrive at their assembly areas, having experienced numerous mechanical problems en route. 1st Company were deployed in reserve behind 12th *Hitlerjugend* SS Panzer Division, 5 miles north-east of Villers-Bocage and 2nd Company was located near Villers-Bocage behind *Panzer Lehr*, 1.5 miles east of Villers-Bocage near Point 213. Battalion Headquarters was collocated with Headquarters I SS Panzer Corps.

13 June. Battle on Point 213 and in Villers-Bocage.

14 June. Island Position Battle.

15 June. The 3rd Company was several days' march behind the rest of the battalion, so did not take part in the Villers-Bocage battle. The 3rd Company arrived at its assembly area near Évrecy and during the night was hit by a heavy bomber strike. Eighteen men were killed and eleven wounded. Two Tigers

burned out. One overturned, killing its crew. The company commander's tank turret was blown off. 138 civilians were also killed.

Tiger Reliability

By the time that the 101st *Schwere* Panzer Battalion had completed its 150-mile march and reached the invasion front between 12 and 15 June, the companies had the following Tigers serviceable out of a strength of fourteen:

1st Company (Commander *Hauptsturmführer* Möbius): 8 Tigers situated; 6 under repair.

2nd Company (*Obersturmführer* Wittmann): 6 Tigers; 8 under repair. One of the Tigers did not take part in the attack due to track damage, another wouldn't start and another was under repair.

3rd Company (Commander *Hauptsturmführer* Schweimert): 4 Tigers at Falaise; 10 under repair. Arrived 15 June.

Battalion Headquarters (Commander *Obersturmbannführer* Westernhargen): 3 Tigers.

The Tiger was *not* significantly less reliable than other German tanks, provided that sufficient time was spent on *planned preventative maintenance*. On a route march, a maintenance stop was required every 8 to 10 miles. Additionally, after three days of action/driving the Tiger required a further day spent in maintenance. These periods were absolutely essential for such complex vehicles and they were all too often ignored, due to a combination of ignorance, senior commanders' demands and tactical expediency.

A broken-down Tiger undergoing a power-pack lift by workshop troops and its crew.

A Tiger of 101 *Schwere* Panzer Battalion towing another broken-down tank.

Typical substantial mechanical defects calculated using figures from two Tiger units, one in Russia and one in Normandy, are as follows:

Brakes, steering and transmission – 34 per cent
Final drives – 25 per cent
Engines – 24 per cent
Radiators – 17 per cent

Minor repairs carried out by company fitters and panzer crews were not recorded, but would also have been a significant contribution to the delay in getting to the battlefield with tracks and road wheels requiring constant attention.

Broken-down Tigers would have to be towed to a place of shelter for work to be carried out. Three of the normal recovery vehicles, the Sd.Kfz.9 tractor, would be required to tow a Tiger. The workshop company in a Tiger battalion was fortunate to have a *Bergepanther* for such tasks and it had its own radio which assisted with speedy tasking.

The fatigue suffered by the panzer crews and mechanics during the battalion's road move to Normandy would have been enormous.

The commander of a Panther company photographed near the Juaye-Mondaye Abbey, 10 June 1944.

7th Armoured Division's Situation Report

The SITREP below was passed to one of XXX Corps' liaison officers at 1945 hours on 13 June 1944.[1]

7 ARMD DIV SITUATION REPORT

22 Armd Bde entered VILLERS BOCAGE without opposition early this morning. They pushed on to the high ground just behind and lost five tks to a tk gun fire.

1/7 Queens cleaned up VILLERS BOCAGE of snipers. The position then began to worsen with enemy attacks starting from the South. TIGER tks penetrated into VILLERS BOCAGE but were driven out.

11 H recced all routes South from VILLERS BOCAGE but were not able to make progress.

Brigadier 22 Armd Bde asked for further inf for holding tk and inf attacks which were now starting from the South, starting on the 213 feature and warming up all the way round South of VILLERS BOCAGE up to TRACY BOCAGE feature and round to the West of it.

1/5 Queens were sent up to 22 Armd Bde to help hold the posn and arrived there at about 1600 hrs. In these attacks 4 CLY lost 20 tks. The remainder of the regt joined 1/7 Queens in the town of VILLERS BOCAGE where things were very confused there, and on Pt 174 during the afternoon. It seemed as if TRACY BOCAGE and VILLERS BOCAGE might be isolated and in fact they were about 1600 hrs. The GOC decided to concentrate everything on TRACY BOCAGE feature 174. That is now being successfully carried out. This Pt 174 dominates the village. The Div attacking has been identified by means of PW as the 2nd SS [*sic*] Pz Div. The axis of supply is precarious as there are small gps of enemy operating on the left flank some of which have had to be silenced by artillery fire. 5 RHA have actually been under small arms fire while manning their guns.

Troops now on the VILLERS TRACY [Island Position] feature are as follows:

4 CLY
5 R Tks
2 Bns Queen's
8 H less one sqn

5 RHA
Bty M 10s.

A number of enemy tks have been knocked out including TIGERS, the exact number is not known.

In the area of GRANVILLE 7664 there are:

1 R Tks
1/6 Queen's
3 RHA.

It is possible that these forces may have to be used to clear the axis or to relieve the forces at VILLERS TRACY. Therefore, inf are needed to attack over this ground and relieve these forces should it become necessary for them to proceed to VILLERS TRACY or to clear the axis.

Patrols of 11 H are reported at following map references:

740596 760602
740585 773565
750588 786578
760620 795590.

The intention tomorrow as regards 11 H is to employ them towards the South in the area bounded by, on the right 73 Grid and on the left rd VILLERS BOCAGE – AUNAY SUR ODON. My intention tomorrow is to hold VILLERS BOCAGE.

German and British Ranks

There are only broad comparisons of the various British and German army ranks as roles and responsibilities varied considerably in both armies.

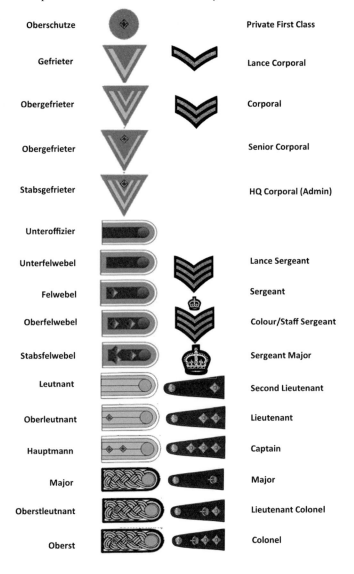

German	British
Oberschutze	Private First Class
Gefrieter	Lance Corporal
Obergefrieter	Corporal
Obergefrieter	Senior Corporal
Stabsgefrieter	HQ Corporal (Admin)
Unteroffizier	
Unterfelwebel	Lance Sergeant
Felwebel	Sergeant
Oberfelwebel	Colour/Staff Sergeant
Stabsfelwebel	Sergeant Major
Leutnant	Second Lieutenant
Oberleutnant	Lieutenant
Hauptmann	Captain
Major	Major
Oberstleutnant	Lieutenant Colonel
Oberst	Colonel

Officers of 7th Armoured Division inspect a panzer knocked out during the fighting on 9 June.

Notes

Introduction

1. WO 219/791, SHAEF/Army Group Records, report dated 16 June 1944. At this very early stage of the campaign this report described Panzer IV as being 'disguised' as Tigers to create trepidation in Allied tank crews! It was, however, also pointed out that the spaced skirts of armour fitted to the Panzer IV to counter hollow-charge weapons and Russian anti-tank rifles were making the tank resemble the much larger Tiger.

Chapter 1 – Planning and Preparations

1. Morgan says he was 'a confirmed Westerner'; that is to say he believed that the war would be won in North-West Europe, not in the Mediterranean as favoured by many other Britons, including Churchill. Morgan, Sir Frederick, *Overture to OVERLORD* (Hodder & Stoughton, 1950).
2. 21 A Gp/1001/C-in-C, dated 14 April.
3. XXX Corps Operation Order Number 1. Volume I, *An Account of the Operations of Second Army in Europe 1944–45*, HQ Second Army, August 1945.
4. The Lorenz attachment was a far more sophisticated coding machine than the Enigma machine that had been cracked earlier in the war. Bill Tutte and Brigadier John Tiltman, in the single greatest intellectual feat of the war, broke the Lorenz code based on twelve rotors rather than three or four.
5. Montgomery of Alamein, *Memoirs* (Collins, 1958).
6. Hills, Stuart, *By Tank to Normandy* (Cassell, 2002).
7. It was Exercise BULLSHEAD. The bull's head was the badge of the 79th Armoured Division, whose beach obstacle clearance capability was demonstrated.
8. Bredin, Speedy, *Three Assault Landings* (Gale and Polden Ltd, Aldershot, 1946).
9. Lewis and English, *8th Battalion, The Durham Light Infantry 1939–1945* (N.&M. reprint).
10. Powis, David, *My World War 2* (Powis Designs, 1999).
11. Neville, Cosmo, 'We landed on D-Day', unpublished account, RHQ Devonshire and Dorset Regiment.
12. Brigadier Cracroft's post-operational report, 8 Armoured Brigade war diary, The National Archives WO 171/613.
13. The nature of the bocage can still be appreciated in places, but today around Point 103 a significant portion of the hedges has been removed for the ease of modern agriculture.
14. Quoted by Stuart Hills.

Chapter 2 – D-Day: 6 June 1944

1. The 50th Division's post-operational report.
2. Saunders, Tim, *Battleground: Gold Beach – Jig Sector* (Leo Cooper, Barnsley, 2001).
3. Armoured Vehicle Royal Engineers, a conversion of a standard gun tank with a demolition gun and the capability to perform a number of engineering tasks.
4. There were no 88mm guns sited to cover Jig Beach. The gun covering the sectors where the SRY landed was a Polish 77mm gun.
5. In British accounts this gun is often described as an 88mm; however, a survey of the German coastal defences by a Combined Ops study team identified it as a Polish 77mm. German maps mark it as a Pak 7.5cm (P).

6. The reserve brigades had been due to land at H + 2½, i.e. 1000 hours.

7. Lewis and English, *8th Battalion, The Durham Light Infantry* (N.&M. reprint).

8. Moses, Harry, *The Faithful Sixth* (County Durham Books, 1995).

9. Of considerable concern was the loss of orders and codes for the next fourteen days in Brigadier Senior's scout car. Lieutenant Colonel Lidwill of 8 DLI assumed command of the brigade at 2230 hours.

10. The 56th (Independent) Infantry Brigade was raised with regular army battalions in March 1944 specifically to come under command of the 50th Division for the invasion as its fourth infantry brigade due to the extent of that division's tasks.

11. The other panzer divisions over which Rommel had control were the 2nd and 116th Panzer, both of which were deployed for operations in the Pas-de-Calais.

Chapter 3 – D+1: 7 June 1944

1. The time it would take for a column of vehicles to pass a single point. Maintaining 100 yards between vehicles because of air attack meant very long columns, further slowed by the necessity of frequently taking cover when Allied aircraft were overhead.

2. US Department of the Army, Historical Division interview with Bayerlein (ETHINT 6612, July 1998).

3. Raised as the 61st Division's reconnaissance regiment, it was transferred to the 50th Division after the destruction of that division's original reconnaissance regiment in North Africa during 1942.

4. A tactical HQ was a small group designed to enable a commander to move around the battlefield to where he could be of greatest influence, communicate and plan. Commanders of armoured brigades were normally mounted in a tank, along with their artillery CO and others as required. The main headquarters was a larger, less mobile affair run by the brigade major.

Chapter 4 – The Advance Begins

1. Described by Captain Hampson of 8 DLI as an 'ungonged brigadier thirsting for blood and glory'.

2. Brouay is one of the many places misspelled (Bronay) on the Allied 1:50 and 25,000 maps.

3. The Auster was known to the Germans as the 'Eisner Tommy' or the 'Iron Tommy' due to it being seemingly impervious to anti-aircraft fire despite its slow speed. One reason is that the German anti-aircraft shell passed through the canvas skin without detonating.

4. The cruisers HMS *Ajax* (8 × 6in), *Argonaut* (10 × 5.25in) and *Orion* (8 × 6in) were firing in support.

5. This is an example of veiled speech, supposedly where the enemy could gain little immediate benefit from the conversation. The *Hitlerjugend*'s Radio Intercept Section had little trouble in 'decoding' such messages and passing target information to their artillery.

6. The Lancers claim that it was hit by an 88mm shell. The only 88mm guns held by the *Hitlerjugend* were the Flak 35/66 which were further back in their anti-aircraft role. The 26 *Panzergrenadiers*' 75mm Pak 41 guns were brought forward as a part of their consolidation of Putot.

7. Captain Keith Douglas was the author of the classic account of the SRY in the North African campaign, *Alamein to Zem Zem*.

8. The communications and flexibility of the Royal Artillery and their interface with the Royal Navy made all the difference throughout the campaign.

9. This was an artillery OP party. To accommodate the additional radios fitted in the turret, the gun was removed and replaced with a dummy.

10. These were fire missions that applied fire from all guns available. 'Mike' targets were regimental shoots, i.e. the twenty-four guns of say 147 Field Regiment; 'Uncle', all seventy-two guns of the division's artillery; 'Victor' shoots were corps: all guns in range from a corps' divisions and its attached Army Group Royal Artillery. 'Whiskey' targets were army and 'Yankee' army group.

Chapter 5 – Advance to Point 103 and Saint-Pierre

1. Several officers and NCOs were subsequently executed for this war crime, but Mohnke was a captive of the Russians and due to the uncertainty regarding the time that Bremer was wounded he was acquitted and he sought refuge in Franco's Spain.

2. Both Germans and Canadians accuse each other of starting this disturbing chain of events and offer evidence of the opposition's guilt. See Saunders and Hone, *12th Hitlerjugend Panzer Division in Normandy* (Pen & Sword, 2021).
3. Attempts to reduce smoke had been under way for many years, but despite shortages of chemicals the Germans reduced the amount of propellant smoke more effectively than the Allies.
4. At the time of the invasion the division was in the process of beginning to redeploy to the Eastern Front. The Panther battalion (I/P130 Panzer Regiment) had already left and was only reported to have rejoined the division on 10 June. Whether some were deployed south of Point 103 during 9 June alongside the *Sturmgeschütz* is possible given that all four companies of II.130 Panzer Regiment were in action on the Tilly-Bayeux road.
5. Bright, Joan, *History of the Northumberland Hussars Yeomanry [102nd Anti-Tank Regiment] 1924–49* (Mawson, Swan and Morgan Ltd, Newcastle-upon-Tyne, 1949).
6. Of a unit's logistic echelons A1, A2 and B, A1 is furthest forward providing immediate replenishment. The tactical situation meant that in this case it was further forward than usual.
7. Such was the air situation at this time that other than specialist platoons and support weapons, most of *Panzer Lehr*'s half-tracks were left at Thury-Harcourt.
8. The 234th Battery was attached to the 50th Division for the invasion from XXX Corps' anti-tank regiment, 73rd Anti-Tank Regiment RA.
9. The equipment and detail of the organization of the anti-tank regiment changed during the campaign as more 17-pounders became available.
10. Lieutenant Colonel Lidwill was still commanding 151 Brigade.
11. Brigadier Bredin's battlefield study presentation to 1 D and D, June 1979.

Chapter 6 – Attack and Counter-Attack

1. I Corps' failure to capture Caen on D-Day did not fundamentally alter Montgomery's plan to draw and fix the Germans in that area but it did create a confined beachhead, which heaped Air Force and media disapproval on him.
2. Lewis and English, *8th Battalion Durham Light Infantry 1939–1945* (M.&N. reprint).
3. HMS *Argonaut* (a *Dido*-class cruiser) was originally designed to carry ten quick-firing dual-purpose guns, but she and several others of her class were modified to carry eight 5.25in guns during refits in 1943 and 1944. The 5.25in weapon had a range against surface targets of more than 24,000 yards, firing an 80lb shell at a rate of seven to eight per minute.
4. Lance sergeant: a senior corporal.
5. With the British 3rd Division having failed to capture Caen, Montgomery planned to launch a two-pronged attack to envelop the city. I Corps was to attack around the city from the east and the 7th Armoured Division from the west. Also, on 10 June the 1st and 2nd US Infantry divisions would attack south to Caumont and St Lô. Delays in disembarking British formations, however, broke the synchronization east of the Orne and a proposed drop of the 1st Airborne Division south of Caen was vetoed by the air commanders as being unnecessary.
6. Cromwells were the brigade's main tank, but each troop had a Sherman Firefly with the 17-pounder gun. Each armoured regiment had forty-three Cromwells, a dozen Fireflies and eleven Stuart light tanks.
7. Unlike ordinary infantry battalions, motor battalions had only three small rifle companies: A, C and I.
8. The battalion had three platoons of two 6-pounders each, which in other infantry battalions would be described as sections.
9. *Ost* battalions were formed from former Red Army prisoners of war who were conscripted into the Wehrmacht. The officers and SNCOs were German. There were some sixteen *Ost* battalions in the invasion area on D-Day; about three battalions per division. They were described as 'a menace' by von Rundstedt.
10. To the mix of weapons should be added the hollow-charge *Panzerschreck* and *Panzerfaust*, which were excellent weapons at close range.

11. Bayerlein confessed in a post-war interview that even though the Germans had occupied Normandy since 1940, they had not considered the problems of fighting in the bocage either. The bocage does lend itself far more readily to defence than offence, but reduced the German advantage in long-range anti-tank fire.
12. Holborne, Andrew, *The 56th Infantry Brigade and D-Day* (Continuum Books, 2010).
13. Not to be confused with Hill 112 south-west of Fontaine-Étoupefour.
14. Pre-arranged 'defensive fire' tasks, usually on likely enemy approaches.
15. The US 987th Field Artillery Battalion had landed on Gold Beach on the evening of D-Day in support of the 50th Division and remained under its command until 30 June 1944.

Chapter 7 – 'Tiger Hill': 11 June 1944

1. 8 Armoured Brigade war diary.
2. A short account of the operations of the 6th Battalion, Green Howards, 6-27 June 1944. TNA 223/31.
3. At this time III/26 SS *Panzergrenadiers* were the only armoured infantry battalioning the *Hitlerjugend* and they had six 75mm guns mounted on Hanomag half-tracks.
4. Hubert Meyer, chief of staff of the 12th *Hitlerjugend* SS Panzer Division and author of the divisional history, is not to be confused with *Oberführer* Kurt 'Panzer' Meyer who commanded the division from 14 June onwards.
5. As CSM D Company, 6 Green Howards, Hollis would be the recipient of D-Day's only Victoria Cross for his actions at the Mont Fleury Battery and again at Crépon.
6. Army Staff College battlefield tour 1968. TDRC.
7. The costly failure of this attack is often contrasted with the success of the 49th Division's attack on Cristot a week later, without recognizing that the *Hitlerjugend* had, in fact, already withdrawn from the village, leaving only outposts there. See Saunders, *12th* Hitlerjugend *Panzer Division in Normandy* (Pen & Sword, 2020).
8. In accordance with German practice, Prinz von Schönburg Waldenburg was posthumously promoted to *Oberstleutnant*.

Chapter 8 – Tilly-sur-Seulles and Essex Wood

1. Pioneers equate to engineers in the British army but they were, as in this case, often used as an additional infantry battalion.
2. Kiln, Robert, *D-Day to Arnhem with the Hertfordshire Gunners: A Personal Account* (The Book Castle, 1992).
3. Interview with Andrew Holborn quoted in '56 Infantry Brigade on D-Day'.
4. Reproduced in the 1947 Staff College battlefield tour documentation.
5. Quoted in Martin, Colonel T.A., *Essex Regiment 1929–1950* (N.&M. reprint, 2016).
6. The company commanders, plus those of specialist platoons and attachments that were to be involved in the attack.
7. Lieutenant Colonel Higson was shortly removed from command as a result of not having the battalion's anti-tank guns up with him. This is despite the supine performance of 22 Armoured Brigade, which did precious little to help the infantry of another brigade.
8. TNA WO 232/77. Staffordshire Yeomanry, Communications within the Infantry Battalion – Lessons from Battle, August 1944.

Chapter 9 – La Belle Épine and Bernières-Bocage

1. Most of the flails had been lost during the landing on 6 June, where they invariably led the breaching teams off the beaches.
2. 79th Armoured Division, as the campaign went on, were adamant that their specialist assault armour should not be used as ordinary tanks, but they conceded that 'In the early days after the landings, with a shortage of armour ashore, needs must.'

Chapter 10 – A Change of Tack: 12 June 1944

1. Staff planning figures for casualties and replacements in offensive operations were intended to be at two levels, 'normal' and 'intense', but such were the levels of casualties such as those being suffered by the 50th Division that a new planning figure was quickly established: 'double intense'.
2. The Germans had magnetic mines, not 'sticky bombs', and applied anti-magnetic *zimmerit* to their tanks until they realized that they were the only army that had magnetic mines!
3. Brigadier Cracroft reported the loss of more than 100 Shermans across his brigade since D-Day.
4. Michael Carver was shortly to be promoted to command the 4th Armoured Brigade. Later he was Field Marshal Lord Carver.
5. 2 Essex had not yet been withdrawn from Essex Wood.
6. German commanders were worried that a significant Anglo-American strike by armoured divisions would deliver a breakthrough.
7. The Achilles version mounted the British 17-pounder gun.
8. Typically 'stand to' at dawn was 0415 hours and in the evening at 2230.

Chapter 11 – Operation PERCH: Villers-Bocage

1. Forty, George, *Battle Zone Normandy: Villers-Bocage* (Sutton, 2004).
2. *Obersturmführer* Michael Wittmann was already regarded as a 'panzer ace', having amassed 117 kills on the Eastern Front and was already a holder of the Knight's Cross with Oak Leaves.
3. See Appendix III.
4. Turret number 234 = 2nd Company, 3rd Platoon, 4th Panzer.
5. The Sherman's nickname among Allied troops was 'Ronson' as it 'lights first time and every time'. The Germans were reputed to refer to the Shermans as 'Tommy Cookers'. It is often thought that the tank's propensity to burn was due to fuel catching fire, but the issue was solved when wet stowage of ammunition was introduced in late 1944.
6. Wilson, Edward, *Press On Regardless* (Spellmount, 2003).
7. Taylor, Daniel, *After the Battle*, Edition 132, 2006; a detailed and closely-argued account of the action to supplement his book *Villers-Bocage Through the Lens*.
8. The Tiger's turret traverse speed was dictated by engine revolutions, so the driver and gunner would work as a team to ensure the speed was appropriate for the task. In action with the engine at maximum revs, a complete circle would take sixty seconds. This compares unfavourably with the Cromwell's fourteen seconds.
9. The 6-pounder armour-piercing discarding sabot (APDS) round, with much greater performance, was only fully in service at the end of the month.
10. An entry timed at 0945 hours in XXX Corps' radio log records a Tiger being knocked out by a 6-pounder.
11. There are no photographs of Tiger 222 or 231 knocked out, probably because it was a 'mobility kill' and therefore recoverable and repairable. Michael Kenny has, however, identified 222 towing 231after the battle.
12. The author was the director of a film that chronicled the events that propelled *Obersturmführer* Wittmann, a knight of the Nazi empire, and a humble shoemaker from Rushden, Northampton-shire, Trooper Joe Ekins, into battle south of Caen. The trailer on YouTube produced praise, balanced by what can only be characterized as vile racial abuse; the one printable comment was 'He was a god.'
13. ULTRA had reported that on the evening of 12 June, the 2nd Panzer Division was still 35 miles south of Caumont.
14. Reconciling the various claims of tank kills is notoriously difficult, but Wittmann's plus six other Tigers are the generally accepted figures; the figures for Panzer IVs range from one to five.
15. *Oberführer* Kurt 'Panzer' Meyer learned this during the actions near the Abbey d'Ardenne on D+1 and at Bretteville on D+2.
16. Lüttwittz, General von. Commander, 2nd Panzer Division in Normandy. US Army intelligence interview B-257.

17. Luttwitz, speaking from memory in an interview with Milton Shulman, quoted 18 June but his own maps in the Bundesarchiv mark their presence days earlier.

Chapter 12 – The Island Position

1. TNA WO 171/336, 30 Corps 'G' Ops war diary.
2. TNA WO 171/1368, 1/7 Queen's war diary.
3. Two medium regiments and one field regiment, plus 3 RHA. The AGRA was still in the process of landing and not yet up to full strength.
4. TNA WO 171/619, 22 Armoured Brigade war diary.
5. TNA WO 171/336, 30 Corps 'G' war diary.

Chapter 13 – 50th Division's Operations: 13–14 June

1. Buckshee, one of the many Hindu words brought into military slang from India, meaning something extra obtained free, especially extra rations.
2. 6 DLI Report, June 1944, WO 223/32.
3. This was the first of nineteen operations and variants that the 1st Airborne Division had cancelled during the summer of 1944 before finally going into action during the ill-fated Operation MARKET GARDEN.
4. The Germans had learned quickly that a withdrawal out of close contact by the British heralded a bombardment or air attack. By moving forward, they not only avoided the fire strike but were able to deploy outposts with which to disrupt the subsequent advance.
5. There are no records of *Panzer Lehr* having armed Panzer IIIs. They were often used as unarmed OP vehicles and there were command variants listed in other divisions. The tank may have been a misidentified Panzer IV.
6. Major Wood 6 DLI and Lieutenant Colonel Woods 9 DLI.
7. Yellow smoke was the most common method of advertising one's presence to enemy aircraft. This method had the advantage of doubling as a tank target indicator.
8. Killin, Robert, *D-Day to Arnhem* (Castlemead Publications, 1993).
9. Moses, Harry, *Gateshead Gurkhas* (County Durham Books, 1995).
10. The sustained fire machine guns were found set up to fire across the front on fixed lines, some with cord attached to their triggers, which enabled the crew to keep firing while still sheltering in their bunkers from artillery fire.
11. Staff College battlefield tour notes. TDRC.
12. There are two theories. One is that this tank was probably captured during the previous days substantially intact and taken into use by the Germans. The other is that at a substantial range it was a misidentified assault gun. The Sherman was, however, a high vehicle and the assault guns held by *Panzer Lehr* had a much lower silhouette.
13. There are two possible explanations for Gunner Bullen's lucky escape and the demolition of a shop. Firstly, all German anti-armour solid shot had HE cores, which detonated after a delay following initial impact. It is therefore plausible that a ricochet with its slight delay could have exploded in the adjacent shop. Alternatively, in a close-quarter action, a tank commander would normally order the loading of the ammunition – HE or AP – he expected to use. In this case, approaching a village, he probably expected to engage infantry and had HE in the breach, which would have to be cleared by firing before reloading with HE.

Chapter 14 – Hiatus

1. *Administrative History* of 21st Army Group.
2. The 9th Dorsets was a home-based holding battalion.
3. After the attack on Hill 112 on 10 July, 4 Dorsets were brought back up to strength with a very large draft of Essex Regiment soldiers.
4. Clay, Major Ewart, *Path of the 50th* (Gale and Polden, 1950).
5. The principle remains early identification, rest and treatment as far forward as possible.

6. Casualties and Medical Statistics, *History of the Second World War*.
7. It is likely that most of such incidents were carried out by French men and occasionally women who had had property, livelihoods and even family members lost to Allied firepower and battle and were angry with them for the destruction wrought on their families. A memorial on Hill 112 details the number of dead suffered by each community in the area during the battle.

Chapter 15 – Tilly-sur-Seulles: 16–18 June

1. 3 RHA war diary.
2. The Radio Link Company fought at Tilly in their conventional role rather than controlling the Borgward radio-controlled demolition vehicles.
3. Madame Pompadour, chief mistress to Louis XV, invented a colour very similar to the purple facings on the uniforms of 2 Essex's antecedents.
4. Their task was the radio link (*Funklink*) to the Borgward radio-controlled demolition tanks. It was to this unit that the much-debated Tigers had been originally attached until replaced by the *Sturmgeschütz*.
5. 'Danger close' was the range within which one's own troops could be hit by shell splinters coming back. In the case of the 25-pounder this was about 100 yards but if the guns were firing from almost directly behind and with momentum carrying most of the shell splinters forward, the advancing troops, could 'lean on the barrage', and get significantly closer.
6. The Mortar, Recoiling, Spigot, 290mm, Mk I or II had a short range, but fired the 290mm 'flying dustbin' demolition round.

Chapter 16 – The Western Flank: 16–19 June

1. Immediate MCs were awarded for single acts of bravery and performance, while periodic MCs, as the name suggests, were awarded for sustained gallantry and achievement.
2. There were no *Jagdpanthers* with their 88mm guns operational on 16 June but 130 *Panzerjäger* Battalion was and they were equipped with the *Jagdpanzer* IV with a 75mm gun.
3. *Zimmerit* is a paste that was applied during the building of panzers to defeat magnetic mines. Later in 1944 the Germans stopped using *zimmerit* when they realized that theirs was the only army using magnetic mines!
4. Calvados, an apple brandy.
5. Wadi Akarit, Western Desert.
6. Ritgen.
7. *Aufklärung Lehr Abteilung* 130.
8. Holdsworth, David and Holdsworth, Diana, *One Day I'll Tell You* (Westfield Publications, 1994), a delightful self-deprecating memoir in which Holdsworth makes no pretence at any martial achievements.
9. Lieutenant Colonel Norrie, originally from the King's Own Regiment (Lancasters), had been a member of Montgomery's staff and was given command of the 1 Dorsets when the previous CO was posted in accordance with Monty's instruction that all COs should be below the age of 36.
10. The 4th/7th DGs' war diary.
11. Admittedly the bocage is particularly thick between Lingèvres and Hottot but 231 Brigade, leaving the tanks behind, contrasts with the successful integration of infantry, tanks and artillery achieved by 6 DLI when outflanking Tilly the previous day.
12. After two days of heavy rain the two streams that cut across the Dorsets' advance were full to overflowing and the only track was in German hands.

Appendix II – 8 Armoured Brigade's Operation Order

1. The National Archive WO 171/1284.

Appendix IV – 7th Armoured Division's Situation Report

1. TNA WO 171/336, 30 Corps 'G' Ops war diary.

A captured Panzer IV. As was common, it has lost its *schurzen* plates covering the hull but those on the turret are still in place.

Index